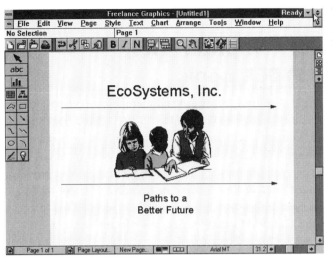

Freelance Graphics for Windows gives you three different ways of viewing your presentation:

Current Page View. This view displays each page—complete with text boxes, symbols, and custom art—the way it appears in the presentation.

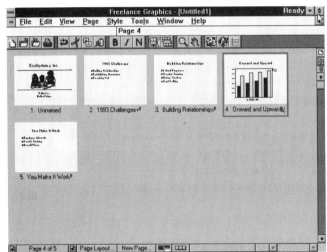

Page Sorter View. This view displays all the pages of your presentation in a reduced size. You can use Page Sorter view to check—and easily modify—the order of the pages in your presentation.

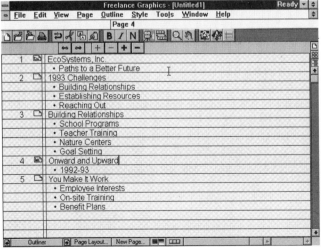

Outliner View. This view displays only the text in your presentation, arranged in outline format on a legal pad. In Outliner view, you can easily change text levels, choose page layouts, and add or delete text.

For every kind of computer user, there is a SYBEX book.

All computer users learn in their own way. Some need straightforward and methodical explanations. Others are just too busy for this approach. But no matter what camp you fall into, SYBEX has a book that can help you get the most out of your computer and computer software while learning at your own pace.

Beginners generally want to start at the beginning. The **ABC's** series, with its step-by-step lessons in plain language, helps you build basic skills quickly. For a more personal approach, there's the **Murphy's Laws** and **Guided Tour** series. Or you might try our **Quick & Easy** series, the friendly, full-color guide, with **Quick & Easy References**, the companion pocket references to the **Quick & Easy** series. If you learn best by doing rather than reading, find out about the **Hands-On Live!** series, our new interactive multimedia training software. For hardware novices, there's the **Your First** series.

The **Mastering and Understanding** series will tell you everything you need to know about a subject. They're perfect for intermediate and advanced computer users, yet they don't make the mistake of leaving beginners behind. Add one of our **Instant References** and you'll have more than enough help when you have a question about your computer software. You may even want to check into our **Secrets & Solutions** series.

SYBEX even offers special titles on subjects that don't neatly fit a category—like our **Pushbutton Guides**, our books about the Internet, our books about the latest computer games, and a wide range of books for Macintosh computers and software.

SYBEX books are written by authors who are expert in their subjects. In fact, many make their living as professionals, consultants or teachers in the field of computer software. And their manuscripts are thoroughly reviewed by our technical and editorial staff for accuracy and ease-of-use.

So when you want answers about computers or any popular software package, just help yourself to SYBEX.

For a complete catalog of our publications, please write:

SYBEX Inc.
2021 Challenger Drive
Alameda, CA 94501
Tel: (510) 523-8233/(800) 227-2346 Telex: 336311
Fax: (510) 523-2373

SYBEX is committed to using natural resources wisely to preserve and improve our environment. As a leader in the computer book publishing industry, we are aware that over 40% of America's solid waste is paper. This is why we have been printing the text of books like this one on recycled paper since 1982.

This year our use of recycled paper will result in the saving of more than 15,300 trees. We will lower air pollution effluents by 54,000 pounds, save 6,300,000 gallons of water, and reduce landfill by 2,700 cubic yards.

In choosing a SYBEX book you are not only making a choice for the best in skills and information, you are also choosing to enhance the quality of life for all of us.

TALK TO SYBEX ONLINE.

Understanding Freelance Graphics® for Windows™

KATHERINE MURRAY

San Francisco • Paris • Düsseldorf • Soest

SYBEX®

Acquisitions Editor: Dianne King
Developmental Editor: Kenyon Brown
Editor: Armin Brott
Project Editor: Brenda Kienan
Technical Editor: Mark Taber
Assistant Editors: Abby Azrael, Michelle Nance
Production and Chapter Artists: Helen Bruno, Ingrid Owen
Screen Graphics Artist: John Corrigan
Page Layout and Typesetting: Len Gilbert
Proofreader and Production Assistant: Lisa Haden
Indexer: Ted Laux
Cover Designer: Archer Design
Cover Photographer: Michael Lamott
Cover Photo Art Directors: Ingalls+Associates
Screen reproductions produced with Collage Plus.

Collage Plus is a trademark of Inner Media Inc.

SYBEX is a registered trademark of SYBEX Inc.

TRADEMARKS: SYBEX has attempted throughout this book to distinguish proprietary trademarks from descriptive terms by following the capitalization style used by the manufacturer.

Every effort has been made to supply complete and accurate information. However, SYBEX assumes no responsibility for its use, nor for any infringement of the intellectual property rights of third parties which would result from such use.

Library of Congress Card Number: 92-83944
ISBN: 0-7821-1231-5

Manufactured in the United States of America
10 9 8 7 6 5 4 3

To Doug, Kelly, Christopher—and our latest release.

ACKNOWLEDGMENTS

CREATING a book is not unlike creating a really important presentation. You envision it, plan it, and ultimately create it, all along the way hoping that your project meets its goals and communicates information in the clearest possible way. Many people are responsible for helping the project stay on course. Special thank-yous go to the following people for helping target and fine-tune the entire process that has become *Understanding Freelance Graphics for Windows*:

- Ken Brown, SYBEX Developmental Editor, for providing clear instructions and perfectly timed doses of encouragement; and Dianne King, Acquisitions Editor, for seeing the book's potential.

- Armin Brott, Editor, for his uncanny ability to make edited text sound more like me than I do. This book is much better because of his involvement. Thanks, Armin.

- The folks at McGlinchey & Paul for providing terrific background information for both Freelance Version 1.0 and 2.0.

- Lotus Development Corporation, for providing pre-release software with technical access for Version 2.0.

- Mark Taber, Technical Editor, for carefully checking all procedures and providing many of the helpful hints we've included here.

- The in-house team at SYBEX: Helen Bruno and Ingrid Owen, Production Artists; John Corrigan, Screen Graphics Artist; Len Gilbert, Typesetter; Lisa Haden, Proofreader; Abby Azrael and Michelle Nance, Assistant Editors; and especially Brenda Kienan, Project Editor, for keeping everything on track.

- And, most of all, thanks to Claudette Moore, for her awesome business ability, keen insights, and warm and friendly set of well-worn clichés.

Contents
AT A GLANCE

CONTENTS

PART TWO   ENTERING, EDITING, AND ENHANCING TEXT

PART FOUR   ENHANCING YOUR PRESENTATION WITH ARTWORK

PART FIVE   FINISHING YOUR PRESENTATION

INTRODUCTION

WELCOME to a new age in presentation graphics. Gone are the days when a manager rushing to a meeting had to spend precious time cutting and pasting charts and text onto a sheet of clear plastic. And those of us gathered around the board-room table no longer have to squint while trying to decipher the illegible scrawl of a manager's wax pencil on the overhead projector.

Today, presentation graphics takes the grudgework out of creating materials that can capture the attention—and imagination—of your audience. Not only can you communicate your materials effectively and professionally, but you can also wow viewers with a myriad of special effects, including animation features, special slideshows, and multimedia capabilities that allow you to mix video and sound.

Whether you want a straightforward little chart or the most complex presentation slide show, Freelance Graphics for Windows was created just for you. The only presentation graphics program that concentrates on the *process* of creating a presentation rather than the number of rote tools you need to get you there, Freelance Graphics for Windows makes creating a presentation as simple and painless as possible.

How to Use This Book

Understanding Freelance Graphics for Windows is a simple, step-by-step tutorial that you can use as a guide to creating effective presentations. Like the software it introduces, *Understanding Freelance Graphics for Windows* takes you through the process of creating presentations in a sequence of logical, what-do-I-do-next? steps.

In each section, illustrations help walk you through the most important steps. In addition, tables are used to present information in a quick-look format and bulleted lists highlight information for quick review. Finally, numbered steps are used throughout the text so you can easily find the tasks you want to try and work through them in a sequential manner.

Feel free to use this book in the most logical progression for you. When you are pressed for time or need a simple reminder on a task you've tried before, you may want to flip through this book as a reference guide. When you've got a few minutes to spare and want to experiment with some of Freelance Graphics' new features, you can use the book as a tutorial guide, helping you learn the hows and whys behind your selected operation, and providing examples and tips to shorten your learning curve.

Who Should Read This Book?

It's no secret that most of us will do almost anything to figure out a computer program without looking at the documentation. So, why are we so lazy? Perhaps it's the prospect of wading through the tons of various manuals, fliers, and inserts that are usually stuffed into a documentation box. Perhaps it's an innate stubbornness that pushes us to tell ourselves "Let's just try one more thing...." Perhaps it's all the experience we've had with manuals—for computers and other hardware items like gas grills and lawn mowers—that are overrun with errors and diagrams that don't tell us anything.

Understanding Freelance Graphics for Windows will help you concentrate on the process of creating your presentations as quickly and cleanly as possible. You'll find the organization, examples, and illustration of this book helpful if you belong to one of the following types of users:

- You are responsible for creating weekly production charts used in the departmental meeting,

- Your time for learning a new software program is limited,

- You need a straightforward, no-frills guide to basic tasks,

- You are new to presentation graphics and want to learn some basic guidelines for creating effective slides,

- You hope to learn more about multimedia and want to master Freelance Graphics in order to produce professional-looking slide shows,

- You have lots of work to fit into an already filled-to-bursting day and want a guide that will help you cut your time and effort investment in learning a new program.

New Features in Freelance Graphics for Windows Version 2.0

Although the first version of Freelance Graphics for Windows was available for only one year, Lotus announced the release of an even more powerful and intuitive version—Version 2.0—in late 1992. Because the focus of Freelance Graphics has always been on the process users find easiest, the designers of version 2.0 added new features in response to user suggestions and made the entire program easier to use and more intuitive (meaning the process of creating charts seems even more natural than before). You'll find a complete list of Version 2.0's new features in Table 1.1 in Chapter 1. You'll also find a more detailed look at these new features in Appendix B.

How This Book Is Organized

Understanding Freelance Graphics for Windows consists of five parts, each adding to your repertoire of Freelance Graphics tasks, and building on your experience. If you have some experience with Freelance Graphics or presentation graphics in general, you may want to skip the elementary sections and go right to some of the more complex operations. Overall, this book is presented in a sequential, process-oriented manner. So, to ensure you learn everything you need to know about Freelance Graphics from the ground up, you may want to follow the part and chapter organization provided. The following sections explain each of the five parts of *Understanding Freelance Graphics for Windows*.

Part 1: Introducing Freelance Graphics

This first part sets up the groundwork for the rest of your Freelance Graphics experience.

Chapter 1 provides you with an overview of Freelance Graphics features, old and new, with a special emphasis on the new enhancements in Version 2.0. You'll meet the typical Freelance Graphics user and learn the basics of creating an effective presentation.

Chapter 2 gives you the boost you need to get started, showing you how to perform Windows basics and work through the Quick-Start tutorial. You'll also get comfortable with the Freelance Graphics work area and learn about the various tools, buttons, icons, and messages.

Chapter 3 takes you through an elementary primer of the features of Freelance Graphics. You learn how to use some of the most important Freelance elements, including using Smart-Masters, working with the different available views, changing displays, starting a slide show, and printing and saving presentations.

Part 2: Entering, Editing, and Enhancing Text

Part 2 gives you the information you need for working with text in your Freelance Graphics presentations.

Chapter 4 shows you how to enter text on your presentation pages. You learn to use the different views as you enter text and make choices about block options.

Chapter 5 shows you how to perform simple text editing tasks (correcting those inevitable typos, among other things) and how to work with blocks of text. Additionally, you'll learn to use Freelance Graphics' built-in spelling checker.

Chapter 6 builds on the text features by providing you with information about controlling text format, setting margins, choosing alignment, enhancing text (by using text styles and fonts), and adding special effects, such as borders.

Chapter 7 rounds out this part by taking a closer look at the outliner view. You'll learn to change text levels, add a new page, move pages of information, and display a selected page. Additionally, the new features of Version 2.0 as they pertain to the outliner are discussed, along with numerous examples and illustrations.

Part 3: Creating, Importing, and Linking Charts

This part shows you how to use Freelance graphics to create and edit charts. In addition to the basic information, you'll learn to import and link charts to existing data files.

Chapter 8 teaches you the basic operations involved in creating and editing a simple chart. Specifically, you'll learn to choose a chart type, work with the screens presented, add titles, edit the chart, and change the chart type. You'll also find a number of chart tips that will help you choose the right chart for your data.

Chapter 9 shows you how to import data from other applications. You may want to copy information by using the Windows clipboard, or you might want to import complete files from other supported applications. You'll also learn to establish a link with other files, change the links you create, and delete unnecessary links.

Part 4: Enhancing Your Presentation with Artwork

This part concentrates on bringing out the artistic talent in all of us—even if we're decidedly non-artistic.

Chapter 10 explores the techniques involved in adding symbols to your presentations. You'll find out what symbols are available with Freelance Graphics, and learn to place, resize, import, and edit the symbols you use.

Chapter 11 focuses on using the Freelance Graphics drawing tools. Specifically, you'll learn about the various tools available—with special attention on the tools new in Version 2.0—and find out about the different options available with those tools.

Chapter 12 shows you how to edit the objects you draw with the art tools. You learn to select, move, resize, copy, paste, and delete objects, and perform other operations. Additionally, you'll find out how to undo the editing changes you've made and to arrange and group objects.

Part 5: Finishing Your Presentation

This final part explores the tasks you need to consider as you near completion for your project.

Chapter 13 explores color considerations, including the new black-and-white toggle available with Version 2.0. Find out about your color choices and choose the palette you want to work with. You'll also learn to substitute colors in the selected palette.

Chapter 14 concentrates on adding the finishing touches to your presentation by providing a series of checklists and suggestions you can use to ensure your presentation flows smoothly, includes the right information, and has an effective appearance.

Chapter 15 goes through the print routine available for printing your presentations. You'll learn to perform a quick print and then to explore each of your printing options. Other considerations, such as choosing paper type, controlling page settings, and evaluating your printout are also discussed.

Chapter 16 completes the book by exploring the SmartShow option. You'll learn to produce snazzy screen shows that capture and hold the viewer's attention. You'll learn how to start a SmartShow and use the various Version 2.0 enhancements, including some with as many as 32 special effects.

Appendices

Appendix A may be the first resource you need to use because it covers the procedures for installing Freelance Graphics for Windows.

Appendix B lists the various new features and enhancements available in Version 2.0.

Now that you know the overall game plan for the book, let's get started! In just a few short minutes, you could be printing your first Freelance Graphics presentation.

PART ONE

●

Introducing Freelance Graphics

If you are new to Freelance Graphics or to presentation graphics in general, this is the place to start. Part One of the book begins with a basic introduction to Freelance Graphics for Windows, with special emphasis on Version 2's new features, and takes you through the hands-on tasks you'll use each time you create a Freelance Graphics chart.

Whether you plan to incorporate sound and graphics or produce something simple, such as a series of charts that show the progress of our economy, Version 2.0 offers you:

- An interface that's easier to use than ever before
- Additional SmartMasters
- The ability to add and print speaker notes
- Many more new or enhanced features.

Also in this part, you'll learn to start Freelance Graphics and begin to explore the screen area and the most important elements of the program.

ONE

An Overview
of Freelance
Graphics for
Windows

f a s t TRACK

● **Do you dread having to give presentations?**   6

Do you hate to spend days learning new programs? Are you
working under a tight deadline? If you answered yes to any of
these questions, Freelance Graphics for Windows is for you.
By providing you with constant on-screen support, a comprehensive help system, and a variety of preview features that
let you see the effects of the options you select, Freelance
Graphics will take you through the steps of how to put
together an effective presentation.

● **Use SmartMasters to get you going fast.**   14

A SmartMaster is a type of template that works interactively
with you, telling you exactly when to add a title, a subtitle, a
symbol, etc. Version 2.0 includes over 65 SmartMasters—in
tastes ranging from conservative to artsy. In some cases,
SmartMasters may be literally all you need to create your initial presentations.

● **Are you a Freelance Graphics Version 1.0 user?**   19

If so, you'll quickly notice the incredible number of enhancements Lotus has made to the program. For a complete list, including chapter reference, see Table 1.1.

● **When you're putting your presentation together,**   **21**

keep in mind who your audience is. The humorous approach you might take with your co-workers probably wouldn't be appropriate for a corporate board meeting. And remember, getting your audience's attention is only half the battle; you need to keep them interested right to the very end of your presentation.

● **If you need a quick overview of the program,**   **21**

the QuickStart tutorial has been improved and now includes an animated introduction and new controls that allow you to work at your own speed.

PICTURE this: You're frantically preparing for a board of directors meeting this afternoon. Your assistant appears in the doorway, holding a purple-and-white shrinkwrapped package. "Someone in Marketing just sent this over," he says. "Thought it might help you create the slides for your presentation."

You look with dismay at the hefty package. *Help?* Seems pretty unlikely. When was the last time you were able to learn a new software program—and produce something usable—in one afternoon?

Lucky for you, the program is Freelance Graphics for Windows. With its easy-to-use interface and clear, no-guess instructions, Freelance Graphics for Windows can lead you through the creation of your entire presentation in less than an hour.

In this chapter, you'll get a bird's-eyeview of Freelance Graphics, you'll find out where you fit in the family of Freelance users, and you'll explore the benefits of using presentation graphics—in particular, Freelance Graphics for Windows—to create more professional-looking presentations with less hassle. You'll discover the important elements of Freelance Graphics and scan through the highlights of the newest release, Version 2.0. Finally, this chapter introduces some basic design strategies that will help you produce effective presentations even a manager would love.

What Is Freelance Graphics for Windows?

No doubt, you are aware that Freelance Graphics for Windows helps you create visual aids to reinforce any type of presentation you may be giving.

Thank goodness, we no longer have to scribble on chalkboards as we talk, or use those awful wax pencils to write (and rewrite) key points on an overhead projector. We can walk confidently into our meetings armed with professional-looking handouts, beautifully produced slides, or a disk containing a slide show we will present to our audience.

Freelance Graphics for Windows makes it all possible. And because the program was designed to be as easy to learn and use as possible, you can produce sleek, sophisticated graphics the first time you use it. You can say to a fellow manager "Just a minute—I want to crank out one more chart" and *mean* it.

From the most simple chart to the most complex multimedia presentation, Freelance Graphics has the capability to help you get the job done. So sit back and relax. You'll have plenty of time to get to your meeting. And, hopefully, you'll have some fun along the way.

Who Creates Presentations?

In creating Freelance Graphics, Lotus Development Corporation adopted a unique strategy that other software manufacturers would do well to imitate: they listened to users. What did users need most? How do ordinary people like us create presentations? Under what circumstances are most presentations created? After extensive research projects, Lotus had a good idea of who Freelance users would be and what they needed most from the product. As the program was being developed, Lotus stayed very close to users' suggestions, and built a program that answered the biggest needs, was simple to use right away, and made even the most boring business tasks almost fun.

Freelance Graphics for Windows, Version 1.0, had been on the market only one year when Lotus decided it was time for an upgrade. Why so soon? Again, Lotus had been listening to users. New features added to Freelance Graphics for Windows, Version 2.0, further ease the burden of creating presentations by giving us more tools, more flexibility, and a wider range of support for producing high-end presentations. (The special enhancements of Version 2.0 are discussed later in this chapter.)

The primary philosophy behind Freelance Graphics is this: users need a program that follows the *process* of creating a presentation—not a toolbox of sophisticated features that may sell the product initially but are of little value to most users. For this reason, the entire process of creating a presentation with Freelance Graphics is simple and more intuitive—meaning it works the way you think it should work—than any other presentation graphics program available.

So who are these users that Lotus paid so much attention to? Typical Freelance Graphics users include the following:

- Business people who create presentation materials rarely—perhaps no more than once a month

- People with little time to learn a new software program

- Users who forget everything about a program after they use it and need to relearn tasks easily

- People with little or no graphics training

- Business people who hate to give presentations

- Users often under the gun, needing to create professional-looking presentations quickly.

Do any of those sound like you? (I fit into several categories.) In today's world of computerized everything, it's next to impossible to learn all there is to know about all the software products we need to master. We have word processors, spreadsheets, databases, communications programs, tax programs, and on and on. There's just too much to deal with. Thank goodness someone has come up with a program that doesn't require us to keep all the commands and menu sequences in our brain's RAM. Instructions are right there on screen, with prompts telling us what to do next, every step of the way.

Whether you need to create only a simple bullet chart every other month or a sophisticated presentation once a week, you'll find that Freelance Graphics for Windows was created just for you. By providing you with constant on-screen support, a comprehensive help system, and a variety of preview features that let you see the effects of the options you select, Freelance Graphics walks you through every step of the process in creating your presentations—a valuable companion when you're stressed out about a part of your job you'd just as soon skip altogether.

Exploring the Benefits of Freelance Graphics

Choosing Freelance Graphics for Windows over other popular presentation graphics programs isn't difficult once you've seen them all lined up side-by-side. Only Freelance Graphics was firmly built on the ease-of-use philosophy. Other programs tend to focus more on the number of features they offer, and not necessarily the usability of those features. This section highlights some of the benefits you'll find as you begin working with Freelance Graphics for Windows.

Focus on Process. Freelance Graphics is based on the process of creating a presentation. In a sense, the program "thinks" the way you do. But what does this really mean as you're sitting in front of the Freelance screen? Simply put, it means you see on-screen prompts—prompts as simple as *Click here to add symbol*—that lead you through every step of the process. You'll never find yourself staring blankly at your monitor, wondering what to do next.

Easy-Access On-Screen Features. The makers of Freelance Graphics for Windows know you don't have time to go hunting through menus and multiple levels of dialog boxes to find a tool you'll use often. For that reason, an incredible number of tools are displayed right on the Freelance work area. In addition to the familiar Windows menu bar, you have a tool box, SmartIcons (which allow you to select commands quickly), and page and view controls—so you can move among the different views Freelance Graphics offers, or from page to page easily (see Figure 1.1).

FIGURE 1.1

The Freelance
Graphics work area

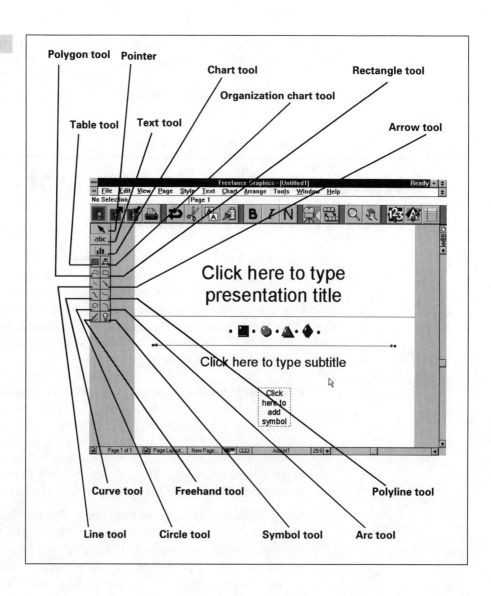

Familiar Windows Interface. For many of us who work with a variety of programs, having a few that look familiar is a great relief. Freelance Graphics for Windows is, of course, a Windows program, so you have the same mouse-based interface, the traditional menu bar, the same minimize and maximize buttons, scroll bars, and conventions you'll find in other Windows-compatible programs. You also gain by using the easy integration of other Windows programs with your Freelance Graphics presentations.

Flexibility for Creativity. Even though Freelance Graphics leads you by the hand through the process of creating presentations, your own creativity won't be stifled. You won't be just plugging data into templates designed by Lotus developers (although you can do that if you really want to). A wealth of tools encourages you to create your own symbols, design eye-catching background art, and use as many varied graph styles as you want.

A Variety of Perspectives. Freelance Graphics gives you several choices for the way in which you view your work. If your brain is primarily text-based—meaning you think better in outline form— you'll really like the Outliner feature that was included in Version 1.0 (but has been significantly enhanced in Version 2.0). The Outliner allows you to create the text for your presentation in, as you might expect, outline form (see Figure 1.2). You can edit, move, and change levels of indentation easily in the Outliner view, and the changes you make are reflected in Freelance's other views, as well. You have the option of working in whatever view is most comfortable for you. Choose from regular Presentation display (the default), the Outliner, or the Page Sorter (in which all pages are displayed in miniature on your screen). Changing from one view to another is easy, too; Freelance Graphics displays the icons on the right side of the work area so you can move among the views with a click of the mouse.

Compatibility with Other Programs. The makers of Freelance Graphics for Windows understand that in addition to using a presentation graphics program, you will also be using other programs. For this reason, Freelance Graphics accepts files created in many other applications—including 1-2-3, Microsoft Excel, dBASE, Harvard Graphics, Ami Pro, WordPerfect, and a variety of popular drawing, painting, and presentation programs. In addition to giving you

FIGURE 1.2

The Outliner view

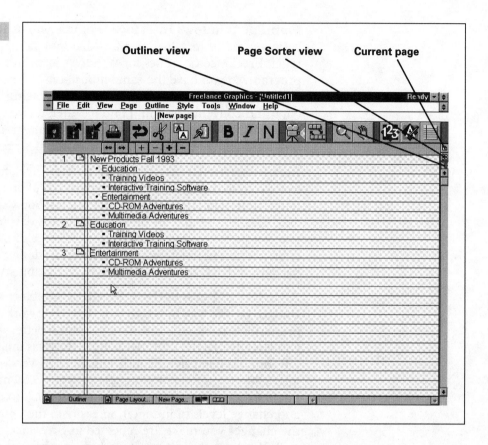

the flexibility of importing these files, Freelance Graphics for Windows supports DDE (Dynamic Data Exchange) with other Windows programs. This means you can link your graphics in Freelance to the original file containing the data—even if the data is in another program. And whenever the data in the original file is changed, the chart is automatically updated.

Professional-Quality Output. The way in which you output your Freelance Graphics presentations will be important to your overall success as a presenter. Will you create color slides to be shown on a projector? Will you display the presentation on-screen? Or will you print your presentation and distribute the pages as handouts? No matter how you plan to resolve this issue, Freelance Graphics has the flexibility to help you meet your goals. Freelance supports printers ranging from 9-pin dot-matrix printers to color PostScript printers. For additional color options, you can set output to a film recorder, a plotter, or a custom slide service such as Autographix.

The points covered here are only a foundation from which to start. As you progress through this book, you'll undoubtedly discover more benefits for yourself. In the next section, you'll learn about some of the elements of Freelance Graphics you'll find important as you create your own presentations.

Important Freelance Graphics Elements

Every program has its own bag of tools and tricks you learn to use over time. Freelance Graphics is no exception. This section introduces you to some of the more important elements in Freelance Graphics—elements you may not have seen before in other programs—terms that need defining, and features you'll use often. Specifically, this section introduces you to the following elements:

- SmartMasters
- SmartIcons
- The Outliner view
- The Page Sorter view
- Page Layout view
- Chart Gallery
- Screen Shows
- QuickStart Tutorial

SmartMasters

In some cases, SmartMasters may be literally all you need to create your initial presentations. A SmartMaster is a type of template that works interactively with you, prompting you to add a title at a specific point, add a subtitle, add a symbol, etc. Over 65 SmartMasters—in tastes ranging from conservative to artsy—are included in Version 2.0. This version added 12 new SmartMasters, along with other enhancement options for working with SmartMaster pages. Even though SmartMasters lay out the entire presentation page for you, don't be fooled; the page is fully customizable, meaning that you can move text and symbols boxes wherever you want and change the look of the SmartMaster to meet your needs. Figure 1.3 shows an example of a SmartMaster.

SmartIcons

If you've used other Lotus applications, you may already be familiar with SmartIcons. A SmartIcon gives you access to menu commands you use often with a simple click of the mouse button. No more long menus to hunt through or shortcuts to remember. Freelance keeps everything right there on-screen for you to use whenever you need.

Freelance Graphics includes many more SmartIcons than can be displayed on-screen at a single time. After you have gained some experience with the program and know which commands you use most often, you can customize the SmartIcon set to display the commands you use most frequently. Freelance also gives you the choice of creating your own custom SmartIcons by using the icon editor included in the program.

The Outliner View

As mentioned earlier, the Outliner view gives you the option to create or work with your pages in outline form. When you create pages by entering text directly in the Outliner, Freelance uses the text to fill in the Add text prompts in the SmartMaster you've chosen. In this way, you never need to enter anything twice—the changes you make in the Outliner are reflected in the current page, and vice versa. By simply clicking on the Outliner icon to the right of the work area, you can change the Freelance display into outline mode.

A Freelance Graphics
SmartMaster

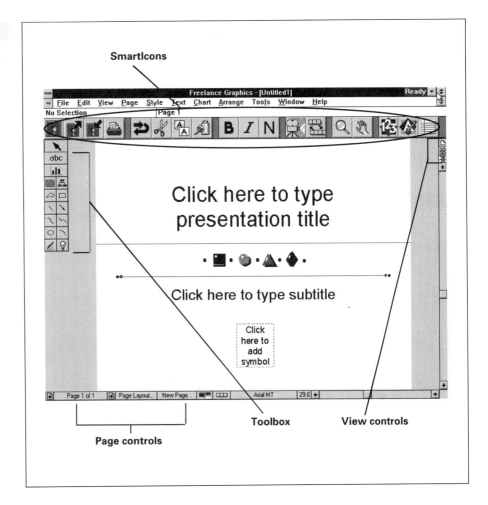

Version 2.0 of Freelance Graphics significantly enhanced the Outliner, adding the ability to collapse and expand the outline, support for Microsoft Word outlines (Ami Pro was already supported), a new feature that lets you select and move blocks of text easily, and the option of printing the outline as created.

The Page Sorter View

The Page Sorter view is true to its name—it allows you to see all the pages in your presentation in thumbnail or lightboard views. By using the Page Sorter, you can review each of your pages while making sure you've put them in the right sequence. Moving pages is as simple as dragging the mouse. You can also add, copy, and delete pages at will. Figure 1.4 shows a sample presentation displayed in Page Sorter view.

FIGURE 1.4

The Page Sorter view

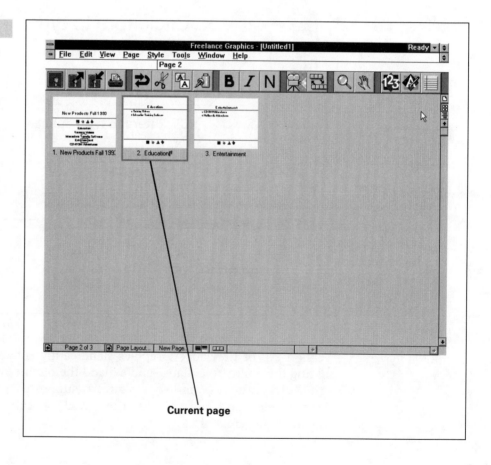

Current page

Page Layout View

What if you want to include a company logo or your department's name on each page in the presentation? Freelance Graphics allows for that, too. By using the Page Layouts view, you can add items—names, symbols, logos, whatever—to every page in your presentation. Everything you create on a Page Layout page is placed in the background. In other words, items you create in current page view will appear "on top" of the background items if they overlap. This gives you the flexibility to include the background items on some pages but not on others.

Chart Gallery

The Chart Gallery is another feature that is a cornerstone of the easy-to-use foundation of Freelance Graphics. With the Chart Gallery, you don't have to reinvent the wheel—all the charts you could possibly want (108 of them!) have already been created and are ready to be used. Choosing a chart you like is as simple as pointing the mouse and clicking.

Freelance gives you pre-drawn charts in the following styles: pie charts, line charts, vertical and horizontal bar charts, 3-D bar charts, segmented and clustered bar charts, area charts, scatter charts, high-low-close-open charts, and a wide range of mixed chart types. New in Version 2.0 are organizational charts, 3-D line charts, 3-D area charts, and radar charts. Figure 1.5 shows you an example of the Chart Gallery.

Screen Shows

Freelance Graphics wouldn't be worth much without some kind of on-screen viewing utility. With Freelance Graphics Screen Shows, you can display your pages at the highest resolution your screen offers.

New SmartShow effects in Version 2.0 include 32 transitional effects, such as dissolves, fades, and wipes, and help increase the professional quality of your presentations. Other new features include the ability to add buttons that turn your presentation into an interactive display, allowing users to move through pages by clicking on a specific button. Multimedia is supported as well, giving you the option of adding video and sound files to your presentations for even more punch.

FIGURE 1.5

The Chart Gallery

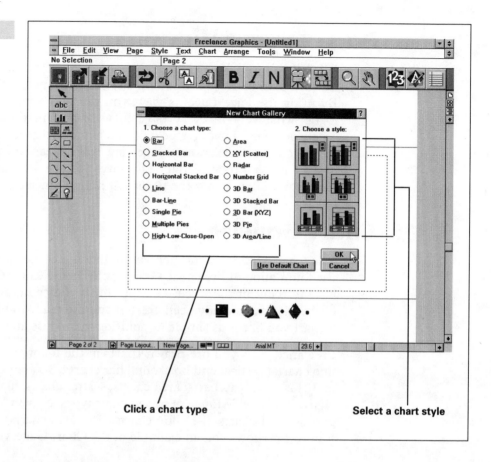

Click a chart type   Select a chart style

QuickStart Tutorial

Any company that puts as much time and effort into researching user response as Lotus does is bound to build a hefty help system into their product. Freelance Graphics, along with its context-sensitive help system (help is always available by pressing F1), offers a terrific QuickStart tutorial that takes you through the process of creating a basic presentation in less than thirty minutes.

The QuickStart tutorial has been improved and now includes an animated introduction and new controls that allow you to work through the process at your own speed. The QuickStart is always available in the Help menu, so if you ever need a refresher course, your teacher is waiting in the wings.

An Overview of Version 2.0

Once again, the makers of Freelance Graphics for Windows remind us that their objective is not to wow us with the number of features they offer, but rather to help us accomplish our goals by providing the easiest, most intuitive presentation graphics program available. Version 2.0 of Freelance Graphics for Windows, released late in 1992, carries on this philosophy. Although some new features have been added, the biggest changes are found in the ease-of-use category—things that enhance features that were already present in Version 1.0. Table 1.1 lists the changes you'll find in Version 2.0 and directs you to the chapter in which they're fully covered.

TABLE 1.1: Version 2.0 Enhancements

FEATURE	DESCRIPTION	SEE CHAPTER
QuickStart	Changes to the existing QuickStart make the tutorial more intuitive and easier for the user to control	2
Tip buttons	Provide users with additional information about the current task	2
New page layouts	Two new page layouts—organization charts and tables—have been added to all SmartMasters	3
New SmartMasters	12 new SmartMasters have been added, two of which have built-in multimedia capabilities	3
Custom page layouts	Version 2.0 enhances the ability to customize pages by letting users make their own "Click here" boxes easily	3
New text features	In Version 2.0, users find an automatic build-slides feature, the ability to use any symbols as text, and the choice of curving text	6, 14

TABLE 1.1: Version 2.0 Enhancements (continued)

FEATURE	DESCRIPTION	SEE CHAPTER
Text notes	Now users can create presentation notes on a 3-by-5 card within Freelance. Notes stay with the presentation file	6
Outliner changes	Users can collapse and expand outlines, print outlines, use outlines from Ami Pro and Microsoft Word, and choose page layouts for text entered in the Outliner	7
New chart types	The Chart Gallery offers additional chart types: 3-D line, 3-D area, and radar charts	8
New importing support	Microsoft Excel files can now be viewed and imported	9
New draw features	A freehand tool, drop-shadows, and an on-screen ruler have been added	11
Color and B&W features	SmartMasters all include color and black-and-white palettes so users can be sure to get the highest quality output for their printer or display type	13
SmartShow features	Screen show features have been enhanced. Buttons allow users to move to other pages in a presentation; multimedia capabilities allow users to add video and sound clips; 32 presentation effects (wipes, fades, etc.) add professional appeal; a VCR-like control panel helps users control presentations on-screen	16

In this section, you've seen some of the elements that make Freelance Graphics different from other presentation graphics programs. But these are by no means all of the special features you'll use as you create your own work—you'll find more features scattered throughout every chapter on this book.

Creating a Good Presentation

Just because the responsibility of creating presentation graphics fell in your lap doesn't mean you're an artist. Most of us aren't. Some of us struggle to produce something that looks relatively "normal."

Once you sit down with Freelance Graphics, you'll feel the heavy weight of creative freedom land squarely on your shoulders. What makes a good presentation good? What if you get up in front of the group and meet with vacant stares or pulled-down eyebrows? How much creativity is too much?

Luckily, you can work within the safe confines of Freelance Graphics and never test the outer limits of acceptability. Real designers put the Smart-Masters together—you can trust them with your titles and charts and count on the fact that they won't steer you wrong. You can even let the SmartMasters tell you what to put where—a title page, a bullet list, a graph, another bullet list—and you'll never have to rely on your own shaky initiative.

If you ever feel a little adventurous and want to wander out from under Freelance's protective wing, a little common sense will help you put together a good—and original—presentation. As you're putting your presentation together, follow these three guidelines:

- Consider your audience.
- Consider the tone of your presentation.
- Consider your tools for presentation.

The following sections take a closer look at each of these considerations and provide you with some questions to examine for your individual projects.

Considering the Audience

Are you going up before a board of directors for a large firm? A small non-profit organization? Stockholders? Advertising executives?

The audience for your presentation will have a lot to do with the content and tone of your work. You won't be presenting a lighthearted romp about mismanagement of office funds to a group of high-level managers; similarly, you won't spend a large amount of time delving seriously into financial matters with managers more concerned with employee productivity.

The audience will also have some bearing on the *type* of presentation you create. If you're teaching a class, title and bullet charts may help reinforce your points better than a series of complex charts. If you are explaining sales trends and hope to motivate a roomful of salespeople, colorful attention-grabbing charts may convey in a glance what would take quite a bit longer verbally.

Before you begin creating your presentation, think about the best way to reach your audience. And remember, once you've reached them, you need to hold their attention.

Considering the Tone

The tone of your presentation is its personality. After you've thought about the audience type and what kind of presentation they might be expecting to see, think about the way you'll present the information. Is the meeting hurried, with only a few moments allotted to each presenter? Or do you have all kinds of time to fill, with plenty left over for questions? These answers will affect whether your presentation must be quick and to-the-point or more relaxed in style and content.

Your company's corporate identity is important. Logos run rampant throughout presentations, and bulleted lists highlighting goals and productivity requirements are a staple. Freelance Graphics gives you the option of adding some "serious" graphics. In other words, you can add, as part of a background, a picture of the world, Canadian and U.S. flags, or other symbols that add a sense of importance to your work. If you want to turn down the intensity a few notches, Freelance also provides many artsy SmartMasters that use geometric shapes and sharp color to give your presentation a more modern, yet relaxed, look.

Remember, the information you are trying to communicate is the most important part of your presentation. Try to resist the temptation to let the special effects Freelance offers overrun the statement you're trying to make.

Considering the Tools

In preparing a typical presentation, we usually find ourselves stuck in comparison mode: one column on the legal pad shows the dream presentation, while the other side shows what's really possible given the limited tools we have at our disposal. Fortunately, Freelance Graphics can solve all the software-related problems. Unfortunately, though, we still have to deal with hardware limitations.

As you create your presentation, daydream a little about how you envision it coming off. Will you be standing before a large crowd? Sitting at a boardroom table? Will you have access to a large-screen monitor (or to a computer at all)? Will you be confined to a slide- or overhead projector?

Think about the tools you'll have for making your presentation and how effective those tools will be, given the type of audience you're addressing. If you are speaking to a large crowd and have only a small-screen monitor on which to display graphs, you will need either to arm-wrestle the AV department for the slide projector and get your boss to pay for slide production, or you'll have to make do with the small screen and print handouts for the audience. (Either way, giving the audience something to take with them—in the form of notes or printed graphs—is good for reinforcing your message.)

The Three C's: Continuity, Conciseness, and Creativity

When you get down to the nitty-gritty of on-screen composition, having a few simple design ideas in mind will help you achieve your goal of producing an informative and successful presentation.

Here's something that sounds like it's straight out of a fourth-grade English class, but it can help keep you on track as you prepare your presentation: The three C's—continuity, conciseness, and creativity—can help you make sure your presentation hangs together, presents your message clearly, and has a spark or two that leaves your audience with the feeling they've seen a more-than-the-ordinary presentation.

Continuity is important for helping readers get the "big picture." Suppose, for example, that your presentation is about new products your toy company is manufacturing for next Christmas. The overall tone is one of excitement and anticipation (after all, your company has done very well in the past fiscal year) and you've been able to put quite a bit of money into research and development to create some new, top-of-the-line toys. Hold on to that enthusiasm—it should carry through your entire presentation. Having four pages about exciting new products, and then throwing in a page showing a drop-off in last year's balloon sales, will throw a wrench into the pattern of your presentation and confuse viewers.

Continuity in tone is often difficult to achieve, especially when you've got both good and bad news to relate to your audience. (It's always better to show the bad stuff first, so the good news washes the bad taste off the palette.)

Visual continuity, on the other hand, is much easier to accomplish. Your presentation will "stick together" with the help of a series of design elements you repeat from page to page or from section to section. Simple items that add visual continuity to your presentations include:

- Company logo
- Company name
- Department name
- Date information
- Graphic design elements, such as boxes, curves, splashes of color, or other items that appear throughout the presentation.

Suppose, for example, that you are creating a presentation that highlights the two best-selling products in your insurance agency. One, a life insurance policy, has been selling well to individuals and business owners. The other, a health policy, targets businesses and has seen a whopping increase in the last twelve months. For each of these products, you want to show three charts: one for last year's sales, one for this year's sales, and one that shows projected sales for the next twelve months.

A presentation without visual continuity might use a different graph type for each chart, leaving viewers struggling to understand what you're talking about, and unable to figure out why you've chosen the charts you did. A visually continuous presentation, on the other hand, would parallel the two products and show, perhaps, a bar chart for each product showing last year's sales, a line chart for both showing this year's sales, and an area chart for next year's sales. Continuity—which comes from using the same type of chart to show the same period of time for each product—helps viewers quickly identify what you're trying to say. Continuity of information will also help your audience retain more of what you've said.

In this chapter, we've covered a lot of ground. First, you learned about the benefits Freelance Graphics for Windows has to offer, and you found out where you—as a new Freelance user—fit into the family of presentation graphics users worldwide. You also learned about many of the important elements you'll be working with as you begin your hands-on experience with Freelance Graphics. Finally, you learned a few pointers that may help as you begin creating your own presentations.

In the next chapter, you'll work through a basic Windows primer and get up and running with Freelance Graphics for Windows.

T W O

Getting Started
with Freelance
Graphics

$fast$ TRACK

● **You can get help at any point in Freelance Graphics**   **41**

by using one of the following methods:

• Press F1 to display context-sensitive help

• Open the Help menu to choose from among the many different help options

• Click on the Help button (which resembles a question mark) to display any available help for the operation you're performing.

● **To exit Freelance Graphics,**   **47**

you can either open the File menu and choose the Exit command, or you can double-click on the control box in the upper left corner of the window.

BECAUSE Freelance Graphics for Windows operates within Windows—that is, you must first start Windows before you can start Freelance Graphics—the first section in this chapter deals with basic Window operations. If you've already had some experience using Windows and feel pretty comfortable with the various procedures for working with the program, you may want to skip ahead to the "Starting Freelance Graphics for Windows" section. If you have never used Windows before or your skills are a little rusty, taking a few minutes now to scan over some of the basics will help you reduce your learning curve in Freelance Graphics.

A Windows Review

As you undoubtedly know, Microsoft Windows is an incredibly popular program—more of an operating environment, really—that allows users to interact with their programs in a manner that is much more comfortable and intuitive than DOS. Rather than having to enter lengthy command lines at an unfriendly DOS prompt, you can use Windows to start applications, work with files, and perform other management tasks with the simple click of a mouse button—something previously available only to Macintosh users.

Windows also offers an umbrella of compatibility for all programs written for that environment. This means that each program (such as Freelance Graphics and Lotus 1-2-3 for Windows) has the same look and feel, as well as similar menus and screen structures.

This section introduces you to some of the basic tasks you'll work with in Microsoft Windows, things that you will be able to use with Freelance Graphics. Specifically, you'll learn the following things:

- Starting Windows

- Understanding the Windows screen

- Using the Keyboard and the Mouse in Windows

- Opening and closing windows

- Resizing windows

- Starting programs from within Windows

- Exiting Windows

Several different versions of Microsoft Windows have been made available to users since the first copy appeared many years ago. The most current version is Windows 3.1, which added some additional features over 3.0 (including multimedia support, which is used by Freelance Graphics).

Here's a quick treatment of procedures you'll often use in both Microsoft Windows and in programs like Freelance Graphics for Windows that run within that environment:

Starting Windows. Starting at the root directory (if you aren't there, type *cd* and press Enter), type *win*, and press Enter. The Windows opening screen, and then the Program Manager, appear (see Figure 2.1).

The Program Manager. The Program Manager helps you manage the programs you run from within Microsoft Windows (that shouldn't come as much of a surprise). Each of the small icons in the Program Manager is a *group window icon*. Inside these icons are the programs you launch from the Program Manager.

FIGURE 2.1

The Microsoft
Windows Program
Manager

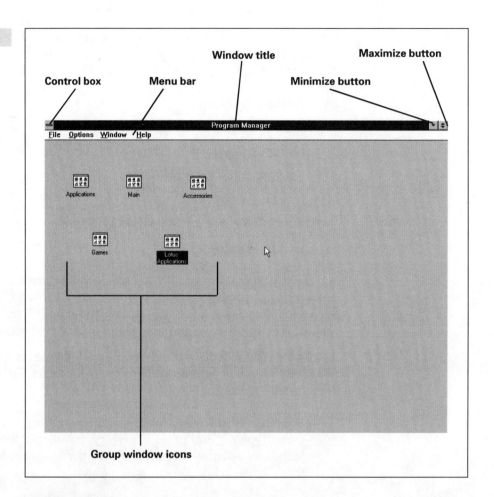

TIP

You can exit Windows quickly by double-clicking on the control box (the small square box in the upper-left corner of the Program Manager) or by pressing Alt-F then X.

Minimizing and maximizing windows. In the upper-right corner of the Program Manager, are two buttons. Click the minimize button (the triangle pointing down) to reduce a window to an icon; click the maximize button (the triangle pointing up) to enlarge a window to its fullest size.

Using the keyboard. Windows provides shortcut keys and key combinations for people who prefer to use the keyboard instead of the mouse. For most operations, you will probably use a combination of keyboard and mouse methods. Table 2.1 lists important keys and key combinations you may use in Windows.

Using the mouse. Windows brought to the PC generation the intuitive point-and-click method of opening menus and selecting commands—something generally associated with the Macintosh world. Table 2.2 lists important mouse operations.

Opening a group window. Position the mouse pointer on the icon you want to open and double-click the mouse button. Figure 2.2 shows the Lotus Application window after the icon has been double-clicked.

Resizing a window. Position the mouse on the border of the window you want to resize. When the pointer changes to a double-headed arrow, press the mouse button and drag the border in the direction you want to resize. When the window is the size you want, release the mouse button.

TABLE 2.1: Important Windows keystrokes

TO PERFORM THIS TASK	PRESS THIS:
To highlight a different icon in the Program Manager	Ctrl-Tab or Ctrl-F6
To open a highlighted group window icon	Enter
To highlight a different program icon in an open group window	← or →
To close an open group window	Ctrl-F4
To open a menu on the menu bar	Alt+ underlined letter

TABLE 2.2: Important mouse operations

TERM	DEFINITION
Point	Move the mouse so that the on-screen pointer is positioned on the item to which you're pointing
Click	Press and release the left mouse button once quickly
Double-click	Press and release the left mouse button twice quickly
Drag	Press and hold down the left mouse button while moving the mouse in the appropriate direction

FIGURE 2.2

The Lotus Applications group window icon

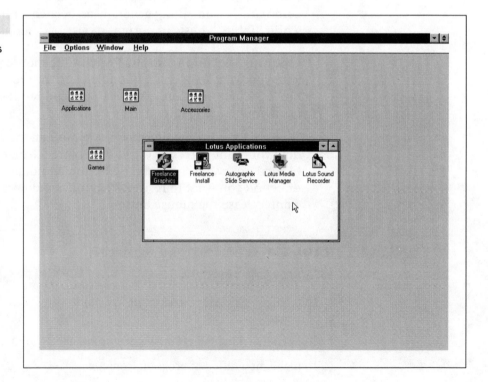

Starting a program. To start a program, first open the group window icon that contains the program. Then double-click on the program icon.

N O T E

When you exit the application program later, you will be returned to the point in Windows where you initially launched the program.

Quitting an application. You can close windows by pressing Ctrl-F4 or by double-clicking on the control box in the upper-left corner. The window is then returned to a group window icon.

Exiting Windows. To exit Windows, open the Program Manager's File menu and choose the Exit command, double-click on the control box in the upper-left corner of the window, or press Alt-F4.

Now that you've been through a basic review of Windows operations, you're ready to try your hand at some basic Freelance tasks.

Starting Freelance Graphics

In the previous section, you learned to open and start Windows applications. Freelance Graphics for Windows is one of those applications. From this point on, we assume that you've already installed Freelance Graphics for Windows on your hard disk. If you *haven't* installed the program, or if you're still wondering whether you have the right hardware and software required to run Freelance, consult Appendix A in the back of this book. Then, when you're ready to get started, come back and join us....

To start Freelance Graphics for Windows, you must first open the Lotus Applications group window by double-clicking on it. Inside the group window are several icons: Freelance Graphics, Freelance Install, Autographix Slide Service, Lotus Media Manager, and Lotus Sound Recorder (see Figure 2.3).

You can start Freelance Graphics for Windows two different ways:

- Position the mouse pointer on the Freelance Graphics icon and double-click the mouse button

- Use the arrow keys to highlight the Freelance Graphics icon (if it isn't already highlighted) and press Enter.

After a moment, the Freelance Graphics for Windows Version 2.0 title screen appears (it's really colorful, too), then disappears and is replaced

FIGURE 2.3

Icons in the Lotus Applications window

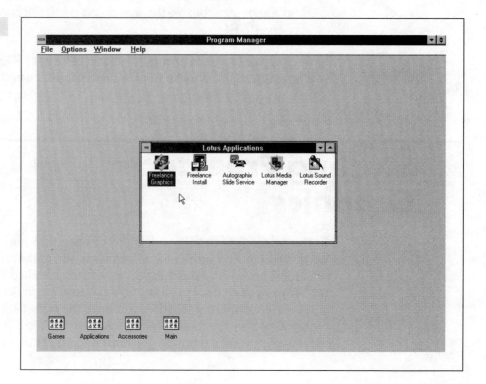

with the Freelance Graphics opening screen. The opening screen asks you whether you want to create a new presentation, work on an existing presentation, or work through the QuickStart tutorial (see Figure 2.4).

NOTE If this is the first time you've started Freelance Graphics for Windows 2.0, you are immediately greeted by the QuickStart Tutorial (the topic of the next section). In subsequent launchings, you'll see the opening screen (from which you will again have the option of choosing the QuickStart).

Later in this chapter, you learn how to find your way around the Freelance Graphics work screen. The following sections show you the wealth of help

FIGURE 2.4

The Freelance Graphics opening screen

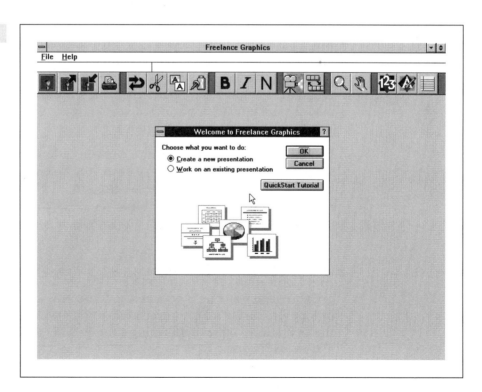

resources Lotus has built into the Freelance Graphics program—something nice to know anytime you're wandering into previously unexplored territory.

Exploring Your Help Resources

As you learned in Chapter 1, Lotus Development Corporation puts a higher priority on user support than probably anyone else in the industry. Freelance Graphics for Windows, Version 2.0, was created in direct response to users' suggestions for improvement. Great care was taken to ensure that the entire process of creating a presentation was as simple—and as fun—as work can ever be.

But try as any manufacturer might, the learning curve involved in mastering a new product can never be completely erased. We still need to discover for ourselves how to select tools, find our way around in the program, open files, save files, manipulate data, and so on. Sure, we can read the documentation (do you know anyone who really does?), but we won't really learn anything until we try it ourselves.

For this reason, Lotus built into Version 2.0 additional enhanced user support features. Version 1.0 had one of the first interactive tutorials available in a presentation graphics program. But Version 2.0 takes the process even further by giving the user more control over the tutorial process. Additionally, you can take a QuickStart tutorial refresher course at any time by simply selecting the tutorial from the Help menu (or by clicking the QuickStart Tutorial button displayed in the opening screen).

And Lotus didn't stop with a state-of-the-art, animated tutorial. A comprehensive, on-line help system brings aid any time you press F1. In addition, Version 2.0's Tip buttons enable you to get extra information about the operation you're performing—things like selecting and formatting text in text boxes.

In this section, you'll individually look at each of the following help resources:

- The QuickStart Tutorial
- The help system
- Tip buttons

A Quick Look at the QuickStart

When you finish installing Freelance Graphics for Windows, you'll be able to take a three-minute tour of Freelance features. This is *not* the tutorial. Instead, it's a quick-look presentation (complete with animation), that highlights some of Freelance Graphics' special features.

When the tour is over, Freelance displays a screen giving you the choice of working through several different tutorial lessons. The QuickStart, in its entirety, takes about thirty minutes and shows you the basics of plugging in text, using the Outliner, choosing chart types, and fine-tuning presentations.

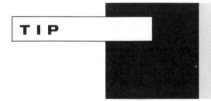

TIP

Remember: if you don't want to take the QuickStart tutorial when you start the program for the first time, you can go through it later by selecting *QuickStart Tutorial* from the Help menu.

The QuickStart begins with a screen offering you six choices:

- Take a Quick Tour
- Create a Title Page and a Bulleted List
- Create a Chart

- Manage Your Presentation
- Use the Outliner
- Create a Table

Figure 2.5 shows the opening screen of the QuickStart.

If you have the time, work through all the lessons. Otherwise, select only those that apply to your current level of expertise. Each lesson is structured in two parts: in the first part, you watch while Freelance Graphics goes through the paces of that particular lesson. In the second part, Freelance Graphics prompts you to perform the tasks yourself.

TIP   You can exit the tutorial at any time by selecting Quit from the QuickStart menu bar.

FIGURE 2.5

The opening screen of the QuickStart

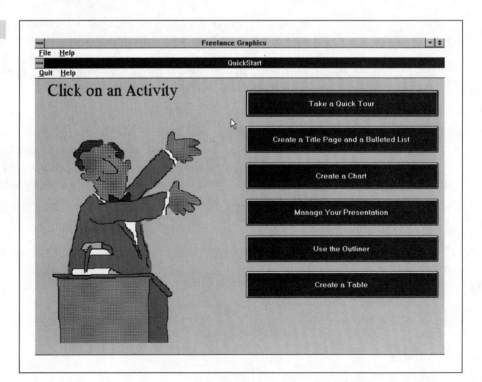

Getting Help

More than just a list of commands and necessary keystrokes, the Freelance help system brings help to you in several different forms. When you're working on a project and are wondering how to use a particular option, press F1 to get an answer. When you are at a loss for your next step in a presentation, you can turn to the Help menu for a list of possible help forums. Figure 2.6 shows the contents of the Help menu. Table 2.3 lists the various help resources in the Help menu and provides a brief description of each.

Of all the help options available in the Help menu, you'll probably start with the Help *Index* or *How Do I?* options. Selecting Index brings up a traditional Windows help screen with the menu bar at the top (see Figure 2.7). Beneath the menu bar are buttons you'll use to navigate through the help system. The Index lists eight different categories of help (each appearing on your screen, if you're using a color monitor, as light green).

FIGURE 2.6

The Help menu options

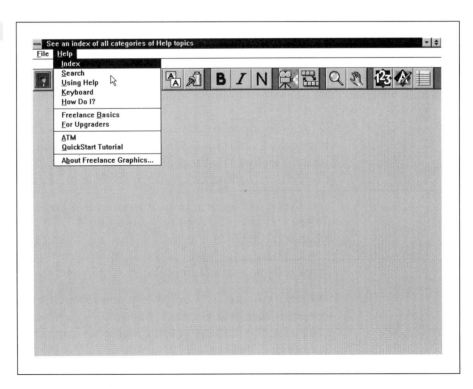

TABLE 2.3: Resources on the Help Menu

OPTION	DESCRIPTION
Index	Displays the main categories of the help system
Search	Lets you specify a topic for which to search
Using Help	Provides you with information on how to use Freelance's help system
Keyboard	Information for keyboard users on important keystrokes to remember
How Do I?	Displays a comprehensive list of specific tasks you perform in Freelance Graphics
Freelance Basics	Introduces elementary operations
For Upgraders	Tells you what's new in the latest version of Freelance Graphics
ATM	Offers help in using Adobe Type Manager
QuickStart Tutorial	Starts the QuickStart
About Freelance Graphics	Displays the current version number

When you move the mouse pointer over one of the categories, the arrow changes to a hand pointer. This means you can click on the category to move directly to that topic. When you are ready to exit the Index, double-click on the control box or open the File menu and choose Exit.

Another amazing help resource is awaiting you in the How Do I? option. When you select this option, you'll find 37 different tasks arranged in alphabetical order. Better than an on-line tutorial, this help resource allows you to go right to the process you need to learn and find out the necessary steps with no extra fanfare. Figure 2.8 shows the How Do I? resource.

Whether you use Help only when you're stuck, or you plan to peruse each option before you get started, you'll have no trouble finding your way around in the help system of Freelance Graphics.

FIGURE 2.7

The Help Index

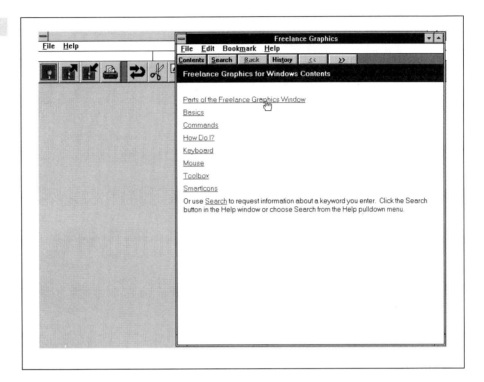

You can get on-line help by using three different methods:

• Press F1

• Press Alt-H

• Click the ? button

Using Tips Buttons

Another nifty feature Lotus built in for user support is Version 2.0's Tips buttons. These buttons appear at strategically placed points in the program—right where you need them most—to give you additional information about a specific action you're performing. For example, when you are adding text to a bullet list chart, a Tips button appears in the text block. When you click on the button, extra information about adding bullets is provided (see Figure 2.9).

FIGURE 2.8

The How Do I? Help resource

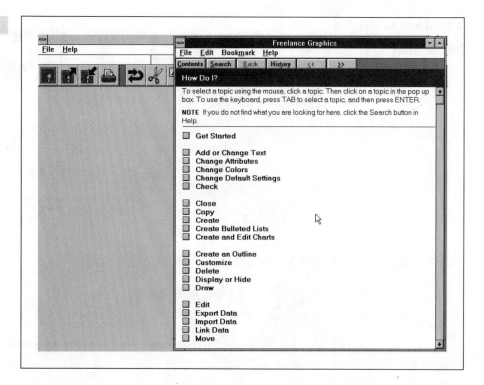

After you review the information provided by the Tips button, click OK to return to the application.

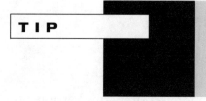

TIP

The Text Tips box includes both a control box and a help box (the help box is marked by ?). You can close the tips box by double-clicking the control box, pressing Enter, Escape, or Spacebar.

As you can see, when you're working in Freelance Graphics for Windows, you're never alone—help is always nearby. The next section introduces you to the basics of the Freelance Graphics screen.

FIGURE 2.9

Text tips provided by
the Tips button

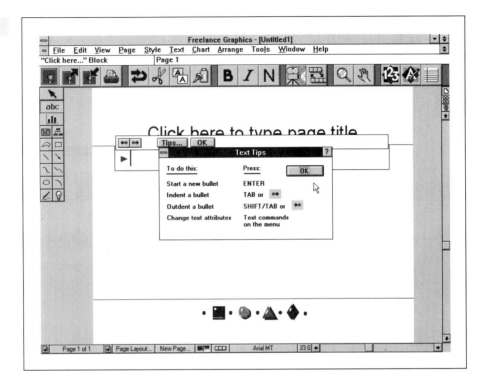

Understanding the Screen Area

Another neat thing about Freelance Graphics is that virtually everything you need is on-screen in front of you at all times. With a wide range of tools, SmartIcons, menus, and view buttons, you can control everything from page layout to type style. This section introduces you to the screen area of Freelance Graphics.

Figure 2.10 shows a typical Freelance screen. The white area in the center of the screen is the page area—in this case, displayed in current page view.

At the top of the screen are the familiar title bar, close box, and Minimize and Maximize buttons that are common to all Windows Applications. Below the title bar, you see the menu bar which contains several more menus than the menu bar in the Program Manager. The Freelance

FIGURE 2.10

A typical Freelance
Graphics screen

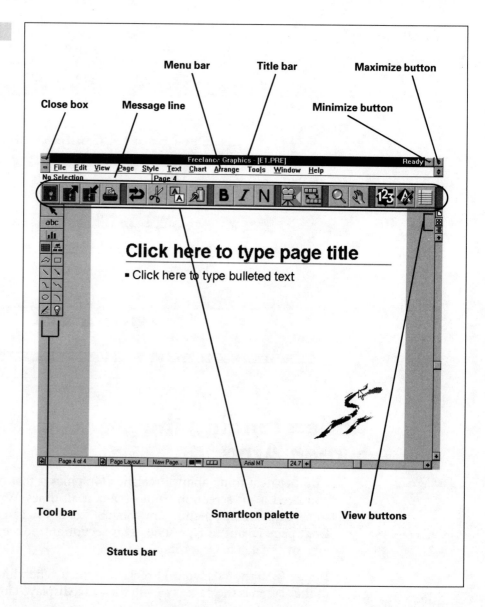

Graphics menu bar contains 11 different menus: File, Edit, View, Page,
Style, Text, Chart, Arrange, Tools, Window, and Help.

Underneath the menu bar, a *message line* tells you what operation you're currently performing (in the figure, this line says No Selection) and shows the number of the current page. The next line contains the *SmartIcon palette*, stretched all the way across the screen. SmartIcons are buttons that enable you to carry out commands you use often without ever having to open a menu. Freelance Graphics contains over 100 different Smart-Icons (only a portion of which are displayed on the screen at one time). As your experience with Freelance Graphics grows, you may want to change some of the SmartIcons shown in the palette or create some of your own. See Chapter 3 for more information on SmartIcons.

Along the left side of the screen, you see the Freelance Graphics *toolbox*. These tools give you everything you need in order to draw and edit objects in your Freelance presentations. Version 2.0 includes a new freehand tool and a tool that allows you to display and hide a ruler.

On the right side of the work area, at the top of the vertical scroll bar, you see three small buttons. These are known as *view buttons*. The top button is the current view. (This button looks as though it has been pressed.) The second button takes you into Page Sorter view, in which all the pages in your document are shown, in thumbnail size, in the work area. The final button takes you into the Outliner—the special text organizational feature in Freelance Graphics that allows you to outline and easily work with text blocks.

Finally, at the bottom of the screen, is the *status bar*. The far-left side of the status bar displays the current page number. When you click on any of the other settings in the bar—Page Layout, New Page, the color palette, the SmartIcon display boxes, the selected font (Arial MT), or font size (29.6)—popup boxes appear, allowing you to choose a different setting.

Exiting Freelance Graphics

Earlier in this chapter, you learned how to start Freelance Graphics for Windows. Now you need to know how to get out. When you are ready to exit the program, first make sure you've saved your file (you'll find out how to do this in Chapter 3). Then follow these steps:

1. Open the File menu by clicking on the menu name or by pressing Alt-F.

2. Highlight the Exit option and press Enter or click on the option. After a moment, you are returned to the Lotus Application group window from which you first started the program.

In this chapter, you learned quite a bit about Microsoft Windows—the operating environment in which you run Freelance Graphics for Windows—and about Freelance itself. We started off with a Windows primer that helped you familiarize yourself with such basic Windows operations as opening, resizing, and working with windows. You learned some of the methods for using both the keyboard and the mouse—techniques that will come in handy as you work with Freelance Graphics.

You learned to start Freelance Graphics for Windows as well as how to access and find your way around the Freelance help system. Remember, just in case you need a refresher course, the QuickStart Tutorial is always nearby.

In the next chapter, we pick up the pace a little. You'll learn all the basic steps involved in creating a simple presentation, from starting out to working with SmartMasters to saving and printing your work.

THREE

A Freelance
Graphics Primer

fast **TRACK**

● **To select a SmartMaster,**

display the Choose a Look for Your Presentation by clicking the Begin a new presentation option in the Welcome to Freelance Graphics screen. Next, highlight the name of the Smart-Master file you want to use. (As you highlight different files, the design of the selected SmartMaster is displayed in the bottom portion of the screen.) After you've highlighted the SmartMaster you want, click OK.

● **To choose a page layout,**

display the Page Layout dialog box by first selecting a Smart-Master set or by clicking on the New Page button in the middle of the status bar (located at the bottom of the screen). Review the different page layouts available and make your selection by clicking on the page layout type to highlight it and then clicking OK to accept your selection.

● **To add and remove SmartIcons,**

first open the Tools menu and select the SmartIcons command. The SmartIcons dialog box appears. The left side shows all the available icons. The center shows the SmartIcons used by default on the Freelance Graphics screen. You can save an icon set you create, delete an icon set, edit individual icons, or change the size of an icon by dragging the icons you want to the center column and then clicking the appropriate buttons on the right side of the dialog box. When you're finished, click OK or press Enter.

● **To add text,**   **73**

> simply click on the text box (One of the "Click here" prompts) when you've decided where the text should go. A text box appears. Type the information you want to include. Freelance automatically places the text in the text font, style, size, and color of the original prompt used in the SmartMaster. When you're through entering text, click the OK.

● **To add a symbol,**   **78**

> first click on the Click here to add symbol prompt. The Add Symbol to Page dialog box appears. Choose the symbol file you want (the symbols are displayed in the bottom portion of the box). In the preview box, click on the symbol you want to use. (Depending on the number of symbols in the symbol box, you may need to scroll through the symbols in order to see all the available choices.) Click on the symbol you want; then click OK.

IN the previous chapter, you were introduced to Windows basics and learned how to start and exit Freelance Graphics for Windows. This chapter takes you through the process of creating a basic presentation—from startup to printing.

Bear in mind that this chapter is provided as a kind of fast-track method of learning basic Freelance commands. You won't find lengthy examples or explanations of various features here. Instead, we show you the easiest way to get up and running quickly. In later chapters, you'll find full discussions of the various tasks with all their options.

As you learned in Chapter 2, starting Freelance Graphics is as simple as starting Windows itself. If you haven't already done so, start Freelance Graphics now by double-clicking on the Lotus Applications group window icon in the Program Manager screen. Then double-click on the Freelance Graphics icon.

After a moment, you see the introductory screen, followed by the Freelance work area displaying the Welcome to Freelance Graphics dialog box (see Figure 3.1). This dialog box gives you two different options: to begin a new presentation or to work with an existing presentation. The first option, Create a new presentation, is selected. For now, click OK.

Working with SmartMasters

We learn most things in life by imitation. If we see an office design that appeals to us, we try to design our office in a similar way. If we run across an advertising gimmick that has been particularly successful, we try to

FIGURE 3.1

The Welcome to
Freelance Graphics
dialog box

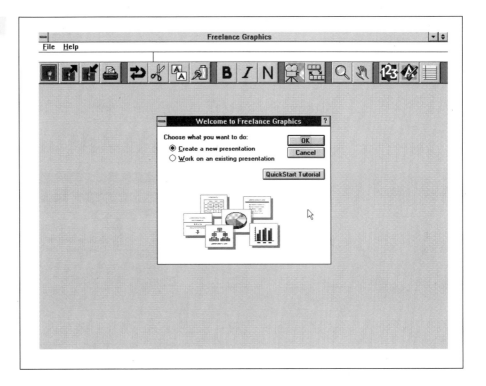

come up with a similar one of our own. Imitation can be a great teacher, showing how others have already done—and been successful at—what you're trying to do.

The process of learning SmartMasters is based on imitation, making the task of creating your own presentations simple and non-threatening. Freelance Graphics provides you with over 65 predesigned presentations—all you have to do is plug in your own text and graphics. You benefit from the expertise of the SmartMaster designers and, in the process, learn to create your own effective presentations.

After you click OK in the Welcome to Freelance Graphics box, the Choose a Look for Your Presentation dialog box appears (see Figure 3.2). It is on this screen that you will choose the SmartMaster for your presentation.

FIGURE 3.2

The Choose a Look for Your Presentation dialog box

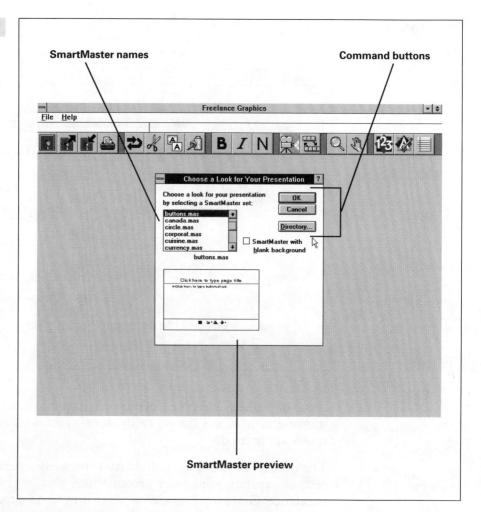

Choosing a SmartMaster

The Choose a Look for Your Presentation dialog box provides you with your options for selecting the SmartMaster you want to work with. In the upper left corner of the box, you see a list box showing several different file names (all ending with the extension *mas*). These are the SmartMaster files you can choose. One of these files, *buttons.mas,* is already highlighted.

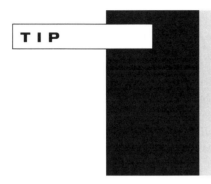

TIP

After you get familiar with Freelance Graphics, you may work with a certain SmartMaster more than others. To select that SmartMaster quickly, without scrolling through the displayed list, simply type the first character of the SmartMaster you want (for example, to select *sketch.mas*, type S). The highlight automatically moves to the first SmartMaster beginning with the character you specified.

In the box beneath the list box, you see a small graphical representation of the highlighted SmartMaster in the above list. This is a preview box. To take a look at some of the different SmartMasters, follow these steps:

1. Select *cuisine.mas* by positioning the mouse pointer on the selection and clicking the left mouse button. The preview area shows a different SmartMaster with a blue background and yellow and white text.

2. Click four times on the down arrow symbols at the bottom of the scroll bar. Our selection, *cuisine.mas,* scrolls up to the top of the list box.

3. Click on *deco.mas.* The preview again changes to reflect the new selection.

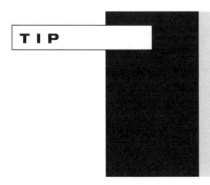

TIP

When the highlighted SmartMaster is shown at the top of the list box, you can scroll through each of the SmartMasters provided by clicking continuously the down-arrow symbol (called the *scroll arrow*) at the bottom of the scroll bar. Each time you click the scroll bar, the highlight moves to the next SmartMaster and the preview changes to display the highlighted file.

The rest of the examples in this chapter are built upon the *sketch.mas* SmartMaster. If you want to follow along with the examples shown here, select *sketch.mas* by clicking on the file name.

When you've chosen the SmartMaster you want, click the OK button. (If you prefer, you can double-click on the SmartMaster name.) After you click OK, the Wait message is displayed in the title bar of the window (right beside the minimize button). A small hourglass cursor appears on-screen, alerting you that Freelance Graphics is working. After a few moments, the Choose Page Layout dialog box appears (see Figure 3.3).

FIGURE 3.3

The Choose Page
Layout dialog box

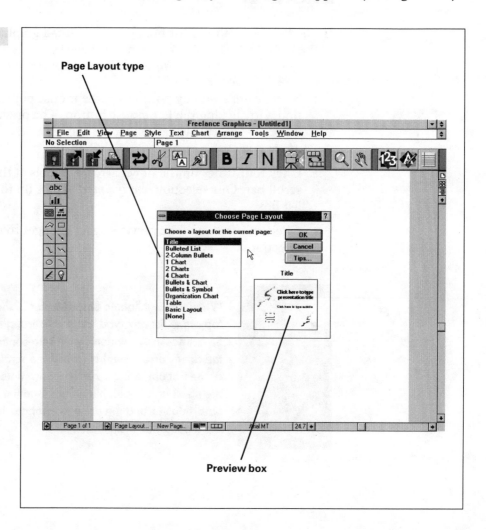

Page Layout type

Preview box

Choosing a Page Layout

As you might expect, the Choose Page Layout dialog box gives you the choice of selecting the type of page you want to create. There are 11 different page layouts listed. Table 3.1 describes the different layouts shown in the Choose Page Layout box.

You can scroll through the various page layouts until you find the one you want (simply click on your choice—there is no scroll bar). When you've got the one you want (for this example, let's choose Title), click the OK button in the upper right corner of the box or double-click on the layout name.

TABLE 3.1: Page layout types

LAYOUT	DESCRIPTION
Title	Used as first page of your presentation; shows large type for title and medium type for subtitle
Bulleted List	Allows you to enter a heading and lines of text for bulleted items
2-Column Bullets	Lets you enter a heading and two columns of bulleted text
1 Chart	Provides a heading and an outline for a chart you create
2 Charts	Provides a heading and outlines for two half-page charts
4 Charts	Shows a heading and space for four charts
Bullets & Chart	Allows you to enter a heading, a half-page chart, and bulleted text
Bullets & Symbol	Similar to Bullets & Chart. Leaves space for a heading, a symbol, and bulleted text
Organization Chart	Leaves space for a heading and a large chart
Table	Leaves space for a title and tabular information
Basic Layout	Provides a title (the rest is up to you)
[None]	Displays a blank page

After a moment, Freelance Graphics displays in full-screen display the page layout you've chosen. As you can see in Figure 3.4, the screen area looks different than it did just a minute ago; now a number of different menus appear in the menu bar (before you selected the SmartMaster, only the File and Help menus were displayed). Additionally, a series of pictures—called SmartIcons—now stretch across the top of the work area.

TIP   If you need to review the different elements of the Freelance Graphics work area, see "Understanding the Screen Area" in Chapter 2.

The next section introduces you to the menus that appear after you've started working with a SmartMaster.

FIGURE 3.4

The work area after you've chosen a SmartMaster

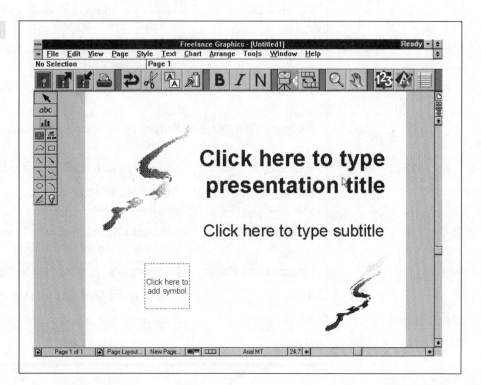

Exploring Freelance Graphics Menus

As Figure 3.4 shows, new menus appear after you've selected the Smart-Master with which you're going to work. Freelance Graphics uses 11 different menus to house the commands you'll work with throughout your Freelance experience. Remember, also, that the SmartIcons shown just below the menu bar represent commands that are also included in the menus. The SmartIcons let you select a command with a simple click of the mouse. You will probably use the SmartIcons to bypass menu operations as you become more proficient with Freelance Graphics.

It's good to start with a basic understanding of the menus, however. In this section, you'll learn

- How to open the Freelance menus

- What each of the menus do

- To select options and close menus

Opening and Closing Menus

Because Freelance is a Windows application, the procedures for opening menus, selecting commands, and scrolling through the display work just like those of any other Windows application. When you want to open a Freelance Graphics menu, choose one of these two methods:

- Position the mouse on the name of the menu you want to open (such as File) and click the mouse button

- Press and hold the Alt key while pressing the underlined letter in the menu name you want (which would be F for File)

A menu opens on the screen (see Figure 3.5). As you'll notice from the figure, there are several interesting things about this menu. Most of the commands are dark, but one (Network Options) is dimmed. While you can select any of the darkened commands, the dimmed ones are disabled and unavailable. Additionally, some of the commands, such as Open, are followed by an ellipsis (...). This ellipsis tells you that when you select the command, a dialog box will be displayed so you can enter more information. A final feature on the menu is the placement of shortcut keys to the right of the command. For example, the Save command shows Ctrl+S in the right side of the menu. This means that you can choose the Save command any time you are working in Freelance by pressing Ctrl and S at the same time.

TIP

When you already have a menu open, you can easily display a different one by pressing the right-arrow key to move to the menu you want. Each time you press the right-arrow key, the next menu to the right is displayed. Likewise, whenever you press the left-arrow key, the menu to the left is opened.

FIGURE 3.5

Opening a menu

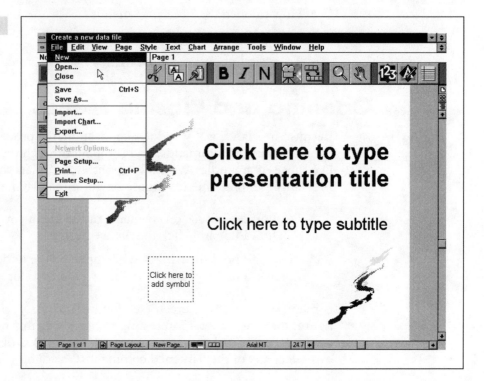

When you select a command (by highlighting it and pressing Enter or by clicking on it), the menu closes automatically and you are either returned to the work area or a dialog box is displayed (depending on the type of command you selected).

To close a menu without selecting a command, use one of these methods:

- Move the mouse off the menu area and click the mouse button
- Press Esc.

Now that you know how to open and close menus, you may want to take a few minutes to familiarize yourself with the placement of the commands in Freelance's menus. The following section provides an overview of the different commands on each menu.

Understanding Freelance Graphics Menus

As mentioned above, the work area of Freelance includes 11 different menus, each of which is organized to help you take care of a certain category of Freelance operations. The menus are as follows:

MENU	DESCRIPTION
File	Includes commands for working with new and existing files. Also allows you to import and export files, print presentations, and control page and printer settings. Additionally, contains the Exit command you use to leave Freelance Graphics.
Edit	Houses the Undo command (which cancels the last operation you performed). Also allows you to cut, copy, paste, and clear items by using the clipboard. From the Edit menu, you can set up links for charts, insert new objects, and edit presentation pages and page layouts.

MENU	DESCRIPTION
View	Allows you to select the different views in which you can display Freelance Graphics. Specifically, you can display full page view, zoom in or out, redraw the screen, select units of measurement, choose display preferences, move to Page Sorter or Outliner view, or access Screen Show commands.
Page	Enables you to add pages, duplicate pages, choose a different page layout, remove links, change page backgrounds, auto-build pages, and add speaker notes to your pages.
Style	Includes commands that affect the style of the object you're manipulating. For example, you can choose default attributes, different SmartMasters, and color and black-and-white palettes. You can also edit your chosen color palette by using the Edit Palette command on the Style menu.
Text	Houses commands you'll use to edit text, select fonts, choose bullet styles, add text styles (**bold**, *italic*, <u>underline</u>, ~~strikeout~~), assign paragraph styles, add a frame, and create curved text.
Chart	Contains commands for selecting, editing, and changing the attributes of charts you include in your presentations. Allows you to add numerous chart options, such as legends, notes, headings, titles, labels, grids, and frames. Additionally, you can control various type settings and placement from the Chart menu.

MENU	DESCRIPTION
Arrange	Provides you with commands for arranging objects in your presentation. Specifically, lets you group and ungroup objects, control layering of objects, specify object spacing, rotate or flip objects, change to points mode (in which you can edit an object), convert objects to different shapes, or crop images.
Tools	Includes commands for starting special tool utilities included with Freelance Graphics. Specifically, you can run the spelling checker, change the SmartIcons displayed, add objects you've created to a symbol library, and change display options.
Window	Provides you with options for changing the look of your screen. Tile displays windows one at a time with no overlapping, while Cascade displays windows in overlapping style. Additionally, this menu shows you the names of any open presentation files.
Help	Includes commands for getting you out of tight places in Freelance Graphics. You can look through the Help index, take the QuickStart tutorial, or choose several other help resources. (For more about getting help, see Chapter 2.)

As you get more comfortable with Freelance Graphics for Windows, you'll find that the process of finding the commands you want comes much quicker. At first, because of the number of menus and the variety of commands on each menu, it's easy to forget where a specific command appears. The next section teaches you the basics of working with dialog boxes.

Working with Dialog Boxes

A feature you've already seen in Freelance Graphics is the dialog box. A *dialog box* is a pop-up window that appears in the middle of your screen, allowing you to enter additional information or select settings. As mentioned in the last section, you can tell which commands display a dialog box because those commands are followed by an ellipsis. Figure 3.6 shows the dialog box that is displayed when you choose the Save As command in the File menu.

At the top of the dialog box, you see the familiar title bar (showing Save As), as well as the close box on the left and the help button (?) on the right. Inside the box, you see several different kinds of settings. The *File name:* box is a text box. (The *File information:* line, at the bottom of the box, is another example.) You can type the name of the file you want by positioning the mouse pointer in the box (currently showing *.pre*) and then typing the file you want. The large rectangular area beneath the text box (which is blank now) will eventually list all the available presentation files in your current directory. The middle box, under *Directories:,* allows you to choose the directory in which you want to work by clicking on the appropriate icon.

On the far right side of the box, you see two command buttons: OK and Cancel. These buttons are used in most dialog boxes throughout all Windows applications. After you've entered all your settings, return to the work area and save the settings by clicking OK (or by pressing Enter). If you want to abandon the changes you've made in the dialog box, click Cancel (or press Esc).

The two circular buttons beneath the command buttons, All files and Current file only, are two examples of *radio buttons.* When you see a set of radio buttons in a dialog box (and they are used frequently), you can select only one from the set of options. Clicking on one option, in other words, moves the highlight to the option you clicked and removes it from the previous selection.

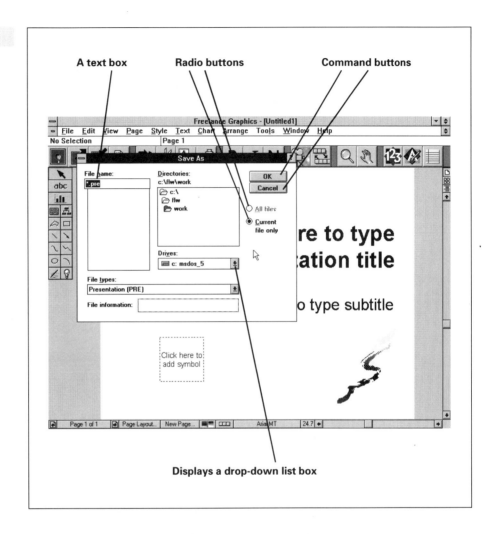

FIGURE 3.6

The Save As
dialog box

The final element in the Save As dialog box is a drop-down list box. The *Drives:* box and the *File types:* box are both examples of drop-down list boxes. You can tell which boxes are drop-down list boxes by the appearance of the down-arrow symbol at the right end of the box. To display the options available in the drop-down list box, click on the down arrow. The list then appears, and you can make your selection by clicking on the item you want or by highlighting it and pressing Enter. Figure 3.7 shows an example of a drop-down list box.

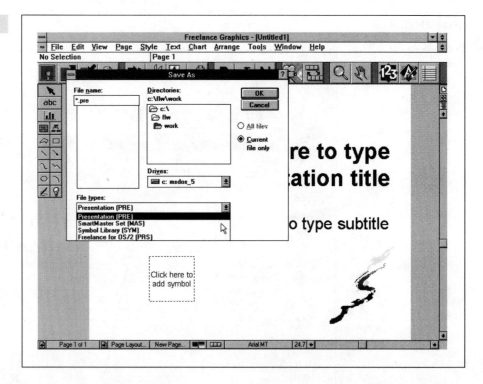

Now that you have a basic understanding of the menu system used in Freelance Graphics for Windows, you're ready to look at the menu alternative: SmartIcons.

Understanding SmartIcons

As you're making your way around Freelance Graphics, you'll find that you use certain commands more than others. In the beginning, you'll use File commands—like New, Open, and Save—more frequently than anything else. As your experience with Freelance grows, you'll begin experimenting with other commands, as well—things that apply only to more advanced text and chart features.

SmartIcons are command buttons that allow you to do in one mouse-click something that might take two or three menu selections. For example, consider the Print icon in the SmartIcon set (the fourth icon from the left). Clicking the Print SmartIcon immediately displays the Print File dialog box. If you used the traditional menu commands, you'd need to open the File menu and then choose the Print command in order to perform the same task.

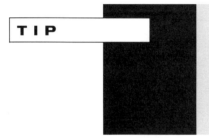

TIP

In the Presentation window, positioning the mouse pointer over the SmartIcon and pressing the right mouse button causes the SmartIcon's function to be displayed in the title bar. You might find this especially handy for those obscure, rarely used icons.

Although Freelance Graphics for Windows only has room to display a limited number of SmartIcons, you can customize the SmartIcon set to include the commands you use most often. Some people, in fact, create different sets of SmartIcons for different purposes. Suppose, for example, that you are working on entering and formatting text for a presentation. One set of commands would apply to that operation. Later, you might add charts, and use an entirely different set of commands. You could create two different sets of SmartIcons and, as your tasks changed, you could change the SmartIcon set you are using.

When you want to change the SmartIcons displayed by default, follow these steps:

1. Open the Tools menu.

2. Choose the SmartIcons command. The SmartIcons dialog box appears, as shown in Figure 3.8.

FIGURE 3.8

The SmartIcons
dialog box

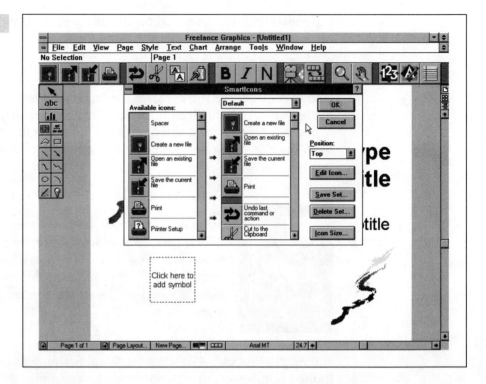

On the left side of this dialog box, you see a list of Available icons. This list—which you can scroll through by clicking the scroll arrow at the bottom of the scroll bar—shows over 100 different SmartIcons you can select for your SmartIcon set. The center list shows the SmartIcons included by default on the Freelance Graphics display. Again, you can scroll through this list as necessary. On the far right side of the dialog box, is a set of buttons which have the following functions:

BUTTON	DESCRIPTION
Edit Icon	Allows you to change the look of an icon included in the SmartIcons set, or a symbol you've created yourself. This button lets you control the color, description, and linked program or function.
Save Set	Lets you save a set of SmartIcons for a specific use.

BUTTON	DESCRIPTION
Delete Set	Allows you to delete a set of SmartIcons you no longer use.
Icon Size	Lets you control the size of the icon displayed (Small for EGA, Medium for VGA, or Large for Super VGA).

Two other items—both drop-down list boxes—appear on the SmartIcons dialog box. The first box, located in the top center of the box, shows the name of the SmartIcon set currently in use. Right now, only the Default set has been created. Once you create additional sets, though, you can select them simply by opening this box and clicking on the set you want to use.

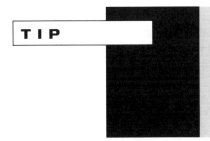

T I P

To switch to a different SmartIcon set, click on the SmartIcon that looks like two rows of square buttons with directional arrows showing movement between the groups (located just beneath the Help menu). Note: You must have created the additional SmartIcon set before selecting this icon.

The other drop-down box, *Position:,* allows you to choose where you want the SmartIcons displayed. When you click the *Position:* box, the following options are displayed:

- Floating
- Left
- Top (this option is selected by default)
- Right
- Bottom

To choose a different display for the SmartIcons, simply click the *Position:* you want. When you select Floating, the icons are displayed as a small pop-up box on top of the traditional Freelance Graphics work area. In order to use the icons, you must enlarge the box (by positioning the cursor on the edge of the box and dragging the border horizontally or vertically). Figure 3.9 shows a floating SmartIcon palette. After you use the Smart-Icon of your choice, you can then reduce the size of the floating icon box and tuck it away in an unused corner of your screen display.

When you choose Left, the SmartIcons are displayed along the far-left edge of the Freelance Graphics screen (to the left of the Tools box). When you choose Right, the icons appear along the far-right side of the screen, to the right of the view buttons and scroll bar. And, as you might expect, when you choose Bottom, the SmartIcons appear below the status line at the bottom of the screen.

FIGURE 3.9

The SmartIcons in "Floating" position

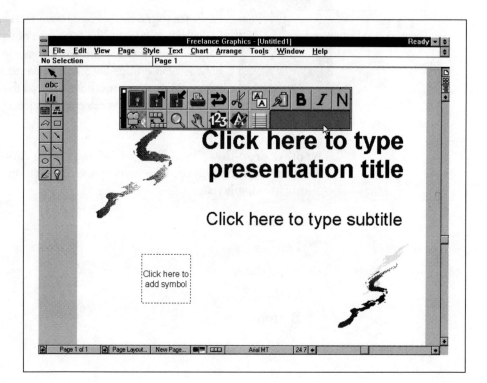

NOTE You can completely suppress the display of SmartIcons, if you choose. To do so, click on the SmartIcon display button (located in the center of the status line at the bottom of the screen, to the left of the typeface box). When you click on this button (the picture looks like three small buttons), a mini-menu appears, giving you the option of Hide or Default (which is displayed). If you hide the SmartIcons and later want to display them, repeat the process and choose Show from the displayed menu.

In this section, you learned to work with the SmartIcons that came with Freelance Graphics for Windows. In the next section, you can put some of your conceptual understanding to work by trying some of the hands-on examples for creating your first presentation.

Adding Text

As you recall, the first thing you did in this chapter was choose a Smart-Master for this work session and select a page layout. The SmartMaster set you chose was *sketch.mas,* a simple design with a few splashes of color. The page layout you selected was a Title page (the logical place to start any presentation). In this section, you'll begin performing some real tasks by interacting with the SmartMaster you've selected. Figure 3.10 shows the Freelance Graphics work area as we begin this tutorial section.

As you can see, Freelance Graphics doesn't leave any guesswork for you. The screen prompts (which tell you where to type title and subtitle text, and where to add a symbols), show you the color and style of the text already chosen. All you have to do is follow the instructions and enter your own text. We'll do this in the next few sections.

FIGURE 3.10

The Freelance
Graphics current
display

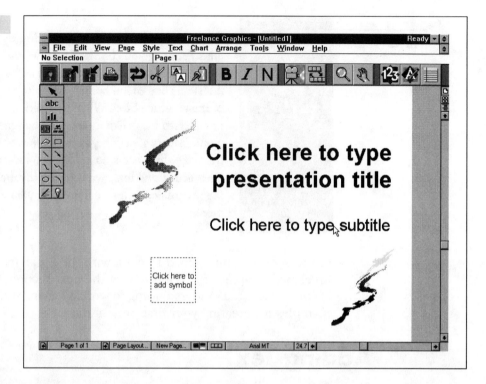

Adding a Title

Let's start by entering a title for the title page. Simply position the mouse anyplace on the title text prompt and click the mouse button. A small text box opens in place of the prompt text (see Figure 3.11).

In this text box, the first thing that catches your attention may be the flashing cursor, blinking at the right side of the box. In the top bar of the box, you see four items: an arrow symbol pointing left, an arrow symbol pointing right, a Tips button, and an OK button.

The left-pointing arrow is a *promote icon*, which you'll use to change the level of text within a presentation. (For example, if you entered text for a bulleted item and then decided you want to use the text as a subtitle, you could click on Promote to change the text from bullet text to the subtitle.)

The right-pointing icon is the *demote icon*, which reduces the text to the next lowest level (for example, changing a subtitle to a bullet text item).

FIGURE 3.11

Displaying a text box
for text entry

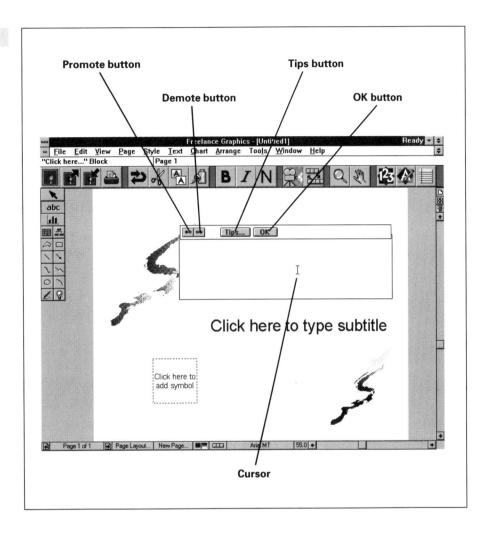

Clicking the Tips button displays a Text Tips box, listing points to consider as you enter text. Finally, the OK button is the button you click after entering the text for the title.

Let's try it. Type

    EcoSystems, Inc.

As you type, Freelance Graphics enters the text—in the font, style, and color shown in the original prompt—in the text box (see Figure 3.12).

FIGURE 3.12

Entering the title text

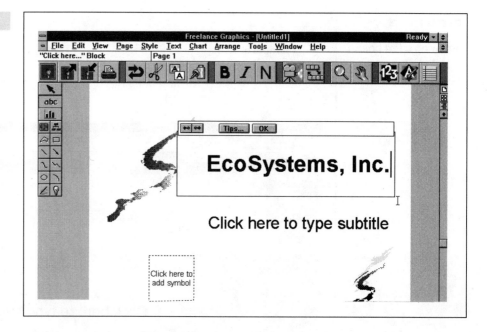

Notice that the text appears from the right edge of the box. This Smart-Master has chosen right-alignment, something you'll learn to change in Chapter 6.

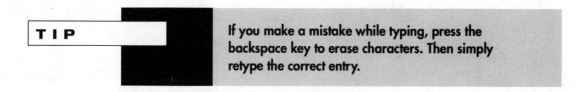

TIP If you make a mistake while typing, press the backspace key to erase characters. Then simply retype the correct entry.

When you've finished entering title text in the text box, click the OK button. The text box is removed, and your title text is placed on the presentation page. Notice, however, that the text box is still selected—that is, eight small black squares called *handles* mark the edges of the text area. These handles appear so you can easily move or resize the text box.

Adding and Resizing a Subtitle

So entering a title is pretty simple, right? That's about as difficult as things get in Freelance Graphics. This section uses the same procedure to enter a different section of text: the subtitle.

Remember how?

1. First click on the subtitle prompt.
2. When the text box is displayed, type Paths to the Future and click the OK button. Again, Freelance Graphics places your text on the page but leaves the text selected.

Suppose you aren't happy with the way the subtitle and title are balanced on the page. The title looks okay, but the subtitle is too far to the right. You have several options for moving the text:

- You can change the justification of the text so that the text is centered in the text box
- You can move the text box
- You can shorten the text box to move the text inward

Let's try the last option. To do so, follow these steps:

1. Position the mouse pointer on the black handle at the right end of the subtitle text box. The mouse pointer changes to a double-headed arrow.
2. Press and hold the mouse button.
3. Drag the mouse inward, to the left. A dotted outline of the text box moves as you resize the box.
4. When the text is placed where you want it, release the mouse button.

Figure 3.13 shows the title page thus far. As you can see, the subtitle has been entered and moved so that it is centered beneath the title text.

Now that you've got the basics of entering text, you're ready to add a symbol to the title page of your presentation.

FIGURE 3.13

The page after the subtitle is entered and centered

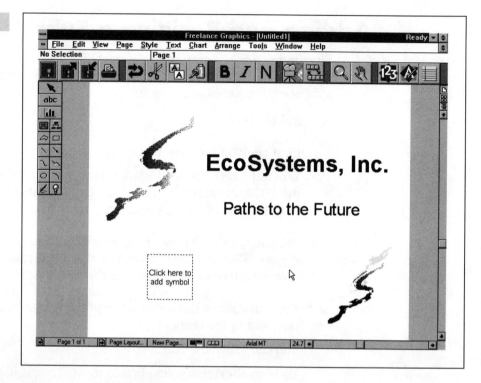

Adding a Symbol

Freelance Graphics for Windows comes with over 100 symbols that can be used as illustrations, as SmartIcons, or as bullets in your bulleted lists. Adding a symbol is no more complicated than adding a title or subtitle.

When you are ready to add a symbol, follow these steps:

1. Click on the symbol box. The Add Symbol to Page dialog box appears, as shown in Figure 3.14. The names of the symbol files are displayed in the *Choose symbol category:* box.

2. Choose a symbol file you want to work with. You can scroll through the different files by clicking on the ↓ at the bottom of the scroll bar. (The symbols in the highlighted file are displayed in the preview window at the bottom of the screen.) For this example, we've chosen *people.sym*.

FIGURE 3.14

The Add Symbol to
Page dialog box

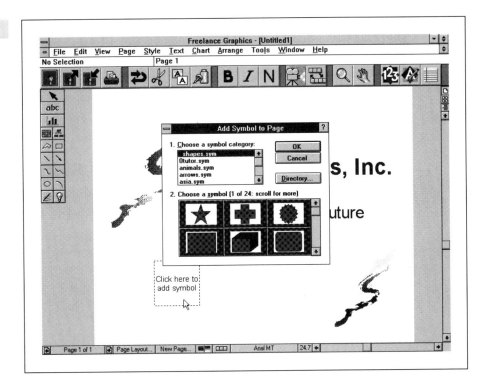

3. After you've highlighted the symbol file you want, you can scroll
   through the displayed symbols by clicking on the scroll bar or the
   scroll arrows to the right of the preview box.

4. Click on the symbol you want.

5. Click OK.

You are returned to the presentation page and the symbol is in place. The
handles are still visible on the symbol and you can now move or resize the
symbol as necessary. Figure 3.15 shows the page after the symbol has
been added and enlarged slightly.

Congratulations! You've completed the first page of your presentation. As
you can already see, Freelance Graphics for Windows makes creating a
presentation so simple that you may find yourself almost looking forward
to your next presentation. (We won't tell your boss.)

FIGURE 3.15

The page after the
symbol has been
added

Starting a New Page

Now that you've mastered the title page, you're ready to move on. This
section walks you through the process of adding a page of bulleted text.

But first things first. Before you can enter any more text, you need to start
the new page. Move the mouse pointer down to the New Page command
in the status line at the bottom of the screen. Click the mouse button. The
screen shown in Figure 3.16 appears. (You've seen this box before.)

Now, instead of choosing the Title layout (like we did last time), we're
looking for the Bulleted List layout. To select the layout, click on Bulleted
List and then click OK (or simply double-click on Bulleted List). A new
page is displayed on the screen, as shown in Figure 3.17.

FIGURE 3.16

The New Page
dialog box

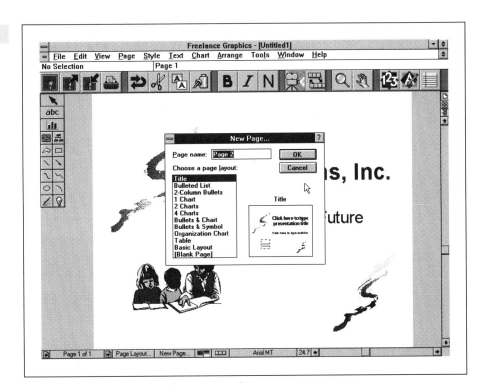

On the new page, you see the familiar title prompt. Beneath the title, a bullet and text in a smaller size appears. The next sections explain how to enter bulleted text on this page. First, however, take a moment and add the following title on your own:

Eco Training Programs

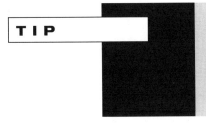

TIP

If you don't remember how to enter a title, follow these steps: Position the mouse pointer on the title prompt. Click the mouse button. When the text box appears, enter the text for the title. When you're finished, click the OK button.

FIGURE 3.17

The new Bulleted
List page

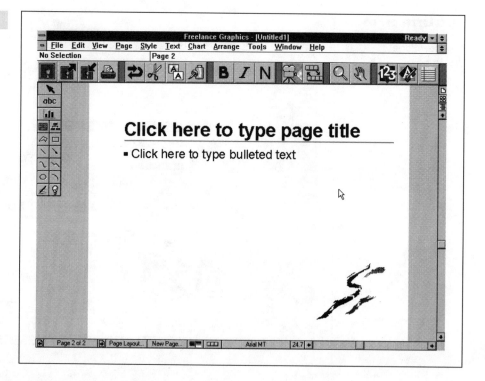

Adding Bulleted Text

When you're ready to add text, position the mouse pointer on the bulleted text prompt and click the mouse button. The traditional text box appears. You will add all the bullets within this single text box. Here's how:

1. Type the first line of text (for our example, type Natural Science Curriculum) and press Enter. The cursor moves to the next line and a second bullet appears.

2. Enter Weekend Workshops for Parents.

3. Enter Hands-On Nature Centers.

4. Enter New "Mothering Nature" Workbooks.

The bullets now appear as shown in Figure 3.18. In the next section, you'll learn to enter second-level bullets.

FIGURE 3.18

The bullets as entered on Page 2 of the presentation

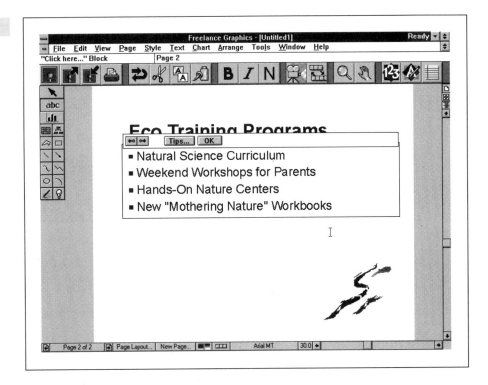

Adding Second-Level Bullets

It seems kind of funny—we've just started working a few pages ago, but we're almost finished. In this section, we're going to add one more bulleted item and two second-level bullets. First, let's add the final first-level bullet:

1. After the New "Mothering Nature" Workbooks line, press Enter.

2. Enter CD-ROM Nature Photo Series. The cursor moves to the next line and displays another bullet.

3. Move the mouse pointer up to the demote icon (the arrow symbol pointing right) at the top of the text box. Click the mouse button. The bullet symbol changes to a dash and is indented another space.

4. Type Mammals and press Enter. The cursor moves to the next line, at the same indentation level.

5. Type Birds and press Enter.

6. Finally, type Lizards and press Enter.

TIP You can also promote and demote text by pressing Shift-Tab or Tab, respectively.

Figure 3.19 shows the completed bulleted list with first- and second-level bullets.

Now that you've learned how to create two different types of pages in Freelance Graphics for Windows, you're ready to experiment with the different viewing options available.

FIGURE 3.19

The completed bulleted list

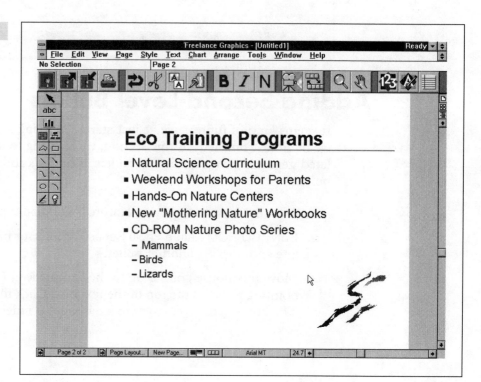

Viewing Pages

Freelance Graphics for Windows provides you with different views from which you can display your work. Specifically, these views are as follows:

VIEW	DESCRIPTION
Outliner view	Shows you only the text in your presentation, organized according to level of subordination (for example, second-level bullets are indented beneath first-level bullets).
Page Sorter view	Shows your entire presentation on one screen, with each page displayed in a miniature size. This allows you to check your entire presentation at once and to easily reorder pages if necessary.
Current Page view	Freelance Graphics's default view and the view you will probably use most frequently. It is in this view that the SmartMaster prompts appear and on which you add symbols, charts, and other graphic elements.

This section also introduces you to some of the settings you may want to investigate as you work with the different views Freelance offers. Specifically, you'll learn how to set display preferences and add a grid to your work area.

Displaying Outline View

Moving from one view to another is easy in Freelance Graphics. As Figure 3.20 shows, you can change from the current page view (which is the default) to the Outliner by using one of two methods:

• Open the View menu and choose the Outliner command

FIGURE 3.20

Changing to
Outliner view

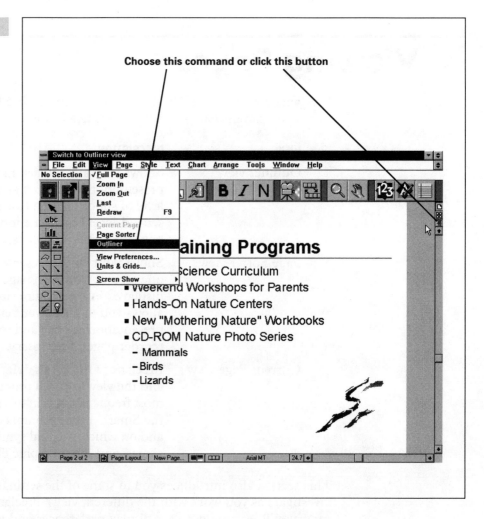

• Click on the yellow Outliner button along the right side of the
screen

Whichever method you choose, Freelance automatically takes you to the
Outliner. The presentation you are working on is displayed in text outline
mode (see Figure 3.21).

Remember the title page we created before the bulleted list? The Outliner
remembers, and displays both pages of the file in Outliner view. The pages

FIGURE 3.21

The presentation in
Outliner view

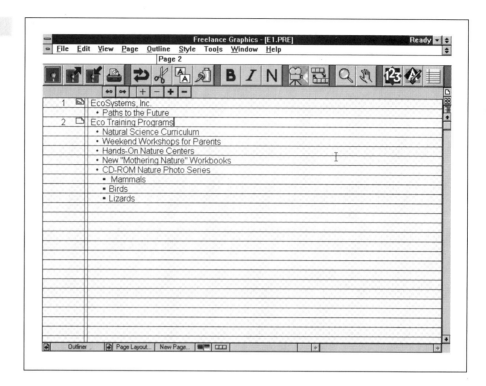

are numbered in the left margin, and small icons are positioned beside
the page titles. Notice the difference between these two icons. The upper-
most icon, beside EcoSystems, Inc., contains a small triangle; but the
second icon is empty. This tells you that the first page includes a symbol,
and the second page does not.

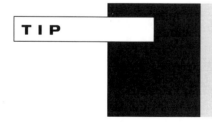

TIP

You can do much more than view your text in
Outliner mode. You can enter new text, move
existing text, use the spelling checker, change text
levels, and perform a number of other operations.
For more about the Outliner, see Chapter 7.

Returning to Current Page View

When you're finished working with the Outliner (or Page Sorter) view, you can return to the current page view in one of two ways:

- Click on the current page icon (the top view button along the right edge of the screen)
- Open the View menu and choose Current Page.

You are then returned to the current page view. Any changes you made while displaying pages in another view are reflected in the current page view.

N O T E If you moved the cursor while you were working in another view, you are returned to the page where the cursor is currently located. For example, if the cursor is positioned on Page 2, when you return to current page view, Page 2 is displayed.

Displaying Page Sorter View

The Page Sorter provides you with a "big picture" view of your presentation. Functioning like a lightboard, the Page Sorter lets you see your entire presentation on one screen. You might want to use this view in some or the following situations:

- You want to make sure your company logo appears on each screen.
- You need to check the order in which you've presented information.
- You want to make sure you haven't used the same chart twice.
- You need to check the consistency of the artwork in the presentation.

- You want to review the sequence of screens before previewing the presentation in a slide show.

As you can probably guess, Freelance gives you two options for changing to Page Sorter view:

- Open the View menu and choose Page Sorter
- You can click on the Page Sorter button (beneath the Current Page button) along the right edge of the screen.

After you select the Page Sorter, Freelance Graphics displays the screens you've selected in the new display (see Figure 3.22). As you can see from the figure, only the two pages we've created are displayed. The second page—which was our current page—is enclosed in a gray rectangle, showing that when you return to current page view, this page will be displayed.

FIGURE 3.22

The presentation pages in Page Sorter view

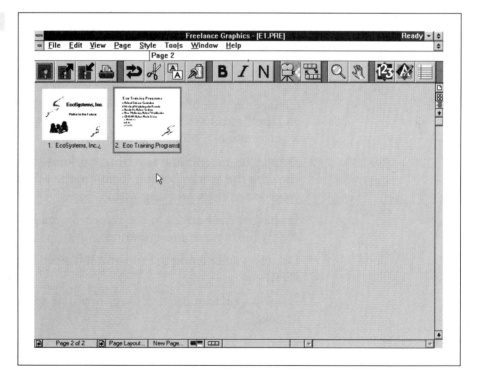

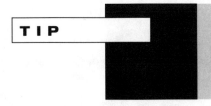

TIP

You can easily reorder the pages in your presentation by dragging the small screens from one place on-screen to another. For more information on using the Page Sorter, see Chapter 14.

Again, when you're ready to return to the current page view, simply click on the current page button or select Current Page from the View menu. Any changes you made in the Page Sorter view are reflected in the current page view, as well.

Choosing Display Preferences

Freelance Graphics for Windows gives you the option of setting some of your own preferences for the way items are displayed. To take a look at the display options you have, open the View menu and choose the View Preferences command. The View Preferences dialog box appears in the center of your screen, as shown in Figure 3.23.

The View Preferences dialog box gives the following options:

- Change the size of the cursor (large or small) that appears when you are drawing in Freelance Graphics (this is known as the *crosshair cursor*). Small is the default.

- Display in the edit line two different kinds of coordinates; one showing the mouse pointer location, the other showing the size of an object you are working with.

- Display at the bottom of the screen the function keys that are usable for the current operation.

- Display a ruler along the top and left sides of the current page view.

- Display a ruler in the text entry box that appears when you click on text.

FIGURE 3.23

The View Preferences
dialog box

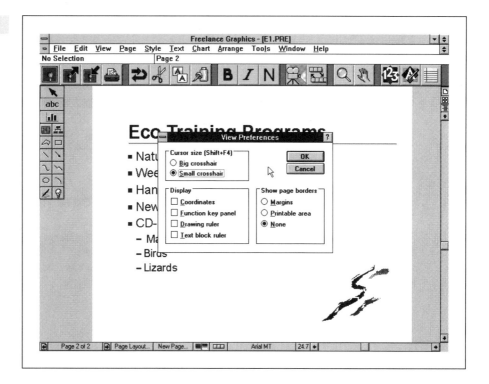

- Display in current page view the margins or border of the print-able area of the presentation (the dashed outline will not appear in print).

To choose any of these items, simply position the mouse pointer on the option you want and click the mouse button. (Notice that the Cursor size and Show page borders options are radio buttons, which means that you can only select one option from each of these groups at any one time.)

Figure 3.24 shows the current page view when all these items have been enabled. The small crosshair cursor has been selected (although it's not shown here because we aren't drawing an object). The Coordinates, Function key panel, Drawing ruler, and Text block ruler have also been selected. In addition, we've elected to show the Printable area of the page.

FIGURE 3.24

The current page
display with selected
view preferences

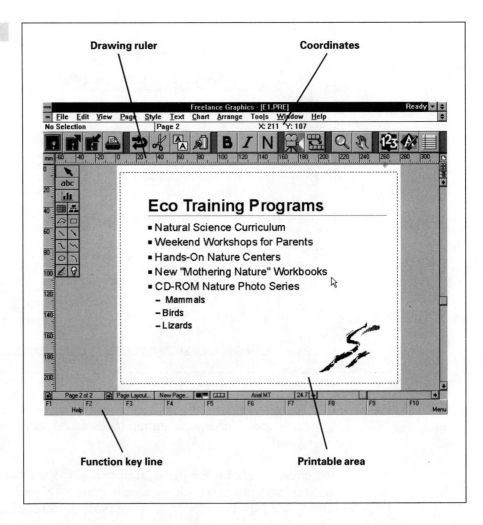

For most of the examples used in this book, you won't need many of these
items. When you are ready to remove extra items, open the View menu and
choose View Preferences again. Then click on the selected options you
want to disable. For now, we'll leave these options enabled, so we can
show you how to change the increment on the ruler, the topic of the next
section.

Changing Units and Adding Grids

You may want to customize the unit of measurement you display in the ruler. Freelance Graphics gives you the following choices:

- Millimeters
- Centimeters
- Inches
- Points
- Picas

Depending on your business needs, you may be more comfortable working in inches, centimeters, or picas. Picas are often used for materials that will be used in the publishing realm, so before you create presentation pages that you plan to incorporate in your company's desktop published newsletter, you may want to check with the production coordinator to see what unit of measure they use.

These options, along with the Grid option, are set in the Units & Grids dialog box. To display the dialog box, open the View menu and choose Units & Grids. The dialog box shown in Figure 3.25 appears.

To select a unit of measurement, position the mouse pointer on the option you want and click the mouse button. These are radio buttons, so only one unit type can be chosen at one time.

In the bottom portion of the dialog box, you see the Grids section. In this section, you can display an on-screen grid or control an invisible "Snap to" grid, which causes the mouse pointer to stick to special coordinates that you set by entering the horizontal and vertical space between increments. This helps you to precisely align objects on your presentation pages.

Figure 3.26 shows the screen display after Inches and Display grid have been selected.

FIGURE 3.25

The Units & Grids
dialog box

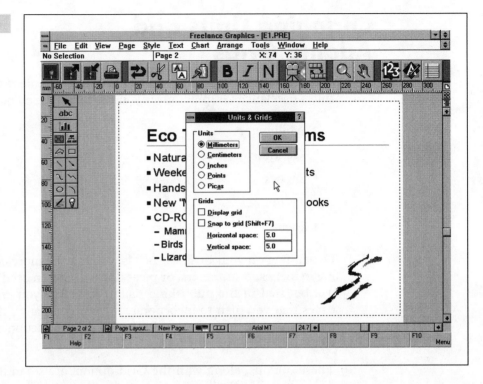

When you want to return the screen to default display, open the View menu and choose Units & Grids a second time. Disable any necessary options (such as Display grid). If you want to hide the ruler display, choose View Preferences from the View menu and select the appropriate command.

In the next section, you'll learn to display a quick slide show of the presentation pages you've created.

FIGURE 3.26

The screen display in Inches with a grid displayed

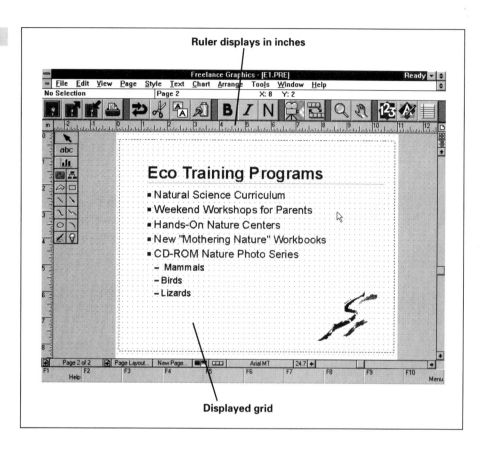

Ruler displays in inches

Displayed grid

Starting a Slide Show

Although we're several pages short of what might be considered a full-length presentation, let's try out the slide show feature of Freelance Graphics for Windows. You can start a slide show two different ways:

- Click on the slide show SmartIcon (the movie camera icon beneath the Window menu name)

- Open the View menu and choose Screen Show, as shown in Figure 3.27.

FIGURE 3.27

Selecting the Screen
Show command

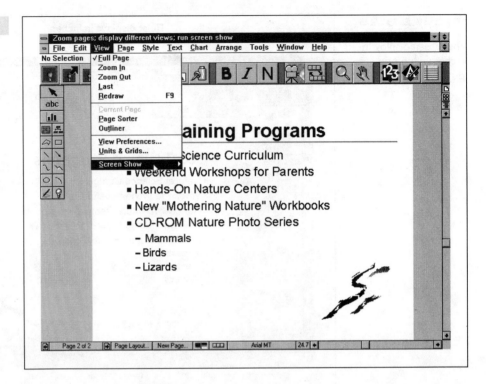

When you choose the Screen Show command, a second set of commands, displayed in a cascading menu, appears to the right of the menu, (see Figure 3.28). The command we are concerned with at this point is the Run command, which starts the screen show. You can also select this command by pressing Alt-F10. (The rest of these commands, along with all of Screen Show's special effects, are discussed in Chapter 16.)

To start the screen show, choose Run by pressing Enter or clicking the mouse button. (That option is already highlighted.) The first slide of your presentation is displayed in full-screen view. To advance to the next screen, press the PgDn or Enter key or click the mouse button. To return to the current page view, press Esc or PgDn when the last page of the presentation is displayed.

FIGURE 3.28

The Screen Show
submenu commands

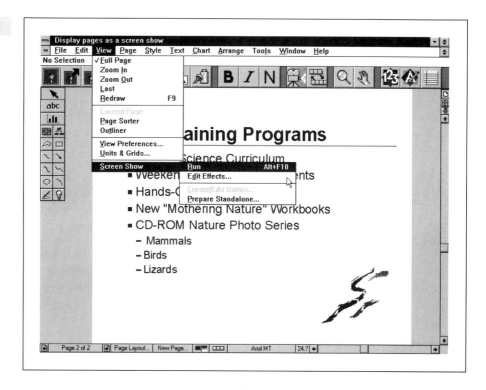

Saving Presentations

You should save the presentation you're working on every once in a while. For best results, don't wait until you're finished with the file before you save it. You never know when a badly timed thunderstorm or a clumsy trip over the power cord will shut down your computer.

Most people save their files after each major step in the creation process. In other words, you might pause to save the file after you select the Smart-Master set and add the first page of text; then again after adding subsequent pages; then again after adding symbols, charts, etc. A good motto is "better safe than sorry"—especially when you're talking about several hours' work. To save your presentation, follow these steps:

1. Open the File menu by clicking on the menu name or by pressing Alt-F.

2. Choose the Save command. The first time you save the file, the Save As dialog appears, as shown in Figure 3.29. If you've saved files previously, they are listed in the list box beneath the *File name:* text box.

3. Type a name for the file (up to eight characters, with no spaces). You don't need to enter an extension (the three letters following the period in the file name)—Freelance Graphics does that for you.

4. If you need to choose a different file type—that is, if you are saving the file to be used in another program—click on the down-arrow

FIGURE 3.29

The Save As
dialog box

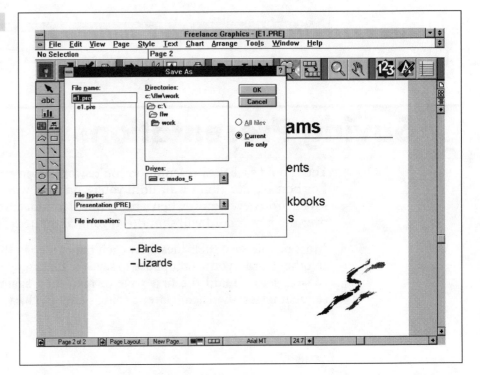

symbol at the end of the File types: line. Choose the file type you want by clicking on it.

5. Check the *Directories:* and the *Drives:* boxes to make sure Freelance will save the file to the correct drive and directory. In Figure 3.29, the file will be saved to the \WORK directory on drive C.

6. Click OK or press Enter to save the file.

The file is then saved in the format you specified. The next time you save the file by selecting the Save command, you will not be asked to enter a file name—Freelance will use the name you specified in the initial save procedure. From this point on, anytime you save the file you can do so by pressing the key combination Ctrl-S. A small pop-up box appears, asking whether you want to replace the file existing with that name. Click Replace to continue the operation, Backup to create a backup file, or Cancel to return to the page display without saving the file.

In the next section, you learn to print the presentation you've created in this chapter.

Printing the Presentation

In Chapter 15, we'll cover all the individual printing options in full detail. In this section, you'll learn to get a quick printout of your presentation. By default, Freelance Graphics for Windows prints one screen on each printed page. To print your presentation, follow these steps:

1. Open the File menu.

2. Choose the Print command. The Print File dialog box, shown in Figure 3.30, appears.

3. Click the Print button.

Freelance Graphics then begins sending your file to the printer. To interrupt printing, press Esc.

FIGURE 3.30

The Print File
dialog box

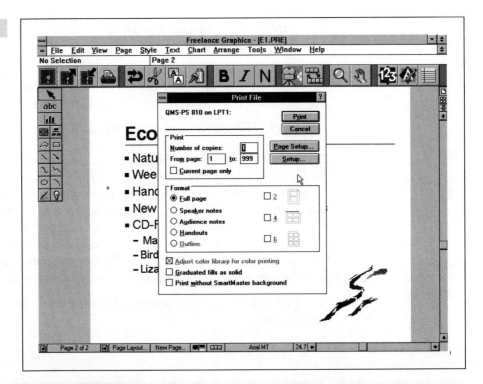

Freelance Graphics for Windows makes it easy to
print multiple copies of presentations, to print only
selected pages, and to choose a number of different
formats for printing (Full page, Speaker notes,
Audience notes, Handouts, and Outline).

If you're having trouble printing, make sure your printer is set up to work
with Freelance Graphics. (Use the Printer Setup command in the File
menu or click Setup in the Print File Dialog box.) If you still don't get a
printout, consult "Printing Troubleshooting Tips" in Chapter 15.

In this chapter, we've covered a lot of ground. Beginning with a basic understanding of the startup procedure for Freelance Graphics, you selected a SmartMaster set, choose Page Layout, and investigated each of the Freelance Graphics menus. You also leaned the basic tasks for creating a presentation, including adding text and symbols, changing views, modifying view preferences, and saving and printing the presentation.

In the next chapter, it's roll-up-the-shirtsleeves time as we start Part Two by learning the different methods of entering text in Freelance Graphics.

PART TWO

●

Entering, Editing, and Enhancing Text

In Part One, you familiarized yourself with Freelance Graphics for Windows. Initially, you learned the basics of Windows and spent some time exploring the various features of Freelance Graphics. In Chapter 3, you worked through a Freelance Graphics primer in which you tried out many of the operations that you'll use in every Freelance work session.

Part Two slows down the pace a bit and takes a closer look at various text operations. In Chapter 4, you'll learn to enter text and to use the various text options available in SmartMaster text boxes and in the Outliner. Chapter 5 continues the discussion by helping you edit individual characters and blocks of text. You'll also learn to use the spelling checker. Chapter 6 teaches you what you need to know about formatting and enhancing your text—from setting indents and controlling alignment to changing fonts, styles, and sizes. Finally, Chapter 7 rounds out Part Two by exploring the various features available when you work in the Outliner.

FOUR

Entering Text

fast *TRACK*

● **The fastest way to start a new page in the Outliner**   120

is to position the cursor at the end of the page preceding the one you want to add (for example, if you want to add a new page 4, position the cursor at the end of page 3) and press F7. Freelance Graphics automatically adds the new page symbol and moves the pointer to the next line.

● **To change text level in the Outliner,**   121

you can use two different methods. To indent a line one level, press Tab. To "outdent"—that is, move the text out one level—press Shift-Tab. You can also change text levels by using the promote and demote buttons. The promote button points to the left and the demote button points to the right. When you click on either of these buttons, the text at the current cursor position moves in the direction you have selected.

IN the previous chapter, you worked through several basic tasks that apply to just about every Freelance Graphics work session. This chapter concentrates on text-entry features—getting your text into Freelance Graphics pages.

Adding Text in Current Page View

If you went through the Freelance primer in Chapter 3, you found out about the direct and simple way to add text in your presentations. At every point on a SmartMaster page, there is a prompt that says *Click here to type subtitle* (or title or bullet text), marking the place at which you will enter the text for your own presentations. Entering text in Freelance Graphics involves two simple steps:

1. Click the place on-screen where you want to add text.
2. Type the text.

TIP

Freelance Graphics gives you the option of setting a variety of text options. For example, you can choose the font, type size, and style of the characters; you can choose the color in which the text will appear; and you can set various attributes for bullets.

The following sections explore each of the basic text-entry steps in more detail.

Replacing SmartMaster Text

Figure 4.1 shows the *forest.mas* SmartMaster title page on which we're going to enter text. (If you don't remember how to select a SmartMaster, see Chapter 3.)

To enter text, follow these steps:

1. Click on the Click here to type presentation title prompt. The text box for that entry appears, as shown in Figure 4.2.

2. Now enter a title for your presentation. For this example, enter EcoSystems, Inc. Notice that as you type, the characters appear from the right edge of the box. This happens because in this

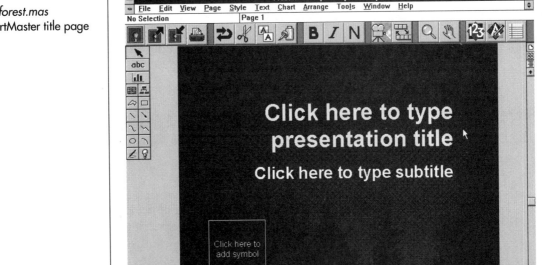

FIGURE 4.2

The text entry box

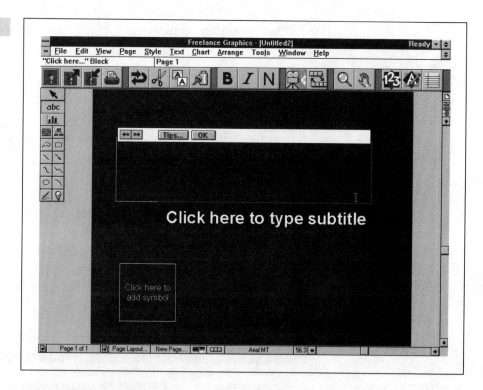

particular SmartMaster the text is right-aligned. You'll learn how to left-align and center text in Chapter 6.

TIP

If you make a mistake while typing, simply press the backspace key to remove the typos; then type the correct text.

If you are using a color monitor, the text appears in yellow against a blue background. For now, let's leave the text settings—font, size, color, and style—the way they are and enter text in another text box.

3. Click OK. Freelance Graphics places the text you typed in the appropriate place on the page (see Figure 4.3). Notice that the text box is still selected—that is, you see eight square handles

FIGURE 4.3

The entered text

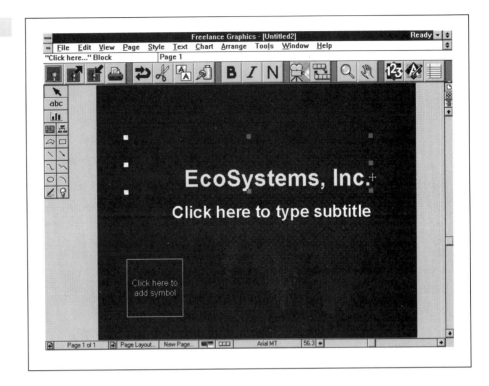

around the perimeter of the text box. You can use the handles to move, resize, or otherwise manipulate the text box.

You can now enter the second section of text by repeating steps 1–3. If your text takes up more than one line, Freelance Graphics automatically wraps the text to the next line for you. *Do not press Enter.* Doing so will tell Freelance you are adding another item in a list (such as a bulleted list) and the text will show up as two separate items in Outliner view. Even if your text wraps to the next line, Freelance will see the text entry as a single item. Figure 4.4 shows a text box that was purposely resized to cause the text to break into two lines.

FIGURE 4.4

A subtitle entry that
uses two lines

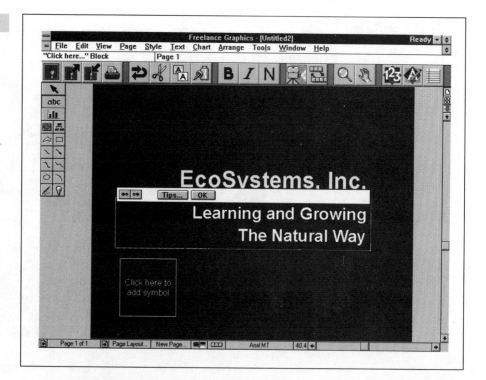

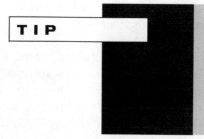

TIP

If Freelance Graphics wraps the line and you don't
like the way it breaks, you can resize the box after
clicking OK. If you drag the left side of the box
inward, for example, the line length for the text will
be shorter. After you release the mouse button,
Freelance will move the text accordingly.

To add another item in the same text box, simply press Enter at the end
of the first item, and Freelance will move the cursor to the next line.

When you click OK, the text is placed on the presentation page (the handles are still visible). You can make any modifications you want by moving
the text, changing the size of the text box, selecting a different font, size,
or style, or even deleting the text at any time from the presentation page
view.

Adding New Text Blocks

Occasionally, you may want to add more text than the SmartMaster leaves room for. Suppose, for example, you want to add a line that shows the date the presentation was prepared.

The procedure for adding your own text block is almost as simple as using the ones the SmartMaster provides. Freelance Graphics gives you a choice for the kind of box you create. If you want Freelance Graphics to place the text in a specific spot and wrap the text if it continues beyond a certain margin, use the text tool to draw a rectangle on the screen. If you *don't* want Freelance Graphics to wrap the text, select the text tool and simply click on the presentation page.

Here's a closer look at the steps for adding a text box:

1. Click on the text tool—the tool that shows *abc*—in the tools row. The pointer changes to the I-beam pointer.

2. If you want to have Freelance Graphics wrap the text automatically, position the pointer at the point where you want to begin drawing the upper left corner of the box. (If you don't want Freelance to wrap the text, place the pointer where you want to begin entering text and click the mouse button. Then enter the text without first creating a box.)

3. Press and hold the left mouse button while dragging the pointer down and to the right. A box with a dotted outline appears as you move the mouse.

TIP

To make a perfectly square text box, hold down the Shift key while dragging the pointer.

4. When the box is the size you want, release the mouse button. Freelance Graphics places a text box in that position in the size you specified (see Figure 4.5)

As you can see, the new text box has the same elements as the SmartMaster text boxes—the promote and demote buttons, the Tips button,

FIGURE 4.5

The new text box

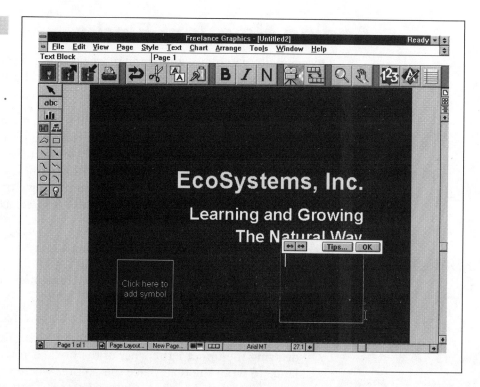

and the OK button. You can now enter your text and click OK to place the text on the page. Figure 4.6 shows the finished title page.

TIP

In many cases, you may find it easier to create a text box in an uncluttered part of the page and then move the box to the desired location. To move a text box, simply click on it. When the handles appear, position the cursor along the border. When the cursor changes into the four-pronged arrow (signifying that the pointer is in the right position to move the box), press and hold the mouse button while dragging the box to the position you want. When the box is in the correct location, release the mouse button.

FIGURE 4.6

The finished title page

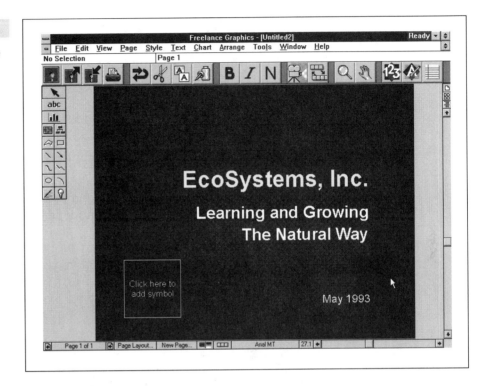

You now know the basics about entering text in current page view. Remember that the Text menu contains many options you can use to edit and further enhance the text in your presentations. (Chapter 5 discusses editing techniques, and Chapter 6 introduces formatting and enhancement issues.) In the next section, you learn how to enter text in the Outliner view.

Adding Text
in Outliner View

In the previous section, you entered text on the title page of your presentation. The Outliner view gives you another perspective from which to view your text. While in the Outliner, you can also enter, edit, and re-organize text. (For techniques other than entering text in the Outliner, see Chapter 7). In this section, you'll learn to enter text in the Outliner view.

First, let's use the Outliner to display what you've done so far. There are two ways to do this:

- Move the mouse pointer to the Outliner button along the right edge of the screen (it's the button above the up-arrow symbol in the scroll bar)

- Open the View menu (by clicking on the menu name or pressing Alt-V) and choose the Outliner command (see Figure 4.7).

Figure 4.8 shows the current presentation. Notice that the entire subtitle, which used two lines in the title presentation page, now takes up only one line. If you had pressed Enter after the word *Growing*, Freelance would

FIGURE 4.7

Selecting the Outliner command

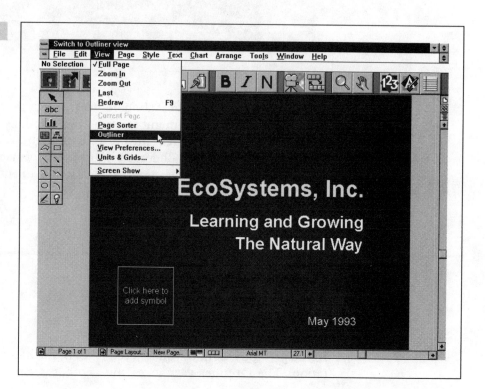

FIGURE 4.8

The presentation in
Outliner view

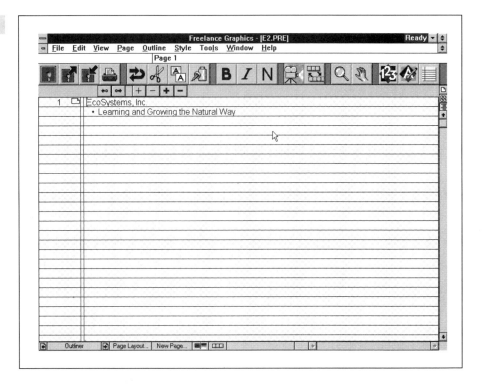

have interpreted the line as two separate entries and would have placed
the Natural Way on the next line, assigning a second bullet to the entry.

The next section introduces you to the Outliner display.

Understanding the Outliner View

Probably the first thing you notice about the Outliner view is the notebook-
like look of the page. Similar to a sheet of legal pad paper, the Outliner
gives you the feeling that you're brainstorming for your presentation,
preparing to design the basic flow of your material.

For many people, working in Outline mode is a comfortable and logical
way to decide what to say next. An outline can help you stay focused on

the progression of information and will help your audience understand where your presentation is going.

Because you've created only one page for the sample presentation, the Outline view displays only one page (and, strangely enough, labels it as "page one"). An open-page symbol tells us that no graphics (symbols, text boxes, or other artwork) were included on the page. (The page icon shows a small triangle, indicating that a symbol or text box has been added to the page. Other types of art—charts, organizational charts, and tables—have their own symbols. More about this in Chapter 7.)

Besides the page symbol, you see the title of the presentation, *EcoSystems, Inc*. The placement of this text is important. This is the first-level text entry. The second line shows a bullet character, followed by the subtitle entered on the presentation page. This text is indented, indicating that it is second-level, or subordinate, text. This text appears in a smaller typeface than the first-level text and is given a supporting role in the presentation page.

In the next section, you will add two more pages to the same presentation while working in the Outliner view.

Positioning the Cursor

When you first display the Outliner view, the blinking text cursor flashes just before the first character in the top line of the outline. You will need to move the cursor to enter new text. You can do this two ways:

- Use the keyboard arrow keys to move the cursor to the end of the entered text; then press Enter to start a fresh line

- Position the mouse pointer at the end of the entered text (after the word *Way*, in this example) and click the mouse button. The cursor moves to the selected spot. Press Enter to move the cursor to the next line.

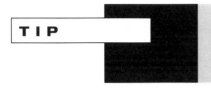

TIP

Use the arrow keys to get to the line you want. Then use the Home or End keys to move to the beginning or end, respectively, of the line.

Notice that when you move the cursor to the next line, Freelance Graphics automatically adds a bullet and positions the cursor even with the text on the line above it (see Figure 4.9). If you want to add another bullet item, this text position is terrific. But what if you want to start a new page with a first-level text item? The next section answers that question.

FIGURE 4.9

The new line ready for text entry

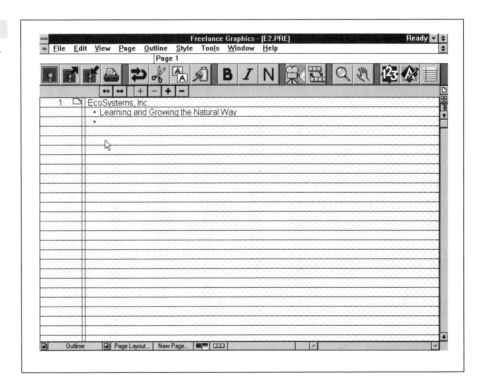

N O T E

The Outliner allows you to specify up to four text levels. The first level is the page title; the second is marked by a round bullet and indented two spaces; the third is marked by a small square bullet and is indented four spaces; the fourth is marked by a dash and is indented six spaces.

Starting a New Page

To start a new page in the Outliner, you can use one of five methods:

- Click on the Promote button (the left-pointing arrow in the row above the first of text)
- Press Shift-Tab
- Open the Outliner menu and choose the Promote command
- Open the Page menu and select the New command
- Press F7.

After any one of these actions, Freelance Graphics removes the bullet and moves the cursor out to the left text margin (see Figure 4.10). Notice that a new page number (2) has been assigned to the line, and an open-page icon appears to the left of the blinking cursor.

Now enter the title for the next page. Type New Products and press Enter. Freelance Graphics displays the typed text and moves the cursor to the next line, adding a second-level bullet by default. The next section explains how to enter subordinate text.

FIGURE 4.10

Starting a new page

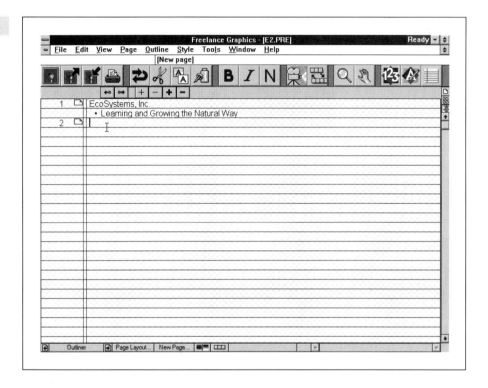

Specifying Text Level

As you saw in Figure 4.10, Freelance automatically adds a first-level bullet underneath a page title. For this example, you may want to go ahead and type another entry (try Educational Videos) and press Enter.

Notice that the cursor moves to the next line, displaying a first-level bullet and positioning the cursor at a point even with the line you just entered. But what if you have subpoints beneath the first-level entry?

To create a second-level entry beneath the first-level entry, you can either press Tab or click the Demote button (the right-pointing arrow in the row above the first text entry). Or, if you prefer, you can open the Outline menu and choose the Demote command. The cursor moves inward two spaces and the round bullet is replaced with a small square one.

TIP

To move the cursor to a superior level, press Shift-Tab, click the Promote button, or choose Promote from the Outline menu. To move the cursor to a subordinate level, press Tab, click the Demote button, or choose Demote from the Outline menu.

You can now enter the text for the second-level entries. Figure 4.11 shows how the Outliner view looks after several more text entries have been added.

FIGURE 4.11

The Outliner view after several text items have been added

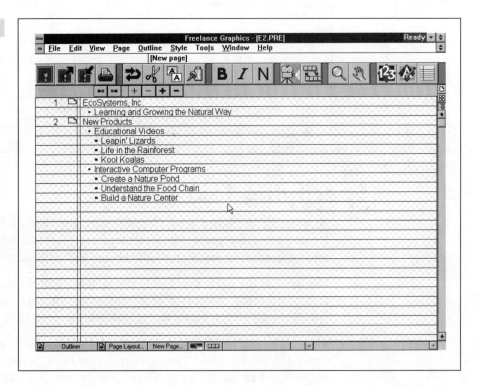

NOTE

Don't forget to save your presentation every so often. Pressing Ctrl-S will save your file to disk in a matter of seconds. (If you've already saved the file, you'll be asked whether you want to replace the one already saved under that name. Click Replace. If you haven't saved the file before, you'll be asked to enter a file name on the Save As dialog box. Type a name and click OK.)

Are you wondering how this second page looks in current page view? Finding out is simple (and it's also the topic of the next section).

Returning to Presentation View

When you are ready to return to normal page display (or presentation view), you have two different options:

- Click on the current page display button at the top of the left scroll bar

- Open the View menu and choose the Current Page command.

After either one of these actions, the current page is displayed. Freelance Graphics moves to the page in which the cursor is positioned, which means that, following the example in Figure 4.11, the second page of the presentation is displayed. Figure 4.12 shows the result of changing back to current page view.

As you can see, Freelance Graphics automatically added all the text on the second page to the presentation. The text is indented as it was on the Outliner screen, but something is different—the bullets that are used are not the ones on the Outliner screen. Not to worry. You can customize bullets and use any symbol in Freelance Graphics (or Lotus 1-2-3 for Windows) as a bullet character in Freelance Graphics. (Chapter 6 explains more about using symbols as bullets.)

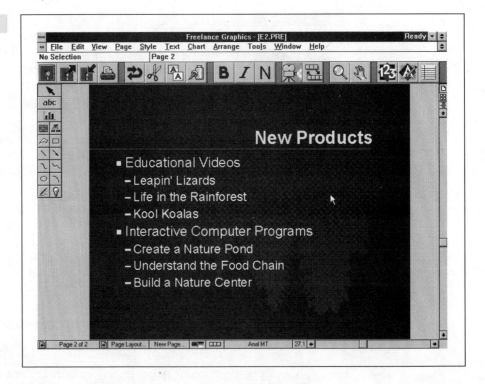

You now know how to enter text both in normal page and Outliner views. As you can see, Freelance Graphics for Windows makes it as easy as possible for you to create a basic presentation.

In this chapter, you've learned the basics of entering text. Starting with a discussion of current page view, this chapter showed you how to replace SmartMaster text with your own. You also learned to add your own text boxes to the SmartMaster page. Finally, you added text in Outliner view and then returned to normal display.

The next chapter shows you how to edit the text in your presentations. Specifically, you'll learn how to work with individual characters as well as blocks of text. You'll also use the built-in spelling checker to make sure you've spelled everything correctly.

Editing Text

*f**a s t*** TRACK

● **To cut a text block,**   **141**

> first, highlight the text block you want to cut. Next, open the
> Edit menu and choose the Cut command. The highlighted
> text block is removed from the current page and placed on the
> clipboard.

● **To paste a text block,**   **143**

> move the cursor to the point at which you want to insert clip-
> board contents, and press Enter, if necessary, to add a new
> line. Next, open the Edit menu and choose the Paste com-
> mand. The contents of the clipboard are then placed at the
> cursor position.

● **To start the spelling checker,**   **147**

> open the Tools menu and choose the Spell Check command.
> Next, tell Freelance whether you want to spell check the
> selected word, the current page, or the entire presentation.
> After you've set any necessary options, click OK or press
> Enter.

IN the previous chapter, you learned to enter text in your Free-lance Graphics presentation. Starting with simple cursor positioning and character-editing tasks, this chapter shows you how to correct typos and other small mistakes. With a discussion on selecting a section of text, known as a text block, you'll learn to highlight and then copy, cut, paste, and delete text in your presentations. Finally, you'll learn how to use the spelling checker to make sense of jumbled spellings.

You'll find that in Freelance Graphics for Windows, you can perform two different kinds of editing operations. The first, simple text editing, involves correcting individual characters. For example, suppose that, as in the sample screen shown in Figure 5.1, you've accidentally misspelled the word *Chameleon*. To correct that typo, all you need to do is position the text cursor at the appropriate point, and add an *h*. That's simple editing—you've modified the word by adding a single character.

Text block editing, on the other hand, makes changes on a larger level. Suppose, for example, that you decide you really don't want to include the line *Ill-tempered Iguanas* in the Leapin' Lizards! presentation page. Removing the line is easy, but before you can delete it, you must first mark the line as a text block. Likewise, if you wanted to copy or cut the text from its position in the page you would need to first mark the text as a block. The following section introduces you to simple text editing.

FIGURE 5.1

An example of a
misspelled word

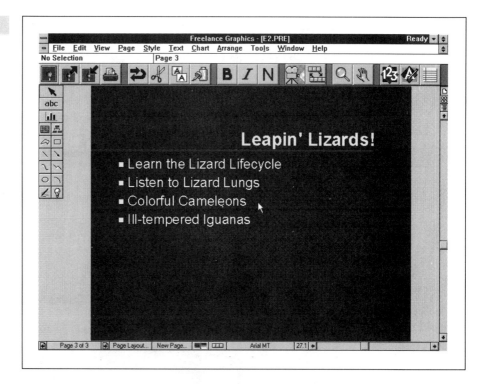

Simple Text Editing

Basic text editing is an easy process to remember. Here are the steps:

1. Select the text box containing the text you want to edit.

2. Open the Text menu and choose the Edit command.

3. Position the cursor at the point you need to edit.

4. Make your changes.

5. When finished, click OK or press Enter.

For now, click on the text box you want to edit. For this example, we plan to edit the word *cameleons*, as shown in Figure 5.1. Eight handles appear along the edges of the text box you selected. Now open the Text menu and choose the Edit command (or press F2). The text box appears and displays the text, ready to be edited (see Figure 5.2).

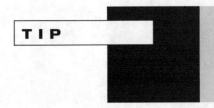

TIP

To change to edit mode without opening the Text menu and choosing the Edit command, simply press F2 after you've selected the text box you want to work with.

The following sections explain how you can move the cursor within the text box and work with both insert and typeover modes.

FIGURE 5.2

Displaying the text to be edited

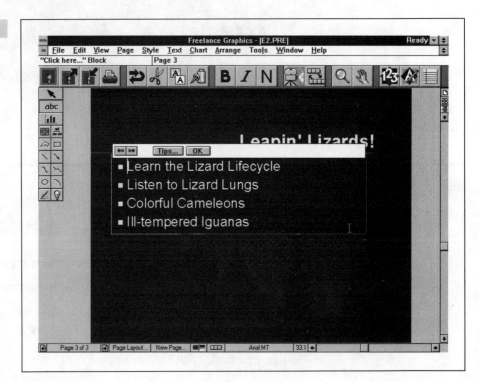

Positioning the Cursor

You can use either the mouse or the keyboard to move the text cursor within the text box. Some keys, such as left- and right-arrow, you've already used; others enable you to move farther, faster. Table 5.1 lists the various keys you can use when you are using cursor-movement keys to position the text cursor.

Of course, you may find it easier to use the mouse to position the text cursor. If you are using the mouse, move the mouse pointer to the position in the text box where you want to place the text cursor; then click the left mouse button. Freelance Graphics instantly moves the text cursor to that point.

TABLE 5.1: Cursor-Movement Keys in Edit Mode

KEY	DESCRIPTION
→	Moves cursor one character to the right
Ctrl-→	Moves cursor one word to the right
←	Moves cursor one character to the left
Ctrl-←	Moves cursor one word to the left
↑	Moves cursor up one line
Ctrl-↑	Moves cursor to beginning of current line
↓	Moves cursor down one line
Ctrl-↓	Moves cursor to end of current line
Home	Moves cursor to beginning of current line
End	Moves cursor to end of current line

Understanding Insert and Typeover Modes

Once you've placed the text cursor where you want to make your correction, you have a decision to make. Will it be easier to type over existing letters or to insert the letters that are missing? How you answer this question will determine whether you use insert or typeover mode.

When insert mode is in effect, any characters you type are inserted at the cursor position. For example, if you position the cursor between the *C* and the *a* in *Cameleons* and type an h when insert mode is active, the corrected word is *Chameleons*.

If, on the other hand, you position the cursor and type the h when typeover mode is active, the word becomes *Chmeleons*. As you can see, the *h* overwrites the original *a*.

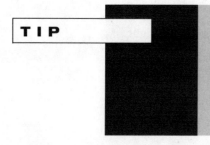

TIP

Freelance Graphics enables insert mode by default. Therefore, any characters you type are inserted automatically at the cursor position. To change to typeover mode, press the Ins key. The cursor changes from a vertical flashing bar to a flashing underline. To return to insert mode, press Ins again.

Let's try an example of basic text editing using insert mode. In the Leapin' Lizards! example, the cursor is positioned automatically before the first character in the text box (in this case, before the word *Learn*). If you're following along, correct the error in the text box by going through these steps:

1. Press the down-arrow twice. The cursor moves to the third line in the text box, before the word *Colorful*.

2. Press Ctrl-→. The cursor now flashes after the word *Colorful*.

3. Press the → key twice. The cursor now flashes between the *C* and the *a* in *Cameleon*.

4. Type h.

The necessary character is inserted at the cursor position, and the word is now correct (see Figure 5.3).

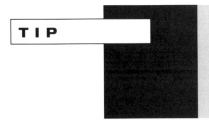

T I P

Remember that even though the examples in this section involve the keyboard, you can easily use the mouse to position the cursor: just point to the place where you want the cursor to appear, and click the mouse button.

FIGURE 5.3

The corrected spelling

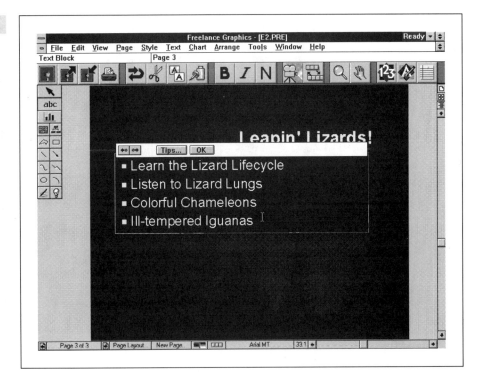

Now let's try an example of editing in typeover mode. Suppose that we feel the word *Ill-tempered* is a bit too negative for our friend the iguana. Let's change that word to *Intelligent,* using typeover mode. Here's how:

1. Assuming the cursor is still in the word Chameleon, press the ↓ key once. The cursor moves to the next line down.

2. Press Ctrl-↑. The cursor moves to the beginning of the word *Ill-tempered.*

3. Press the Ins key. This changes Freelance Graphics into typeover mode. The cursor changes to a blinking underline.

4. Type Intelligent. The characters you type overwrite those that were already there, except—oops—a single letter remains (see Figure 5.4).

FIGURE 5.4

Editing in typeover mode

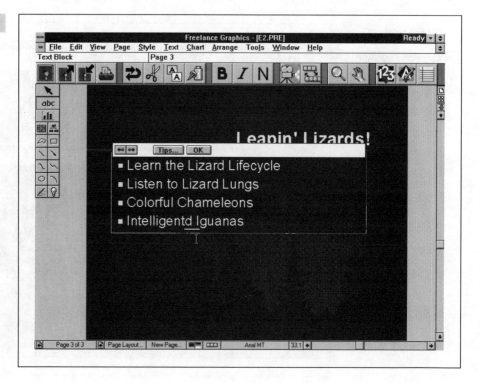

5. Press the Del key to remove the unnecessary letter. Now the text is correct.

6. Click OK or press Enter to accept your changes and return to the page display.

TIP

If you double-click on a word (anywhere in the word), the whole word will be selected. Then, just start typing the replacement word. Don't worry about stray letters, Freelance automatically deletes the entire old word and replaces it with whatever you're typing.

You can also do simple editing in the Outliner view. Use the same techniques for positioning the cursor—point and click with the mouse, or use the keyboard cursor-movement keys—and then correct the characters as necessary. Insert and typeover modes work in the Outliner, as well.

Now that you understand more about simple editing techniques, you're ready to investigate a bigger subject: block editing.

Working with Text Blocks

Another type of editing you'll perform in your Freelance Graphics documents includes block editing. We're not talking about the traditional, stack-em-up-and-knock-em-down kind of block—we mean a block of *text*.

What exactly *is* a text block? Simply put, a text block is any amount of text you mark, or highlight, from one character to an entire presentation. For most of your Freelance uses, a text block will probably range from a word to a line of text.

When will you use text blocks? You may think you've learned the basics of editing your presentation text, but there are many more operations you'll perform that require the selection of a block first. For example, suppose you want to copy a line of text. How will Freelance Graphics know which line you want to copy? You need to highlight the text first, thus marking it as a block. Block operations include the following:

- Copying text
- Cutting text
- Deleting text
- Changing the font, style, or size of text
- Changing the color of text
- Adjusting the margins or alignment of text

Some of these operations—such as changing font, color, and margins—are beyond the scope of this chapter and are more fully discussed in Chapter 6. In the following sections, you'll learn to select text blocks and then copy, cut, paste, and delete blocks you highlight.

Selecting Text Blocks

The first task you need to master is the selection of the text block itself. You can use both the keyboard and the mouse to select text (although the mouse method is noticeably easier).

If you're using the mouse, follow these steps:

1. Click on the box containing the text you want to select.

2. Open the Text menu and select the Edit command.

3. Position the I-beam pointer at the place you want to begin highlighting.

4. Press and hold the mouse button.

5. Drag the mouse until the text you want is highlighted. (You can select a few characters, a word, a phrase, or an entire text box.)

6. When you've selected the text you want, release the mouse button.

Figure 5.5 shows the sample Leapin' Lizards! page with a selected text block.

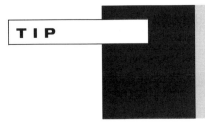

TIP

Here's a faster way to select a block. Position the I-beam pointer where you want to start. While holding down the Shift key, click where you want your selection to end. Everything in between the I-beam and the click is selected.

Once you've highlighted the text block you want to work with, you can perform a number of editing operations, which are the subjects of the following sections.

FIGURE 5.5

A selected text block

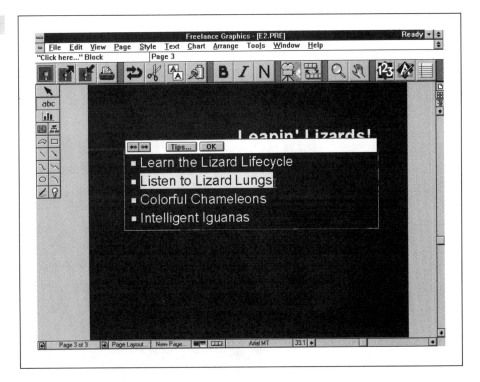

Copying Text Blocks

You might want to copy a text block, for example, when you are creating a new presentation page that will include the same text already found on another page. Copying saves you the trouble of retyping text you've already entered.

When you copy a block of text, Freelance Graphics places the text on an "invisible" clipboard. Later, you'll use the Paste command to place the text you've copied. To copy a block of text, follow these steps:

1. Select the text block you want to copy.

2. Open the Edit menu.

3. Choose the Copy command (see Figure 5.6).

Freelance Graphics then makes a copy of the highlighted text and places the copy on the clipboard.

FIGURE 5.6

Selecting the Copy command

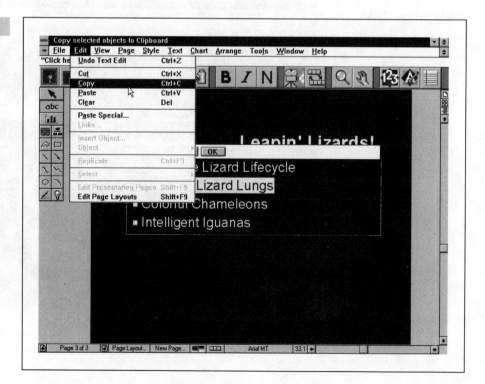

T I P To bypass the menu selections necessary for the Copy command, use the Copy SmartIcon or press Ctrl-C or Alt-E, then C.

Understanding the Clipboard

The clipboard—albeit invisible—performs a very real function in Freelance Graphics. Anytime you copy, cut, or paste an item in Freelance, you'll be working with the clipboard. Here are a few tips and reminders for dealing with the clipboard:

- You can place only one item on the clipboard at one time. (Subsequent items replace the last item placed on the clipboard.)

- If the commands that use the clipboard—such as Copy, Cut, or Paste—are dimmed, you can't select them at the current time. If Copy or Cut is gray, check to make sure you've actually highlighted the block you want to work with. If Paste is dimmed, there is nothing on the clipboard to paste, meaning you haven't used the Copy or Cut command before selecting Paste.

Cutting Text Blocks

Cutting text is a particularly good option if you want to move text from one place to another. Suppose, for example, that you want to move the line *Listen to Lizard Lungs* from the second item on the Leapin' Lizards! page and make it the last item on the page. The first part of this process involves removing the text from the current page—that's the Cut part—which places the removed text on the clipboard for safekeeping.

To cut text from a presentation page, follow these steps:

1. Highlight the text you want to cut.

2. Open the Edit menu.

3. Choose the Cut command.

Freelance Graphics then cuts the text from the page and places it on the clipboard. As you can see from Figure 5.7, the bullet still remains. (If you want to delete the bullet as well, press the backspace key.)

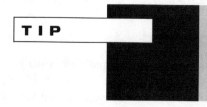

TIP

To skip the menu selection process of the cut procedure (opening the Edit menu and choosing the Cut command) by using any of the following: the Cut SmartIcon, Ctrl-X, or Alt-E, then T.

In the next section, you'll learn to replace the text line you've cut from the example.

FIGURE 5.7

The text box after a text block has been cut

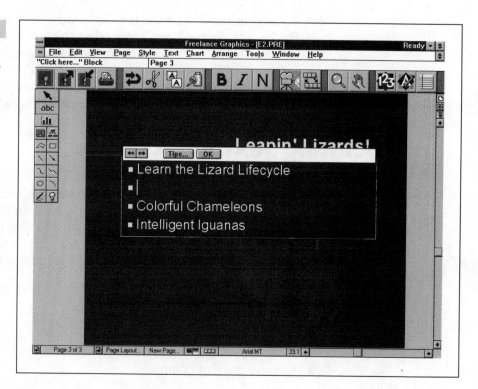

Pasting Text Blocks

As you might expect, cutting and pasting go hand-in-hand. Once you cut (or copy) something to the invisible clipboard, you need some means of placing that something back into your presentation. The Paste command inserts the contents of the clipboard at the cursor position. In this example, we'll move the cursor down to the last line of the Leapin' Lizards! page and paste in the text cut in the last example.

To paste a text block on a presentation page, follow these steps:

1. Move the cursor to the point at which you want to insert clipboard contents. (For this example, press down-arrow as necessary to move the cursor to the end of the *Intelligent Iguanas* line.)

2. Press Enter, if necessary, to add a new line.

3. Open the Edit menu.

4. Select the Paste command.

The contents of the clipboard are placed at the cursor position, as shown in Figure 5.8.

TIP   Rather than opening the Edit menu and selecting the Paste command, you can use the Paste SmartIcon, Ctrl-V, or Alt-E, then P.

Deleting Text Blocks

At first glance, *delete* might not seem a whole lot different than *cut*. Both procedures, after all, remove the selected text block from the page. One, however, stores the text on the clipboard, while the other throws the selected block away. As you learned in the last section, Cut saves the information lifted from the page and saves it for a Paste operation later. Clear, on the other hand, removes the selected text and sends it to never-never land—meaning that you'll never-never see it again.

FIGURE 5.8

Pasting clipboard
contents on the page

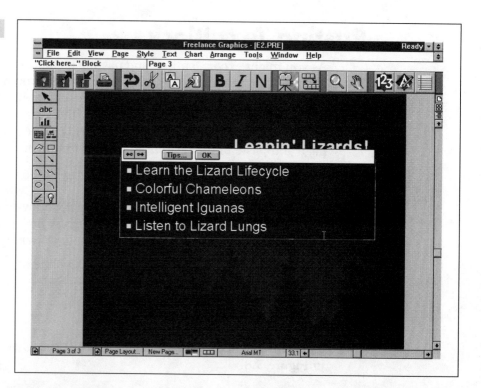

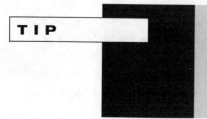

TIP   Paste can also be used to delete and replace blocks of text. Copy the desired text. Then select the block you want to delete. Finally, execute the Paste command. Presto! The old text disappears and is replaced by the text you copied.

To clear a text block, follow these steps:

1. Highlight the text block you want to clear.

2. Open the Edit menu.

3. Choose the Clear command.

The information you selected is removed from the page instantly. Since you cannot retrieve cleared text, be sure to take a second look at the text before you delete it.

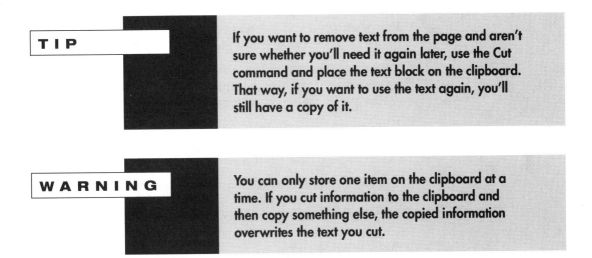

T I P

If you want to remove text from the page and aren't sure whether you'll need it again later, use the Cut command and place the text block on the clipboard. That way, if you want to use the text again, you'll still have a copy of it.

W A R N I N G

You can only store one item on the clipboard at a time. If you cut information to the clipboard and then copy something else, the copied information overwrites the text you cut.

Using Undo

Life would be so much easier if everything came with an Undo command. If you took the wrong exit on the freeway, you could push an Undo button on your dashboard and the mistake would be instantly wiped away. If you said the wrong thing in a board meeting, you could select an Undo command and wipe the remark from everyone's minds.

Freelance Graphics for Windows knows that we don't do everything right every time. And for that reason, the program gives us the option of reversing our most recent decisions. Did you really want to move that line from the beginning of the presentation to the end? No? Well, that's easy enough to correct with the Undo command.

But, like all things in life, even Undo can't safeguard us from everything. Here is a list of things to remember before you use the Undo command to bail you out:

- Undo enables you to reverse the last operation you performed. For example, if you cut text to the clipboard and then thought better of it, selecting Undo places the text back on the page.

- Selecting Undo several times allows you to reverse actions that preceded your most recent one. Depending on the operations you've performed, you may be able to reverse the last ten actions.

- You can select Undo by opening the Edit menu and choosing Undo, by pressing Ctrl-Z, or by clicking on the Undo SmartIcon (to the right of the Print icon in the SmartIcon palette).

- You can use Undo with both editing and graphics work.

To undo your last editing operation, follow these steps:

1. Open the Edit menu.
2. Choose the Undo command.

TIP

To get around the menu selections and use Undo, press Ctrl-Z or click the Undo SmartIcon (to the right of the Print SmartIcon).

Now that you know how to reverse your most recent actions (Freelance's actions, anyway), you're ready to move on to the utility that takes the guesswork out of your spelling tasks.

Using the Spelling Checker

Once you've entered the text for your presentation, take a few minutes and get to know Freelance Graphics' spelling checker. This spelling checker will dutifully check every word in your text pages, tables, charts, and speaker notes to ensure that things are as accurate as possible.

How does it work? The spelling checker has an incredible built-in dictionary, containing thousands of commonly used words and in which it looks up virtually every word in your text. If a Freelance encounters a word in your presentation that isn't in the dictionary, the program displays a screen telling you where the word is found, gives the context of the word (with the questioned word underlined), suggests a possible replacement, and lists alternative words or spellings. For each of these found words, you'll tell the program whether you want to add the word to the dictionary (so Freelance won't have to ask you about the same word next time), skip over the word, replace the word with the displayed word, or cancel the spell operation.

Beginning the Spelling Process

You can start the spell checker from any point in your Freelance Graphics presentations. Whether you are currently working in presentation page, Page Sorter, or Outliner view, here's how to start the spelling checker:

1. Open the Tools menu.

2. Choose the Spell Check command (see Figure 5.9).

TIP

You can bypass the menu selections and begin the spelling checker by pressing Ctrl-F2.

FIGURE 5.9

Choosing the Spell
Check command

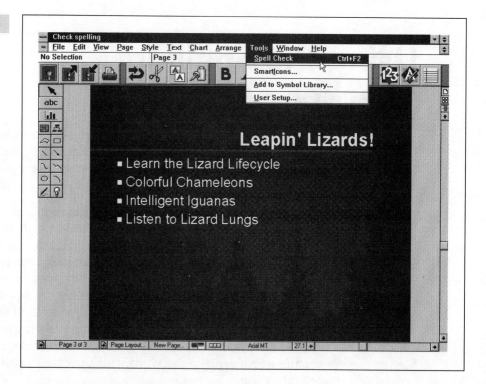

The Spell Check dialog box appears, as shown in Figure 5.10. In this dialog box, you can specify how much of the presentation you want to check. At the top of the box, you see three options, allowing you to choose whether you want to check a selected word or words, the current page, or the entire presentation (including tables, notes, and charts). As you can see, Current page is selected by default. To spell check the entire presentation, click the radio button in front of Entire presentation.

Notice that in the bottom half of the box, you have three options that allow you to specify which additional items—Data charts, Organization charts, and Speaker notes—you want to include in the spelling operation. When the option box shows an X, the text in that particular item will be spell-checked. To add (and remove) the X, click in the appropriate box.

Along the right side of the dialog box are several more buttons. You should recognize OK and Cancel—they are present in just about every dialog box you see. The next section introduces you to the wonders behind the Options button.

The Spell Check
dialog box

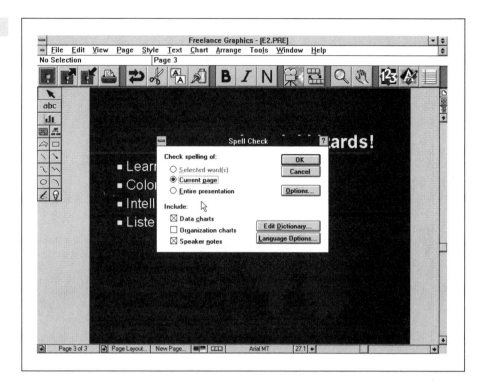

Exploring the Spelling Options

Clicking the Options button displays a screen of Spell Check Options that
you can select to better control the way your presentation is checked (see
Figure 5.11).

The Spell Check Options dialog box gives you the option of looking for
words mistakenly used used twice (did you catch that one?), checking
for words that include numbers, checking all words with initial caps, and
including words from a user dictionary you can customize for your own
business's language.

Table 5.2 lists the options in the Spell Check Options box and provides a
brief description of each.

After you've selected the options you want from the Spell Check Options
dialog box, click OK to return to the main Spell Check screen.

FIGURE 5.11

The Spell Check
Options dialog box

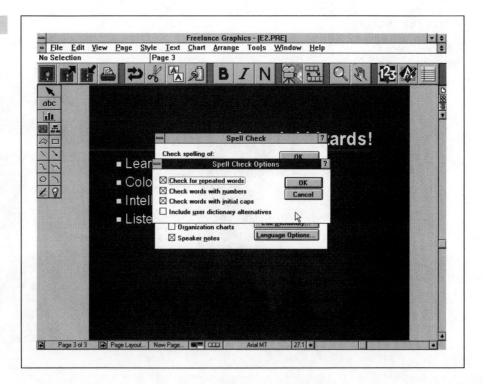

TABLE 5.2: Options in the Spell Check Options Box

OPTION	DESCRIPTION
Check for repeated words	Looks for words that have been accidentally repeated in the presentation (common occurrences include double-use of the words *the*, *and*, *you*, *to*, *for*, and *of*)
Check words with numbers	Displays the Spell Check dialog box whenever a word that includes a number is found. For example, the word *4KidsClub* would be displayed, but *fourteen* would not.

TABLE 5.2: Options in the Spell Check Options Box (continued)

OPTION	DESCRIPTION
Check words with initial caps	Stops at all words with initial capitalization, including proper names, business names, and titles (such as *Murray*, *Sybex*, or *Product Manager*). If your work includes many such names, and you don't want to check the accuracy of the spelling, you may want to disable this option by removing the X. This will speed the spelling process.
Include user dictionary alternatives	This option allows you to add-in words that you enter in your own custom dictionary. For example, in many businesses there are terms that are common to that industry but are not often found in common-usage dictionaries. In the computer industry, for example, RAM and ROM are common, but in a traditional language dictionary, they can often cause the speller to stumble. To save time and trouble, you can create your own user dictionary with words unique to your industry. Then, when Freelance spell checks the presentation, words in your dictionary are checked and passed over when their accuracy has been assured.

Understanding the User Dictionary

The next button in the Spell Check dialog box is the Edit Dictionary button. As you might expect, this button takes you to a new dialog box in which you can add words to a more specialized dictionary that contains terms unique to your industry (see Figure 5.12).

FIGURE 5.12

The Spell Check User's
Dictionary dialog box

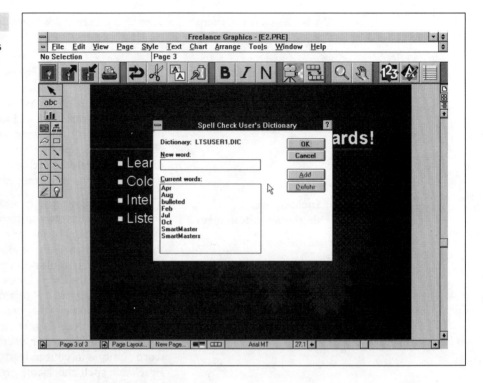

To add a word to the user dictionary, follow these steps:

1. Click in the *New word:* box. The blinking cursor is positioned in that box.

2. Type the word you want to add.

3. Click the Add button on the right side of the dialog box.

Freelance Graphics then adds the word you specified to the user dictionary *ltsuser1.dic,* the file shown at the top of the dialog box. The word is removed from the *New word:* box and is alphabetized in the *Current words:* list in the bottom of the dialog box. You can add as many words as necessary by repeating the process.

You can also use this same dialog box to delete words from the user dictionary. Here's how:

1. Click on the word you want to delete. The word will appear highlighted.

2. Click the Delete button. The word is immediately deleted from the *Current words:* list.

3. Click OK or press Enter to return to the Spell Check dialog box.

Choosing Languages

The final option in the Spell Check dialog box is the Language Options button. This button displays another dialog box, Spell Check Language, that allows you to choose another language for the words you're checking. You can choose from either American or British. You can also choose other dictionaries, if you've created them, from this dialog box.

To make a selection, click on the dictionary you want and click the OK button or press Enter. Freelance Graphics then uses the dictionary you specified when you begin the spell check routine.

Spell Checking the Presentation

Now that you've explored all the various options and buttons in the spell checking procedure, there's nothing left to do but click OK. Figure 5.13 shows the dialog box that appears when the spelling checker encounters a word it doesn't recognize.

At the top of the dialog box, you see the location in the presentation where the word was found (*Page 1 of 3*). Below the location is a box showing the culprit: *EcoSystems.* The *Replace with:* box provides you with an alternate word (which, in this case, oddly enough, is the same word).

Beneath the *Replace with:* box, the Alternatives box lists other spellings (in this case, other capitalizations and punctuations). In the bottom right corner of the box, you see a series of six buttons. Table 5.3 lists each of these buttons and provides a brief description of each.

FIGURE 5.13

The Spell Check
dialog box

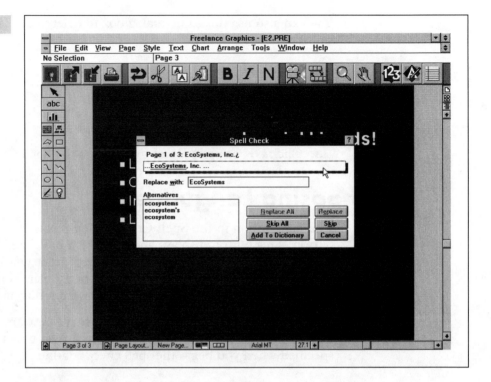

TABLE 5.3: Spell Check Command Buttons

BUTTON	DESCRIPTION
Replace All	Replaces all occurrences of the found word with the word displayed in the *Replace with:* box
Replace	Replaces only this occurrence of the found word
Skip All	Skips all occurrences of the found word without making corrections
Skip	Skips only this occurrence of the found word
Add To Dictionary	Adds the found word to the user dictionary
Cancel	Cancels the spelling operation

After you make your selection, Freelance Graphics continues the checking process, stopping on each unrecognized word and displaying alternate spellings. When your entire presentation has been checked, Freelance displays a small dialog box that tells you *Spelling check complete*. Click OK or press Enter to return to the presentation page.

In this chapter, you've learned a lot about simple editing tasks as well as more complicated text block editing operations. You also learned the ins and outs of the spelling checker that Freelance Graphics for Windows shares with its sister programs, Ami Pro and Lotus 1-2-3.

In the next chapter, you'll learn how to change the look of your text by working with formatting and text enhancement.

SIX

Formatting and
Enhancing Text

fast TRACK

● **To change the justification of text,**   **165**

first click on the text box containing the text you want to change; then open the Style menu and choose Attributes ["Click here..." Block]. When the Paragraph Style menu appears, click on the paragraph style you want to modify. Then click on the button that corresponds to the way in which you want the text aligned (left, centered, right, or justified). Click OK. The text is then realigned according to your specifications.

● **To align text vertically within the text box,**   **167**

display the Paragraph Styles dialog box. Then click on the Vertical justification setting you want (Top, Middle, or Bottom). Click OK.

● **To turn word wrap off and on,**   **168**

first display the Paragraph Styles dialog box by double-clicking on the text box you want (or by opening the Style menu and choosing the Attributes command). Next, move the pointer to the Word Wrap option. To turn off word wrap, click in the box, removing the X. To turn on word wrap, repeat the process. This time, when you click in the Word Wrap box, the X will appear, indicating that the feature has been enabled.

● **To change the style of selected text,**   181

first display the text in edit mode (click on the text box and press F2). Next, highlight the text you want to change. Now, click on the SmartIcon that represents the style you want to use (B for Bold, I for Italic, or N for Normal), or open the Text menu and choose the appropriate style.

● **To change bullet style,**   190

first click on the text box containing the bullets you want to change. Open the Text menu and choose Bullet. When the Text Bullet dialog box appears, click on Style: Select any character you want (if you want to use a symbol, click on Symbol at the bottom of the list and make your selection from the Use Symbol as Bullet dialog box). To choose a color, click on Color: and select the color you want from the displayed palette. To choose a size, click on the *Size:* box and make your selection from the drop-down list of available bullet sizes. When you've finished making choices, click OK or press Enter.

● **To add speaker notes,**   198

first display the page to which you want to add the note. Then open the Page menu and choose Speaker Notes. The Speaker Note dialog box appears on the screen. Type your text as necessary, making any editing or enhancement changes by using the commands in the Edit and Text menus. To return to the page, click OK or press Enter.

IN the previous chapter, you learned various techniques for editing the text you've written for your presentation. This chapter shows you how to change the look of the text by making changes to the way it's formatted as well as to the font, size, and style of the text you've chosen.

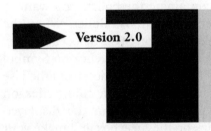

Version 2.0

The symbols-as-bullets feature and the speaker note capability are new with Freelance Graphics for Windows, Version 2.0. You can now use any symbol as a bullet character and you can add speaker notes to help you give your presentation.

Formatting Text

Formatting, simply put, is the process of arranging text on the page. Will your subtitle be indented? Do you want the presentation title to be centered or aligned to the right? These issues and more will be explored in this section.

A few of the items you've already seen—margins, columns, tabs, and justification—all fall under the general heading of formatting. This chapter reviews the settings already in effect (the SmartMaster you choose takes care of formatting automatically) and provides you with the information you need to change format specifications.

N O T E

This chapter continues working with the *sketch.mas* SmartMaster you first saw in Chapter 3. In the examples that follow, illustrations are used to show formatting and enhancement changes. If you want to follow along, feel free to create the examples used in the figures. Otherwise, work on something of your own that will allow you to get some hands-on practice with formatting and text enhancement tasks.

Understanding Paragraph Styles

Most of the formatting options you'll use are found in the Paragraph Styles dialog box. This box, which contains many different options, controls the way Freelance Graphics formats and displays three different paragraph styles.

You'll use the Paragraph Styles dialog box to set global options—that is, to make choices that will affect all text on all pages in the level you choose. For example, if you change the Level 1 paragraph style to New Century Schoolbook 36-point bold type, all text formatted in that level will be assigned that font and style. (More about fonts and styles later in the chapter.) In other places in this chapter, you'll learn to make these changes for selected bits of text. Remember, however, that when you want to make major changes—like changing the font, color, or alignment—to all text in a particular paragraph style, use the Paragraph Styles dialog box.

What exactly is a paragraph style? If you've worked with some popular word processing programs, you may already be familiar with paragraph styles. A paragraph style is a group of settings—which control spacing, alignment, and font issues and that can be applied to a particular paragraph. For example, suppose you want the text in your bullet list to be centered, 30-point Times. You want to include a small amount of space just before the item so the list is spaced well. A paragraph style can take care of these settings for you.

Without any interaction from you, Freelance Graphics automatically places the text you enter in one of three paragraph styles—one for each of the text levels available in bulleted lists. Paragraph styles make working with formatting and text enhancement options easier. Rather than having to go through each page of your presentation and select the settings you want in each text box, you can change the paragraph style assigned to a particular text level. All text in that level is changed to reflect your new settings.

You can use up to three levels of bullets in a bulleted list. The first paragraph style (Level 1) corresponds to the first-level indent; the second paragraph style (Level 2), to the second-level indent; and the third paragraph style, (Level 3), to the third level indent. You can change any or all of these paragraph styles so that each time you enter text for one of these levels, the new settings go into effect. Table 6.1 shows the settings used for each of the paragraph styles.

TABLE 6.1: Paragraph style settings

PARAGRAPH STYLE	SETTINGS
Level 1	Typeface: Arial MT Size: 30-point Text color: Black Bullet: Square Bullet color: Red Bullet size: 30-point Justification: Left Vertical just.: Top Word wrap: On
Level 2	Typeface: Arial MT Size: 26-point Text color: Black Bullet: Dash Bullet color: Red Bullet size: 26-point Justification: Left Vertical just.: Top Word wrap: On

TABLE 6.1: Paragraph style settings (continued)

PARAGRAPH STYLE	SETTINGS
Level 3	Typeface: Arial MT
	Size: 30-point
	Text color: Black
	Bullet: Triangle
	Bullet color: Red
	Bullet size: 30-point
	Justification: Left
	Vertical just.: Top
	Word wrap: On

As you can see, the difference between these three styles is minimal. Levels 2 and 3 are unique only in that they use different bullet characters. You control all these settings (and enter your own) by using the Paragraph Styles dialog box, which is the subject of the next section.

Introducing the Paragraph Styles Dialog Box

The first step in understanding paragraph styles—and in formatting the text in your presentation—is to display the Paragraph Styles dialog box. In this box, you'll find everything you need to change the way text is placed on your presentation page. To display the Paragraph Styles dialog box, follow these steps:

1. Click on the text box with which you want to work.

2. Open the Style menu.

3. Choose the Attributes ["Click here..." Block] command.

TIP You can bypass the menu selections and display the Paragraph Style dialog box quickly by double-clicking on the text box.

The Paragraph Styles dialog box appears, as shown in Figure 6.1. In this box, you see the familiar close box in the upper left corner; a help button in the upper right corner; and several different groups of options. The top portion of the box enables you to choose which paragraph style you want to work with. The second group of options contains the various attributes for the selected style. On the bottom left side of the box, you see options for controlling justification and word wrap.

On the right side of the box, a group of buttons appear. The Spacing & Indents button takes you to yet another dialog box, containing many of the options you'll use in changing the format of your text.

FIGURE 6.1

The Paragraph Styles dialog box

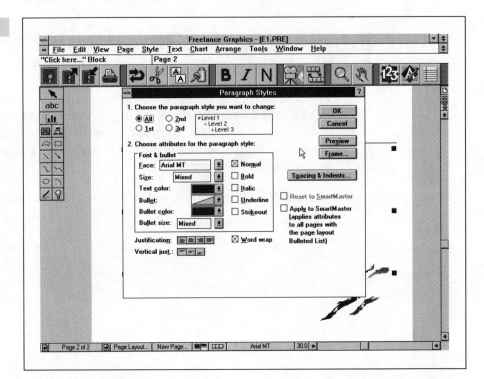

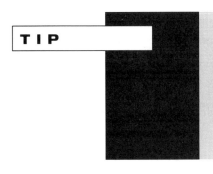

TIP

You can use the Default Attributes command in the Style menu to set default paragraph style attributes for the entire presentation before you begin. When you choose this command, a dialog box almost identical to the Paragraph Styles dialog box appears, and allows you to modify the default settings as necessary.

In the following sections, you'll learn how to control the following formatting options from within the Paragraph Style dialog box:

- **Justification**, in which you choose whether you want the text to be left aligned, centered, right aligned, or justified (more about this in a minute)

- **Vertical justification**, in which you decide whether you want the text to be placed at the top of the page, in the center, or at the bottom of the page

- **Word wrap**, which controls whether Freelance Graphics wraps long lines of text to the next line or extends the text to the edge of the text boundary.

Choosing Justification

The term *justification* may seem like a strange word for the alignment of text, but that's what it controls: the way your text is aligned within the text box. Remember back in Chapter 3 when we entered text in a text box? The text was right-aligned, meaning it appeared from the right side of the box. With Freelance Graphics, you have a choice of four different types of justification:

- **Left-aligned**, in which the text is aligned along the left margin but not the right

- **Centered**, in which the text is centered between the left and right margins

- **Right-aligned**, in which the text is aligned along the right margin, but the left margin remains ragged, and

- **Full Justification**, in which small spaces are inserted between words so the text aligns along both the left and right margins

Figure 6.2 shows how the example page looks when the bulleted items have been centered.

Looks a little strange, doesn't it? You'll probably want to experiment with the different settings and find the one that helps you present your material in the best way.

In your presentations, you may use any combination of settings to align your text. You could, for example, center a title, left-align bullet text, and right-align a note in the bottom right corner. The four buttons after the *Justification:* option show you, in miniature, the format adopted by each setting. To choose a new justification for the selected text, click the button you want.

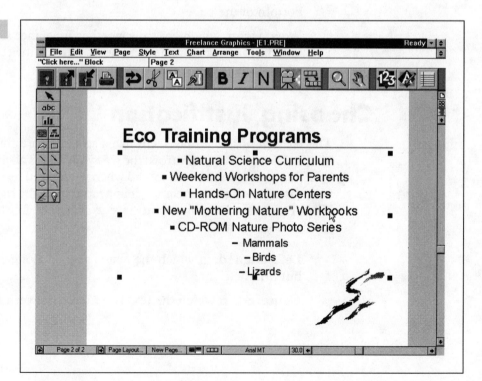

T I P

Click the preview button to view the results of the change without clicking OK and returning to the presentation page. The change is displayed, but the text has not actually been moved. A small pop-up Preview box appears, listing three buttons: OK, Change, and Tip. Click OK if you want to keep the new setting you entered; Change if you want to return to the Paragraph Styles dialog box; or Tip to find out more about using Preview.

Specifying Vertical Placement

Another type of justification option is available in the Paragraph Style settings. Rather than control alignment between the left and right margins, the Vertical justification option allows you to change the way the text is placed within the vertical confines of the text box. In other words, you can specify whether you want the text to be placed at the top, middle, or bottom of the box.

Setting vertical alignment is important when you are trying to space out the text used in a page that contains several text boxes. Rather than jumble everything together, you can control the way the text is placed within the text box so your page is uncluttered and easy to read.

To choose a vertical alignment for your text, look carefully at the graphical icons that represent your choices. The first choice aligns the text at the top (this is the default). The second choice aligns text in the middle of the box, and the last choice places text at the bottom of the box.

After you've made your selection, you can preview the change by clicking the Preview button. Choose OK in the displayed Preview box to accept the changes, Change to return to the Paragraph Style dialog box without making the change, or Cancel to cancel the operation.

TIP

You can select more than one text box at a time by holding down the Shift key while clicking on the boxes you want. By selecting more than one text box at a time—whether you're planning on changing the format, font, size, style, or color of text—you can change the settings for all selected text at once.

Controlling Word Wrap

You may not think of it as a formatting feature, but word wrap—and whether is it enabled—affects the way your text appears within the text box. Consider, for example, the new page shown in Figure 6.3. In this example, we want to enter the text Environmental Changes in the displayed text box. The problem? The words are too long to fit on one line.

FIGURE 6.3

Illustrating word wrap with a new example

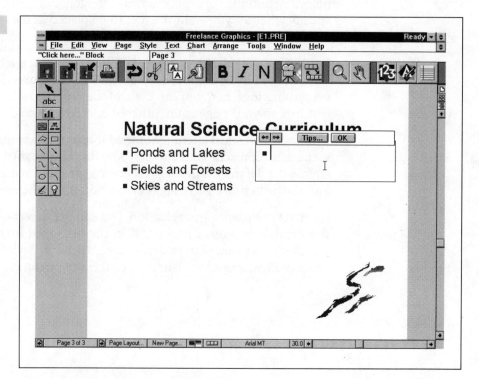

Because Freelance uses word wrap by default, the word Changes is automatically bumped to the next line without any action on your part. Figure 6.4 shows the entered text.

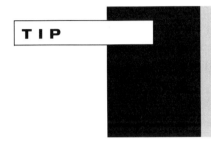

TIP

Even though Freelance Graphics wraps text automatically when word wrap is turned on, the program still considers the text as a single entry. Thus, when you look at the presentation in the Outliner, the entire entry will be on one line even though two were used on the presentation page.

To turn off the word wrap feature, begin once again at the Paragraph Styles dialog box. The Word Wrap option is to the right of the Justification settings. It is a simple checkbox, meaning that when an X appears in the

FIGURE 6.4

The text with word wrap in effect

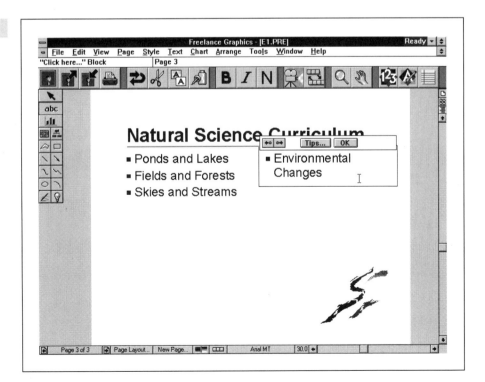

box, the feature is turned on, and when the box is blank, the feature is turned off. To turn off word wrap, click in the Word Wrap box. The X disappears. You can then preview the text box to see whether you want to keep the change you've just made. Figure 6.5 shows the text in the box when word wrap has been disabled.

What happens when you enter text that cannot possibly fit all on one line of your text box? The text box expands to accommodate your entry, perhaps even extending off the presentation page area.

Seems a little silly, considering that this text won't be printed or displayed in its entirety. It makes you wonder why you would ever want to disable word wrap, doesn't it? Here's a possible answer.

Freelance Graphics uses standard margin settings, keeping the text away from the edge of the page for a logical, well-balanced presentation look. In some cases, the text you enter may be one or two characters too long to fit all on one line. In such a case, you may want to disable word wrap for

FIGURE 6.5

The text when word wrap is disabled

that text box so that the text you're working with will fit within the space you've allotted for it. In situations where the text will cut into the margin space or beyond the printable area of the page, you'll probably find that rethinking your page layout and using word wrap is a better alternative.

Now that you've covered the formatting aspects of the Paragraph Style dialog box, you're ready to go another level deeper—to Spacing & Indents. The next section tells you how.

Modifying Spacing

In the middle of the right side of the Paragraph Style dialog box, the Spacing & Indents button appears. This button takes you to yet another dialog box in which you control—you guessed it—the spacing and indents of the text in the chosen text box. Go ahead and click on the button now. The screen shown in Figure 6.6 appears.

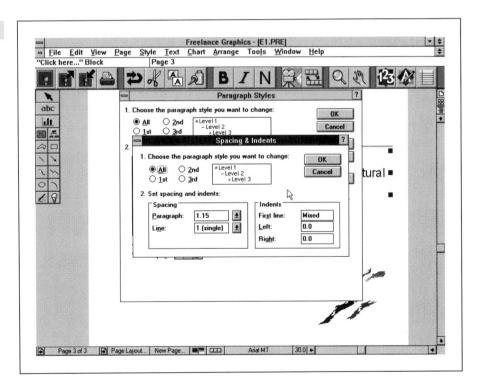

The first section of this dialog box should look familiar—it's the one that lets you specify which paragraph style you want to work with. (*All* is the default.) You can change the spacing for all paragraph styles in the presentation, or you can select only the level with which you are currently working.

Setting Paragraph Spacing

The *Paragraph:* spacing setting controls the number of lines between paragraphs. The default value is 1.15 lines. To modify this setting, follow these steps:

1. Move the pointer to the Spacing options box (or press P, if you're using the keyboard rather than the mouse).

2. Click on the down-arrow symbol to display drop-down list of available paragraph spacing settings (see Figure 6.7). If you're using the keyboard, you can press the down-arrow key to display each of the available choices in the setting box.

FIGURE 6.7

The drop-down list box of paragraph spacing choices

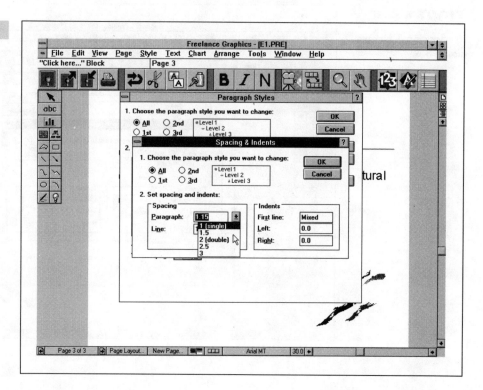

3. Highlight the choice you want.

4. Click OK.

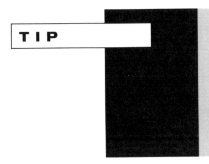

TIP

Freelance Graphics considers each individual text entry—marked by a carriage return at the end—as a paragraph. This means each bulleted item is in a paragraph by itself, even though several bullets may occupy the same text box. If you press Ctrl-Enter, Freelance will move to the next line *without* creating a new paragraph.

You are returned to the Paragraph Styles dialog box. Preview the change, if you like, by clicking the Preview button. Otherwise, you can return to the presentation page by clicking OK or pressing Enter. Figure 6.8 shows

FIGURE 6.8

The changed paragraph spacing

a preview page in which the spacing for the selected box has been changed to 2.5. Notice the Preview options in the center of the screen.

If you want to change the setting, click the Change button or press C. Otherwise, to accept the changes, click OK or press Enter.

Setting Line Spacing

You can set the *Line:* spacing option from within the Spacing & Indents dialog box. This setting controls the amount of space inserted between lines in a paragraph that has wrapped to more than one line. For example, remember the Environmental Changes entry, earlier in this chapter? The long version of that entry covered three lines on the right side of the page (see Figure 6.9).

How many spaces do you want to separate each line? To display the Spacing & Indents dialog box, go through the now-familiar routine of double-clicking on the text box, and clicking the Spacing & Indents button on the

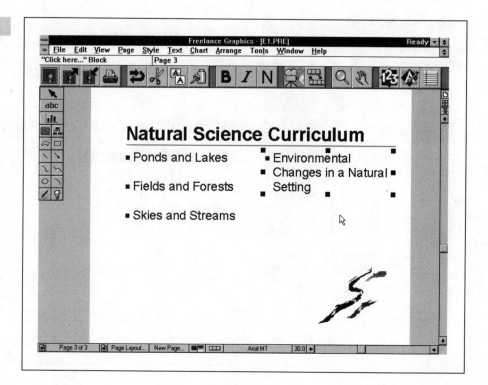

FIGURE 6.9

A multiple-line text entry

right side of the Paragraph Style dialog box. When the Spacing & Indents box appears, follow these steps:

1. Move the mouse pointer to the *Line:* setting (or press N).

2. Click on the ↓ at the end of the box to display a drop-down list of line settings. (If you're using the keyboard, press the down-arrow key to scroll through the available choices).

3. Highlight the setting you want or type a new setting of your own.

4. Click OK or press Enter. You are returned to the Paragraph Styles dialog box.

You can now preview your changes or go on back to the page by clicking OK or pressing Enter. Figure 6.10 shows the selected text box after the line spacing has been changed to 1.5.

FIGURE 6.10

The modified line spacing within the text box

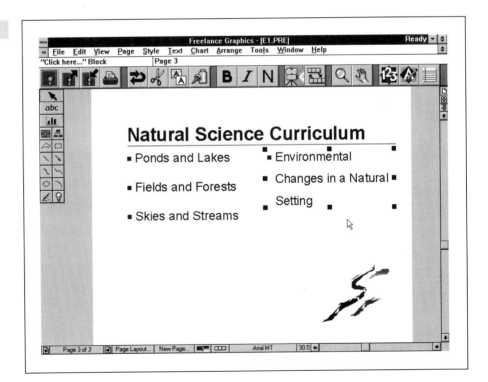

TIP

In a "real" presentation situation, you would use spacing to contrast the three bulleted items on the left side of the page with the one bulleted item on the right side. In this case, having less space for the multiple-line entry would probably be better. This would lead the reader's eye through the entire entry rather than make him or her stop at the end of each line. Effective use of spacing also helps reduce the guesswork.

Setting Indents

The *Indent:* settings is on the other side of the Spacing & Indents dialog box. Indents, as you probably remember from high school typing class, are those annoying little spaces we insert at strategic points in our documents. (I say "annoying" because I always forgot them and my teachers always remembered....)

Nevertheless, indents can be helpful in formatting text. In traditional business-style prose, a five-character indent is standard and lets readers know when a new paragraph begins. Other types of indents are used to help control the format of text. These indents include:

- **First line indent,** in which you specify an amount by which only the first line in a multiple-line text entry is indented

- **Hanging indent,** in which the first line of text literally "hangs out" and subsequent lines are indented

- **Left indent,** in which the entire left edge of the text is indented by the amount you specify

- **Right indent,** in which the right edge of the text (all lines) is indented by the amount you specify.

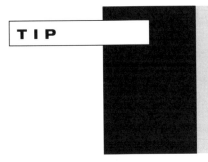

TIP When you specify an indent setting, you'll be using the units of measurement you specified earlier. If you don't remember which unit of measure you chose—millimeters (mm), centimeters (cm), inches (in), picas (p) or points (pts)—you can display the current settings by opening the View menu and choosing the Units & Grids command.

Since Freelance Graphics uses them as its default, the examples that follow will use millimeters as their unit of measurement.

Setting a First Line Indent

You can specify a first line indent whether you've got many lines of text in an entry or a series of single-line items. The effect, however, will most likely be lost for single-line entries (readers would have no subsequent lines to compare the first line with, so who would know the line is actually indented?). First line indents look good when you have multiple lines that have wrapped around in a single text box.

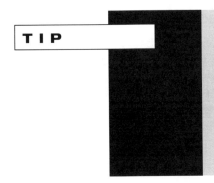

TIP When specifying a first line indent, make sure that the amount you enter is larger than the left indent, if you use one. For example, if you specify a *First line:* indent of 5.0 millimeters and a *Left:* indent of 5.0, the First line indent won't appear because both lines will be indented the same amount. In order for the *First line:* indent to appear, enter 10.0 or 12.0, thus offsetting the 5.0 indent for the left margin.

To add a first line indent, follow these steps:

1. If you haven't already done so, display the Spacing & Indents dialog box. (Do this by double-clicking on the text box you want to modify; then click the Spacing & Indents button.)

2. Select the *First line:* indent option by clicking on the setting or typing S.

3. Enter the number of millimeters you want to include in the indent.

4. Click OK or press Enter. You are returned to the Paragraph Style dialog box.

You can now preview your changes or click OK to return to the presentation page. The modification you made may be hard to see, depending on the type of measurement you are using. Repeat the process until you get the kind of contrast you are trying for.

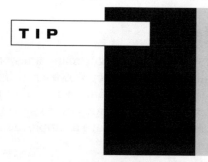

TIP

If you're having trouble seeing the indents you've added, display the ruler to make sure the changes are actually taking place. To do so, open the View menu and choose the View Preferences command. When the View Preferences dialog box appears, click Drawing ruler (in the Display options). Then click OK or press Enter.

Creating a Hanging Indent

A *hanging indent* is a special kind of indent that is used to call attention to the beginning of a text item by having the first line hang out into the left margin. Specifying a hanging indent is no more complicated than entering a first line indent that is smaller than the left indent. For example, the following setting (based on millimeter measurement) would create a hanging indent:

First line:	6.0
Left:	12.0
Right:	0.0

The hanging indent is often used to call attention to multiple-line entries, but, as you can see from Figure 6.11, it is not very effective here.

FIGURE 6.11

An example of a
hanging indent

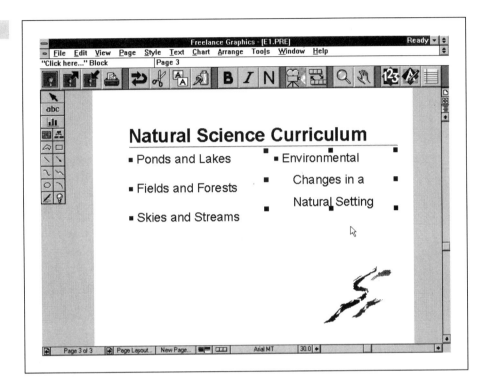

After you specify the indents, click OK to return to the Paragraph Styles
dialog box. You can then preview your changes by clicking the Preview
button, or return to the page by clicking OK or pressing Enter.

Setting Left and Right Indents

Now that you understand first line and hanging indents, left and right indents should be a piece of cake. As you know, Freelance Graphics sets up
margin settings that you can use as-is or change to meet your needs. These
margins are displayed in the File Page Setup box that appears when you
open the File menu and choose—no surprise—Page Setup. To specify the
margins for the page, choose Top, Bottom, Left, and Right margins. (If
you need a refresher course on setting page options, consult Chapter 3.)

The left and right indent settings you enter in the Spacing & Indents dialog box affect the spacing within the text box—*not* the entire page. If your text box butts up against the edge of the page, the page margins set in the File Page Setup box remain in effect, and any indents you specify are added to the original margins.

To specify left or right margins, follow these steps:

1. Click in the box to the right of the indent you want to set (*Left:* or *Right:*). If you prefer, you can type the underlined letter for the appropriate selection.

2. Type a value that represents the amount of space by which you want to indent the text. The *Left:* value will indent text along the left edge of the text box. The *Right:* value indents text from the right edge.

3. Click OK. The Paragraph Style dialog box is displayed, and you can preview the page or click OK to accept changes.

That just about does it as far as formatting goes. You can also manually move boxes around on the page, and arrange text, charts, and other graphics any way you want. But these topics fall under the heading of "arranging," which will be covered in Chapter 14, "Fine-Tuning Your Presentation."

The rest of this chapter concentrates on enhancing the look of your text.

Enhancing Text

When you're working with a new program for the first time, just getting the text entered correctly can be a major accomplishment. So, it may be a while before you have to worry about changing the look of the text your chosen SmartMaster provides. SmartMasters are so thorough, in fact, that all the text enhancement options—font choice, alignment, color, style—are already programmed in.

At some point, however, you'll feel comfortable enough to try your own hand at mixing and matching different type styles and fonts. In this section, you'll learn to do the following things:

- Change the style of selected text
- Curve text
- Specify a different font
- Choose a new text size
- Work with bullets
- Add a text frame
- Add speaker notes

NOTE A few quickie definitions: A font is one size and style of a particular typeface (for example Times 24-point bold text). A style is a particular type setting that serves to highlight the text (styles include boldface, italic, normal, underline, and strikeout). Size refers to the size of the characters in that font, measuring from the base of the character to the top of the character's highest point.

The following section starts things off by showing you how to change the style of text you select.

Changing the Style of Selected Text

A style can communicate a lot about your text: **bold** jumps out at the reader; *italic* emphasizes defined terms or important concepts; <u>underline</u> reinforces a section of text.

Boldfacing Text

As you might expect, the first step you'll need to take when you decide to boldface a section of text is to select the text you want to change. Here's how:

1. Display the text in edit mode (click on the text box and press F2).

2. To highlight the text, position the mouse pointer at the place you want to begin highlighting.

3. Press the mouse button and drag the mouse until the text you want is selected.

4. When the text is highlighted, release the mouse button.

TIP   You can highlight a single word quickly by positioning the pointer anywhere in the word and double-clicking the mouse button.

There are three different ways to place the selected text in boldface style:

• Open the Text menu and select the Bold command.

• Press Ctrl-B.

• Click on the bold SmartIcon (indicated by the big B in the Smart-Icon palette).

After you perform any one of these actions, the text is placed in boldfaced type. Figure 6.12 shows the text box with the word *Natural* in boldface type.

Although this section explains how to change the text style for selected text, you can also change the style, font, and size of text globally—that is, for *all* the text in your presentation. You make these changes in the Para-graph Styles dialog box. Global text enhancements are discussed later in this chapter.

FIGURE 6.12

Boldfacing selected text

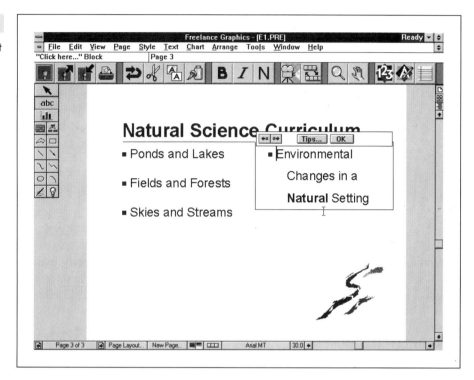

Italicizing Text

Specifying italic text style follows pretty much the same pattern: display the text in edit mode, select the text you want to change, and choose one of these methods:

- Click the italic SmartIcon (I)
- Open the Text menu and choose Italic
- Press Ctrl-I

The text is then formatted in italic text style.

TIP

Text changes that concern only selected text override global settings. For example, if you choose Italic type in the Paragraph Style dialog box, but you've already boldfaced the word Natural, the entire text entry except the word Natural appears in italics. The style settings chosen for Natural are preserved as you selected them.

Applying Other Styles

Other styles are available in Freelance Graphics, as well. You can choose Underline or Strikeout for those specialized uses that require something other than boldface or italic text. To specify underline, you can open the Text menu and choose Underline or press Ctrl-U; to specify Strikeout, you must open the text menu and choose Strikeout.

Returning Text to Normal Style

After you specify a style for selected text, you can easily return to "normal" style—that is to regular text without boldface, italic, or any other enhancement.

Use any of the following ways to return to normal style:

- Open the Text menu and choose the Normal command
- Press Ctrl-N
- Click the normal SmartIcon (N)

The text you highlighted is then returned to normal style. If you had selected global settings, those settings would be overwritten by your selection.

You now have the ability to create curved text—something other presentation graphics packages only dream about. By adding curved text to your presentations, you can create snazzy logos or other special effects. You can format text in the shape of an oval, a curve, a triangle, in diagonal lines, bell curves, and a variety of other shapes. For more information about using text as graphics, see Chapter 11.

Working with Fonts

So now you know how to change the look of the selected text. But what if you want to change an entire typeface? A font, as discussed earlier in this chapter, is any one size and style of a particular typeface. A typeface, also called a type family, is a "brand" of type—characters that all belong to one family that have the same basic formation. Here's a list of the different fonts available with Freelance Graphics for Windows 2.0:

- Arial MT (this is the default font used in Freelance presentations)
- Arial
- Avant Garde
- Bookman
- Courier
- Courier New
- Helvetica
- Helvetica Narrow
- New Century Schoolbook
- Palatino
- Symbol
- Times
- Times New Roman

- Wingdings
- Zapf Chancery
- Zapf Dingbats

Not all of these fonts are actual letters—Symbol, Wingdings, and Zapf Dingbats are actually typefaces that contain various symbols and dingbats (arrows and other small graphical characters).

NOTE   Any font available in Windows 3.1 is also available in Freelance Graphics.

The following section explains how to select a new font for your text.

Selecting a New Font You can set a new font from within the Paragraph Styles dialog box (if you want to change the font for all pages in the presentation) or from the Font dialog box. As usual, though, before you do anything else, you first need to select the text you'll be changing. Here's how:

1. Click on the text box you want to work with.

2. Press F2 to change into edit mode.

3. Highlight the section of text you want to modify. Now you can choose the new font by following these steps:

   1. Open the Text menu.

   2. Choose the Font command. The Font dialog box appears, as shown in Figure 6.13.

   3. Scroll through the typefaces shown in the *Face:* box in the upper left corner of the dialog box by clicking on the scroll arrows along the right side of the bar. As each typeface is highlighted, the bar at the bottom of the dialog box shows you what the typeface looks like.

   4. When you've found the typeface you want, click OK.

FIGURE 6.13

Selecting a new font

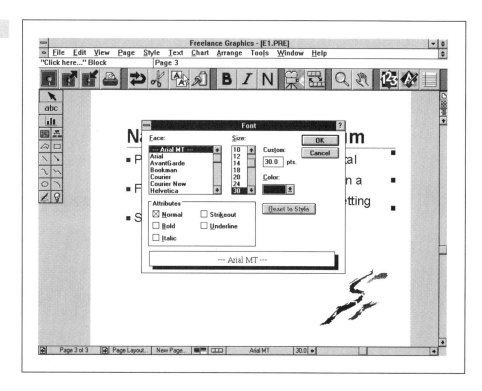

You are then returned to the page and the highlighted text is displayed in the new typeface.

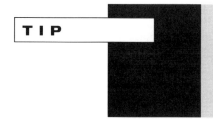

TIP

You can also set the attribute, or style, of the text from the Font dialog box. These styles go into effect for the entire highlighted section of text and will override any settings you entered in the Paragraph Styles dialog box.

Freelance Graphics provides you with another quick way to select a new typeface. In the status bar, at the bottom of the page, you see several things: the page number, a Page Layout button, a New Page button, a color palette, a series of six squares (that's the SmartIcon display button), and a box showing the name of the current typeface (which, by default, says Arial MT). You can display a list of all available typefaces by clicking on this button, as shown in Figure 6.14. To use this shortcut, first highlight the text you want to use, and then click the button. When the list is displayed, make your choice. The highlighted text is then automatically changed to the typeface you specified.

The next section tells you how to change the size of the text used in your presentations.

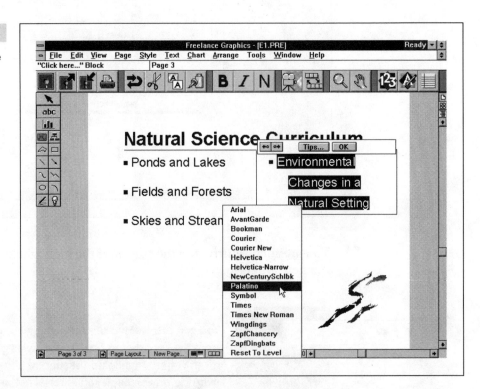

Changing Text Size

As mentioned earlier, a font really consists of one typeface (which we've already taken care of) in a specific style and size. You know how to choose the typeface and the style. In this section, you learn to specify the size.

As you've probably noticed, the Font dialog box contains two different settings that control the size of your text. First, click on the text box you want and press F2 to enable edit mode. Now highlight the necessary text, open the Text menu, and choose Font. There's that Font dialog box again.

To the right of the *Face:* box, you see the *Size:* box. This is a logical place to change the size of a font, right? In this box, you see an incredible number of font sizes, ranging from 8 to 72 points. (There are 72 points per inch.) To choose one of the sizes from the *Size:* box, simply highlight the one you want and click OK. To the right of that box, you see a smaller box with the label *Custom:*. In this box, you can enter whatever size you want and click OK or press Enter.

NOTE Depending on the type of printer you're using with Freelance Graphics, you may or may not be able to produce all these fonts in every size. For more information on the capabilities of your individual printer, consult your printer's manual.

Another easy method of selecting size without ever leaving the presentation page is offered, again, in the status bar. Beside the button that allowed you to select the typeface is a button that shows the currently selected size. When you click on this button, a list of available sizes appears, as shown in Figure 6.15. Click on your selection, and the highlighted text is changed instantly.

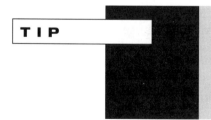

TIP Here's a neat trick for changing the text size: Select the text box with the text you want to change; Hold down the Shift key; Resize the text box in the usual way. Freelance automatically scales the text size as it size changes the size of the box.

Now that you're comfortable working with fonts, styles, and sizes, you're ready to tackle something a little more complicated that straight text: let's start sprucing up those bullets.

FIGURE 6.15

Selecting a new text
size from the status bar

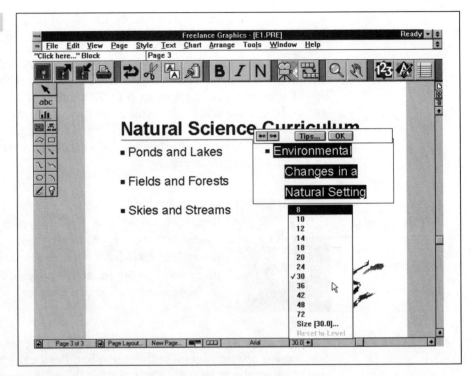

Choosing Bullet Characters

It's no secret that bullets can be pretty boring. Those asterisks, round bullets, and dashes remind us of monotonous chemistry teachers and computer science majors with a passion for flowcharts. But bullets can have personality—especially now that you're using Freelance Graphics Version 2.0. In the old days, you could only choose between a limited number of bullet types, but now you can use any symbol—from Freelance Graphics, Lotus 1-2-3, or Ami Pro—as a bullet character. This section helps you choose different bullet types and make choices about the type, color, and size.

Selecting Bullets

But first things first. Select the text you want to bullet, open the Text menu, and choose the Bullet command. The Text Bullet dialog box appears, as shown in Figure 6.16.

FIGURE 6.16

The Text Bullet
dialog box

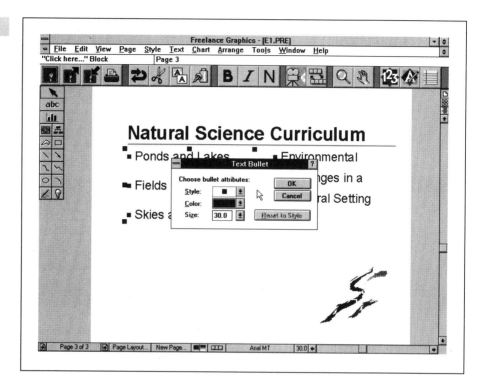

In this dialog box, you'll choose the style, or type, of bullets you use, the color of the bullet characters, and the size of the bullets. You can also use symbols as bullets from within this dialog box. All of these tasks are discussed in the following sections.

Choosing a Bullet Style

As soon as Text Bullet dialog box is appears on your screen, you are ready to choose a style for the bullet character. To display your options, click on the down-arrow beside the *Style:* box. A long drop-down list of bullet characters appears, as shown in Figure 6.17.

To select a new bullet style, simply click on the choice you want. You can also choose None, if you prefer, and Freelance Graphics will automatically move the text to the right in the text box, making up for the room ordinarily used by the bullet characters. You can also choose the Symbol

FIGURE 6.17

Viewing bullet choices

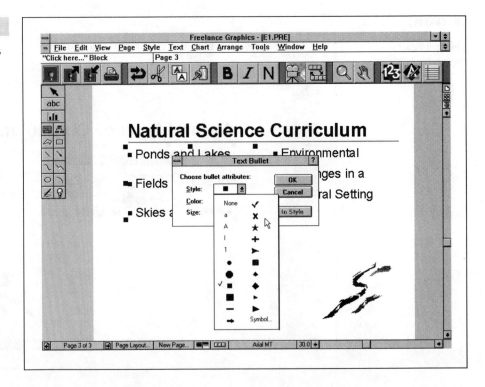

option to display another screen of choices (symbols, this time). We'll discuss using symbols as bullets later in this chapter.

For now, make your selection by clicking on the bullet style you want (for this example, we chose the star). Now, let's choose a color.

Choosing a Bullet Color

Ordinarily, we think of bullets as being more functional than decorative. But Freelance Graphics provides you with an incredible rainbow of colors to use with your chosen bullet style.

When the Text Bullet dialog box is displayed, you can view the color palette by clicking on the down-arrow symbol beside the *Color:* box. As Figure 6.18 shows, a beautiful range of colors appears in a palette on your screen. You can click on the color choice you want (in this case, we chose an electric blue). You are then returned to the Text Bullet dialog box.

FIGURE 6.18

Choosing a color
for bullets

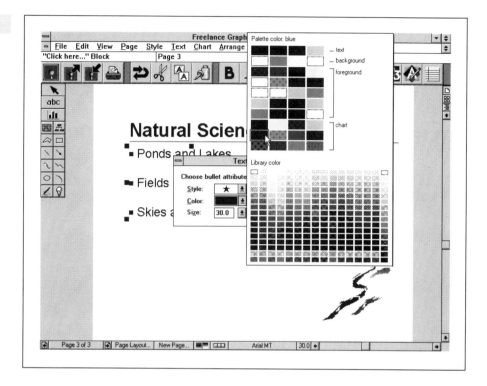

Choosing Bullet Size

The final choice in the Text Bullet dialog box involves selecting a size for
the bullet character. A word of warning, though: a little goes a long way.
Fight the temptation to create huge bullets—even if you've used a really
cool symbol or are particularly fond of the color you've found. Bullets are
meant only to draw the reader's eye to the text—the text itself should do
the rest.

When you're ready to choose a size for your bullets, click on the *Size:* box
in the Text Bullet dialog box. A drop-down list of bullet sizes appears (this
list is similar to the size boxes you've seen concerning fonts). Choose the
size you want and the box closes.

Now all that's left to do is to click OK. After you do so, the bullets are
changed in the selected text box. Figure 6.19 shows the modified bullet
style, color, and size.

FIGURE 6.19

The bullets after
modification

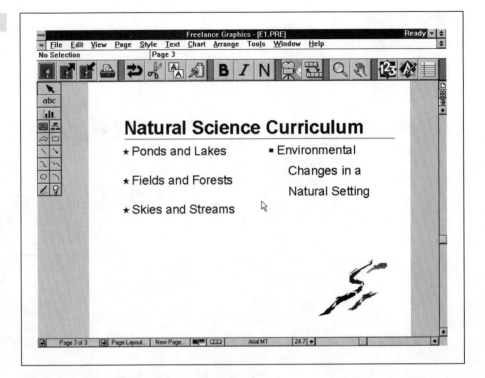

Using Symbols as Bullets

To choose a symbol as a bullet character, follow these steps:

1. Select the text box you want to change.

2. Open the Text menu.

3. Choose the Bullet command. The Text Bullet dialog box appears.

4. Click on the down-arrow beside the *Style:* box. A drop-down list of bullet types appears.

5. Click on Symbol in the bottom right corner of the list. The Choose Symbol for Bullet dialog box appears as shown in Figure 6.20.

6. Scroll through the symbol files as necessary (each time a new file is highlighted, the symbols in that file are displayed in the bottom half of the dialog box).

FIGURE 6.20

Using a symbol as a
bullet character

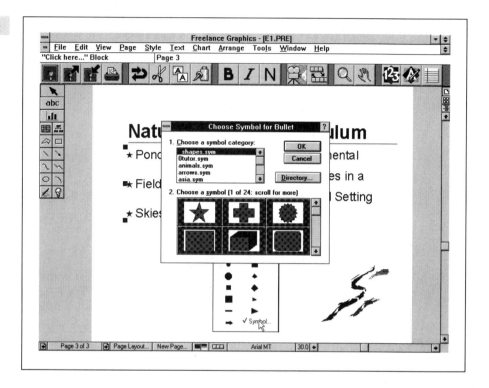

7. When you find the symbol you want, click on it to select it. (For this example, we chose the big red button in the *buttons.sym* file.)

8. Click OK to return to the Text Bullet dialog box. The symbol you chose will appear in the *Style:* box.

9. Click OK to accept the changes and return to the page.

Figure 6.20 shows the page with the new symbol inserted as a bullet character. You can further modify these bullets, if necessary, by changing the color or the size.

Another type of enhancement you might like to make is to surround a specific block of text with a *text frame* (just a fancy way to say border). Text frames are the subject of the next section.

Adding a Text Frame

A frame can help set off the text inside the frame and can also draw the reader's eye from other points and make him or her focus on the boxed text. With the available frame options, you can choose the width of the frame itself, the inside or outside color or pattern, and the style of the edge.

To add a text frame to a text box, follow these steps:

1. Click on the text box you want to frame.

2. Open the Text menu.

3. Choose the Frame command. The Text Frame dialog box appears, as shown in Figure 6.21.

4. In the Edge options, click on the Color setting. The familiar color palette appears. Choose the color you want to use for the edge of the frame. You are returned to the Text Frame box.

FIGURE 6.21

The Text Frame dialog box

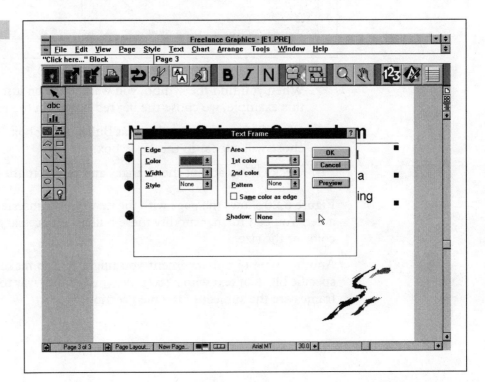

5. Click on the Width setting. A drop-down list of available widths appears. The thinnest line has been chosen as the default. Make changes, if necessary, by clicking on the line thickness you want.

6. Click on the Style setting. This displays a drop-down list of line styles. Choose either None, a solid line, or several variations of broken lines. Make your selection by clicking the appropriate selection.

7. In the Area section, you can specify the colors for the inside of the frame. Freelance Graphics allows you to specify two different colors, which gives you the option of showing a variety of fade patterns (covered in the next step). Make sure you choose two colors that will work well together. Clicking on either setting brings up the color palette so that you can make your choice.

8. The Pattern section allows you to choose the pattern for the color mix on the background of the frame. For example, click on the Pattern setting. The pop-up box of patterns shown in Figure 6.22

FIGURE 6.22

Choosing a pattern for the color selections

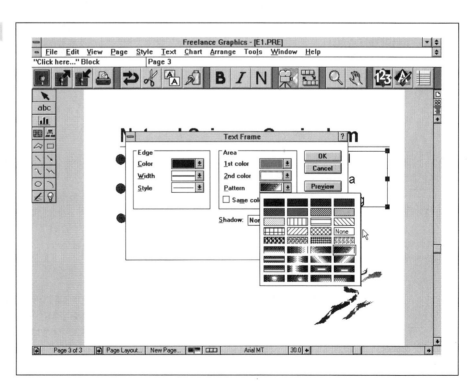

appears. By selecting the appropriate pattern, you can blend two colors in such a way that one gradually changes into the other, creating a sophisticated special effect.

When you've finished specifying settings, you can preview the frame by clicking the Preview button. Or, if you prefer, you can click OK to return to the page. Figure 6.23 shows an example of a frame with an area that blends two contrasting colors.

FIGURE 6.23

A color-filled text frame

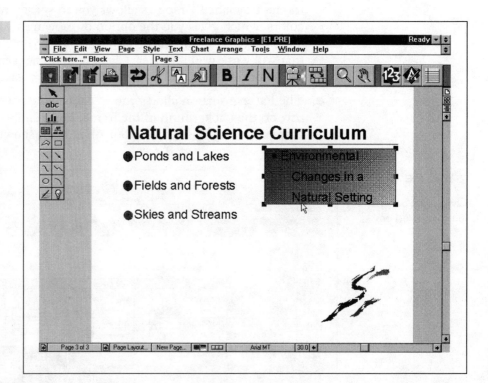

Adding Speaker Notes

Having a great, professional-looking presentation isn't going to do you much good if you get up in front of people and forget what you're going to say. Speaker notes can give you—in traditional 3-by-5 card style—the extra push you need when you get stalled on a certain point or forget what to discuss next.

The speaker notes you create stay with the current page. You can enter text, edit the note, and print it as necessary.

Here's how to add speaker notes to your presentation:

1. Open the Page menu.

2. Choose the Speaker Notes command. A notecard appears inside a Speaker Note dialog box, as shown in Figure 6.24.

3. Enter the text for your speaker note. You can use commands in the Edit menu to copy, cut, or paste text. You can use commands in the Text menu to change the font, style, and size of text. If you like, you can use the Default menu commands to change the font, bullets, and size of all text in the speaker notes.

FIGURE 6.24

The Speaker Note dialog box

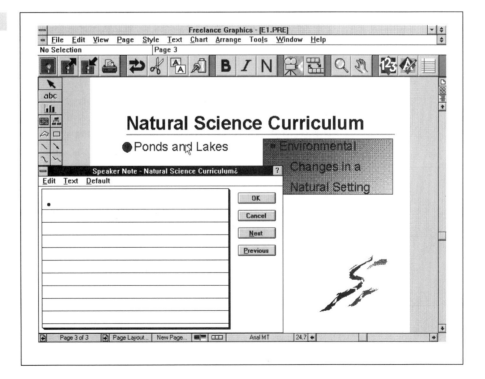

4. Click OK to add the note. If you prefer, you can click Next to move to the speaker note associated with the next page or Previous to move to the note for the preceding page. (If you haven't already added text for the notes on these pages, the note boxes will be blank.)

After you click OK, the Speaker Note dialog box closes and you are returned to the current page.

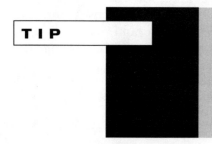

TIP When you want to print speaker notes, use the Print command in the File menu. When the Print File dialog box appears, move the pointer to the Format options and click the Speaker notes radio button. Change any other options as necessary. When you're ready to print, click the Print button.

In this chapter, you've learned a wide range of techniques for formatting and enhancing your text. Specifically, you used the Paragraph Styles dialog box to make changes to all the text in a selected style throughout your presentation. You also learned to use the Font, Bullet, and Frame commands in the Text menu to make changes to selected text. Finally, you learned to add speaker notes to your presentations.

In the next chapter, we finish up Part Two by exploring the various capabilities of the Outliner.

SEVEN

Working
with Text in
Outliner View

f a s t ~~*TRACK*~~

● **To change to Outliner view,**   208

you can either click on the Outliner icon (just above the ↑ at the top of the scroll bar along the right edge of the screen), or open the View menu and choose the Outliner command.

● **To enter text in the Outliner,**   211

first position the cursor at the point at which you want to enter text. (If you want to add a new page first, position the cursor at the end of the line after which you want to add the page. Then press F7.) Now simply type the text you want to add.

● **To change text levels,**   215

use one of these three methods: Press Tab to indent the level (that is, move from a first-level to a second-level entry), or Shift-Tab to outdent the text (move from a second-level to a first-level entry), or click on the Promote or Demote buttons, or open the Outline menu and choose the Promote or Demote commands.

● **To delete information,**   **218**

you can either highlight the text and press Del, or you can click on the item (bullet or page) and press Del or select Clear from the Edit menu. Clear leaves a blank line, while Del removes both the text and the line.

● **To print an outline,**   **228**

Open the File menu and choose Print or click on the Print SmartIcon. When the Print File dialog box appears, click on the Outline radio button in the Format options. Finally, click Print to start printing.

IN the previous chapter, you mastered many of the tasks you'll use to change the way your text looks to those who will be seeing your presentation. This chapter concentrates on changing the way your text looks to *you*.

Specifically, in this chapter, you'll learn to display text in the Outliner, enter and edit text, move text sections and entire pages, and collapse and expand the outline you create (new features with Version 2.0). Additionally, you'll find out how to print your outline and how to use outlines from other popular programs like Ami Pro and Microsoft Word.

An Outliner Overview

The Outliner allows you to get a bird's-eye-view of your presentation by showing your text in outline form. From the outline, you can easily review the way information flows through your presentation. In a sense, the outline gives you a kind of roadmap for checking the logical progression of your topics. For example, Figure 7.1 contains an outline flaw. Can you tell where the error was made?

The problem with this outline is that the topics are out of order. In other words, we say we're going to discuss topics in a certain sequence and then we deviate from that sequence. For example, notice that on Page 2, the first three topics are Natural Science Curriculum, Weekend Workshop for Parents, and Hands-On Nature Centers. This page serves as a kind of table of contents for the rest of the presentation. Page 3, as you can see, picks up on the first topic, Natural Science Curriculum. Page 4, however, deviates from the sequence by including Hands-On Nature Centers before Weekend Workshops for Parents, which appears on Page 5.

FIGURE 7.1

A problem outline

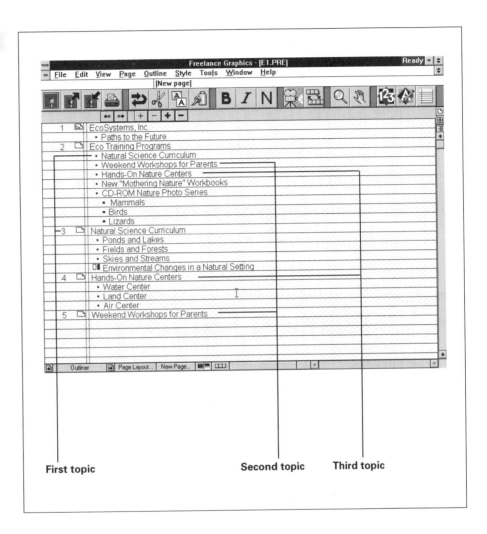

First topic   **Second topic**   **Third topic**

This flaw may not be readily apparent in current page view, but it is enough to confuse your audience. By looking over the outline carefully in Outliner view, you can make sure your presentation is as clear and well-organized as possible. Later in this chapter, you'll learn to correct the error by moving Page 5 so it follows Page 3.

If you're working with long outlines, it may be particularly helpful to see only the page titles or first-level headings of the outline. Version 2.0 of Freelance Graphics for Windows incorporates a new collapse and expand feature, which enables you to collapse the outline to show only selected information and later to expand the outline as necessary. This version of the program also allows you to print the outlines in expanded form.

But more than anything else, the Outliner view gives you the ability to focus on the real meat of your presentation—the words you'll be using to communicate with your audience. By ensuring that your topic is discussed in a logical, understandable manner, you can help your audience get the message—loud and clear.

Displaying Outliner View

As you may recall, displaying the presentation in Outliner view is as simple as clicking a button. To change to Outliner view, use one of these methods:

- Open the View menu and choose the Outliner command
- Click on the Outliner icon in the vertical scroll bar along the right edge of the screen.

The Outliner view appears. Depending on the number of pages you have entered, you may see a long outline or only a page or two. The flashing cursor is positioned at the beginning of the page that was current when you were displaying presentation view.

TIP

You don't need to create pages before using the Outliner. In fact, you can create an entire presentation in Outliner view. Simply start a new presentation by choosing the SmartMaster you want to use, and, after you choose the initial Page Layout style, click the Outliner icon. You can then type the text as necessary for the presentation. When you're finished entering text, you can change to Page Sorter view or return to current page view.

Although you've seen the Outliner screen before, there are several special features you should be familiar with. Figure 7.2 shows a blank Outliner screen.

As you work with text in the Outliner, you will need to know the location and function of these features:

- Promote and Demote icons
- Expand page button, Collapse page button
- Expand outline button, Collapse outline button
- View buttons
- Page Layout button.

Here's how all these buttons are used:

BUTTON	FUNCTION
Promote and demote	Changes the text level of text in your outline
Expand and collapse	Changes the depth of information displayed in the Outliner
View	Changes back to Current page view or Page Sorter view
Page Layout	Selects a page layout for pages you add in Outliner view

FIGURE 7.2

Exploring the Outliner screen.

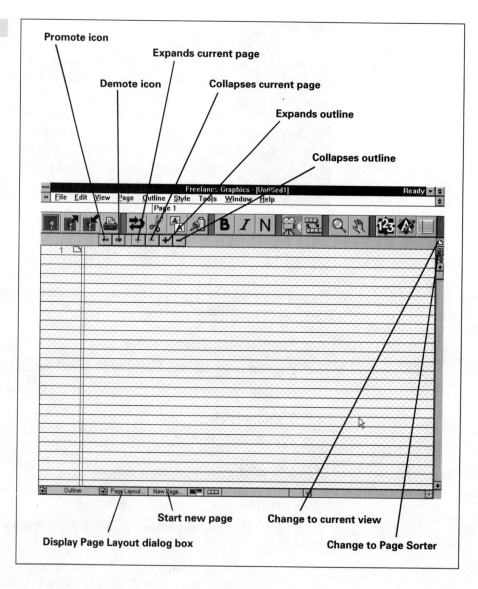

The sections that follow explain each of these features in more detail.

Working in the Outliner

You'll find a variety of text operations that you can carry out in the Outliner. You can enter or edit text, copy, cut, and paste text, move pages or text sections, collapse and expand outlines, and print the outline you create. This section introduces you to each of these tasks.

A Review of Text Entry

Here's a review of the method you learned in Chapter 4 for entering text in Outliner view:

1. Position the cursor at the point you want to enter text.

2. Click the mouse button.

3. Type the text.

4. Press Enter.

The process of indenting and "outdenting" text in the Outliner is discussed in subsequent sections. For now, though, you're concerned only with getting the text you want in the outline.

As mentioned earlier, the Outliner places all text after the title page in bulleted list form by default. You do have another option, however. If you chose a two-column bulleted list when the Page Layout dialog box was displayed, you can enter a second column of bullets for a two-column bulleted list. Freelance automatically inserts a new icon (two small rectangles—one white, one black) to show you where the second column of bullets begins within the page (see Figure 7.3).

In some cases, you'll be entering text from within the Outliner and you'll need to tell Freelance where you want the second column to begin. First, start the page as usual, and enter the bullets for the right column. Then, when you want to add the second column of bullets, follow these steps:

1. Position the cursor at the point after which you want to add the second column of bullets.

FIGURE 7.3

The second-column
icon for bulleted lists

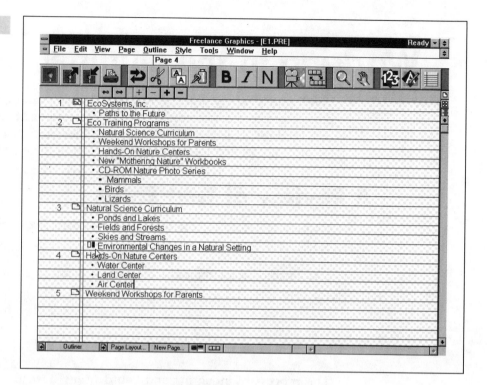

2. Open the Outline menu.

3. Choose the Make Second Column command (see Figure. 7.4).

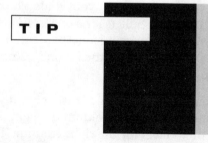

TIP

To change a regular bulleted list into a two-column bulleted list, position the cursor in the page you want to change and click the Page Layout button in the status bar at the bottom of the page. When the Page Layout dialog box appears, select the 2-Column Bullets layout type and click OK.

FIGURE 7.4

Adding a second
column of bullets

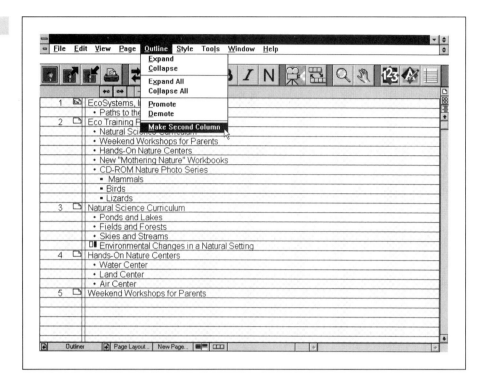

Freelance adds the second-column icon to the beginning of the line, and you can enter the bullets for the second column as necessary. Figure 7.5 shows the outline after a second column of bullets has been added.

The first line of bullet text in the second column shows the second-column icon. Bullets entered beneath that point are shown as first-level bullets.

FIGURE 7.5

The outline after
second-column bullets
are added

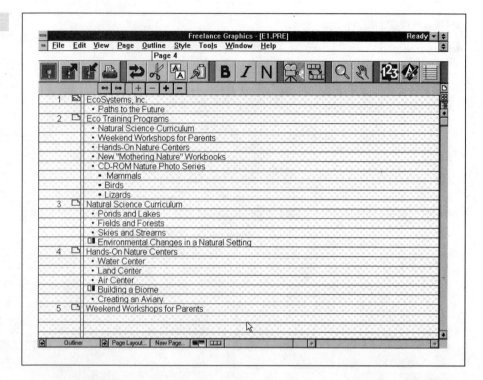

TIP

The Outliner uses a single font—Arial—to display text. You cannot change text style, font, or size from within the Outliner. If you want to make stylistic changes to your text, return to current page view by clicking the appropriate icon or by opening the View menu and choosing Current Page.

Editing Text in the Outliner

Editing text in the Outliner is simple, as well. If you're performing character-based editing (meaning that you need to correct the spelling of a word or change punctuation), simply position the cursor at the point you need to make the change, use the backspace key to delete any incorrect characters, and retype the correct information.

If you need to make changes to blocks of text—perhaps for copying, cutting, or pasting purposes—you can work in the Outliner in much the same way you do in the text box on a presentation page. Simply use the cursor to highlight the text you want to work with (double-click inside a word to highlight that word, or drag the mouse to highlight longer sections of text). Then open the Edit menu and choose the appropriate editing command for your operation. For a review of text editing, see Chapter 5.

The paragraphs that follow provide you with more information about additional editing procedures.

Changing Text Levels

As you're looking over your outline, you may see places where text is not organized the way it should be. Perhaps one text level is indented when it should be parallel with the preceding level. This is the case in Figure 7.6.

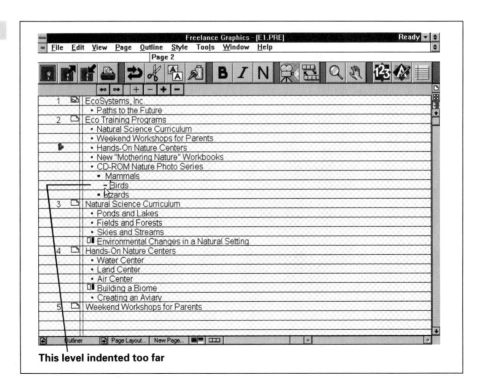

FIGURE 7.6

A problem with text indentation

This level indented too far

As you can see, the topic *Birds* should be parallel with both *Mammals* and *Lizards*. You can easily move *Birds* out to where it belongs by using one of the following methods:

- Position the cursor in the line to be changed and press Shift-Tab

- Position the cursor in the line to be changed and click the Promote button (the button pointing left in the line above the text area)

- Position the cursor in the line, open the Outline menu and choose the Promote command.

If you want to move the text inward—that is, indent the text another level, you can use one of these methods after positioning the text cursor in the line you want to change:

- Click the Demote button (the one that points to the right)

- Press Tab

- Open the Outline menu and choose the Demote command.

All three of these actions have the same result—the text is indented another level.

NOTE Freelance automatically assigns a paragraph style to each text level. For example, level 1 text (first bullet) is placed in a certain font, style, alignment, and color. Level 2 text (secondary bullets) are formatted in a completely different style. When you change to current page or Page Sorter view, these paragraph styles will be applied to the text you enter in the Outliner. See Chapter 6 for a review of how to change paragraph styles.

Adding a New Page

You can easily add a new page in the Outliner. First position the cursor at a point after which you want to add the blank page. You then have several options:

- Click the New Page button at the bottom of the screen
- Press F7
- Open the Page menu and choose the New command.

Freelance adds a blank line and places the page number and page icon to the left of the text entry area. Figure 7.7 shows the outline after a blank page has been added.

FIGURE 7.7

Adding a blank page

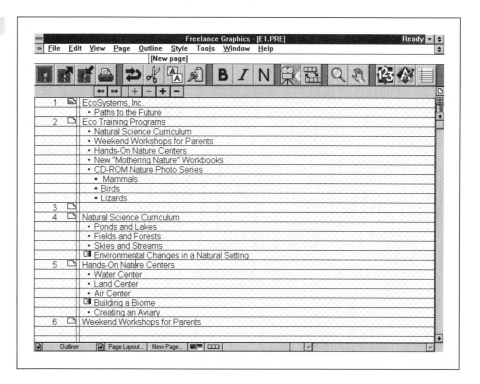

T I P   Double-clicking on the page icon in Outline view automatically takes you to the current page view.

Deleting Pages

Whether or not a page currently includes text, you can delete it by clicking the page icon and then pressing Del. After you initially click in the page icon, the entire box is selected in a rectangle, as shown in Figure 7.8. You can then press Del to delete the page.

After you press Del, a Delete Page dialog box appears, informing you that carrying out this process will delete the selected page forever. Click OK to continue the deletion or click Cancel to abandon the procedure.

FIGURE 7.8

Deleting a page

![Screenshot of Freelance Graphics outline view showing pages: 1 EcoSystems, Inc. / Paths to the Future; 2 Eco Training Programs with sub-items Natural Science Curriculum, Weekend Workshops for Parents, Hands-On Nature Centers, New "Mothering Nature" Workbooks, CD-ROM Nature Photo Series with Mammals, Birds, Lizards; 3 (selected empty page); 4 Natural Science Curriculum with Ponds and Lakes, Fields and Forests, Skies and Streams, Environmental Changes in a Natural Setting; 5 Hands-On Nature Centers with Water Center, Land Center, Air Center, Building a Biome, Creating an Aviary; 6 Weekend Workshops for Parents]

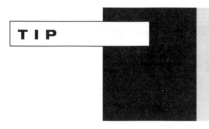

Moving Text in the Outliner

Because one of the biggest benefits of using the Outliner is the perspective it gives you on the full scope of your work, it seems only logical that you would need some way to make necessary changes. As usual, Freelance makes it easy to move information—sections of text, whole pages, or even groups of pages—around within the Outliner. The following sections explain each of these procedures.

Moving Text Sections

The first step in moving a text section—whether that section is a single bullet entry or an entire page—is to select the section with which you want to work. For example, suppose while working with the Outliner shown in Figure 7.8, that you want to move the line *Environmental Changes in a Natural Setting* to a page of its own, Page 6. Here's how:

1. Click on the icon to the left of the text entry. A rectangle encloses the text line, indicating that it is selected.

2. Move the mouse pointer to the left edge of the text line.

3. Press and hold the mouse button. The pointer changes to a large triangle (see Figure 7.9).

4. Move the triangle downward, to the line following Page 5. A dark line accompanies the triangle as you move the mouse, showing where the line will be positioned.

FIGURE 7.9

Preparing to move text

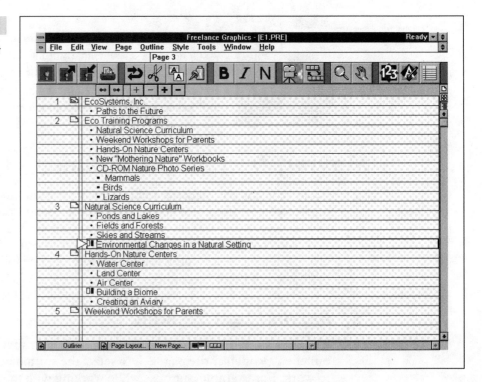

5. Release the mouse button. The line is moved to the new location (see Figure 7.10). As you can see, we still need to make this a new page by clicking the Promote button.

TIP

Clicking on the page icon selects everything on that page. Clicking on a single bullet item selects only that bullet.

Moving Pages

The process for moving pages is basically the same as for moving sections of text, but the method of selection is a little different. There are two basic

FIGURE 7.10

The newly moved line

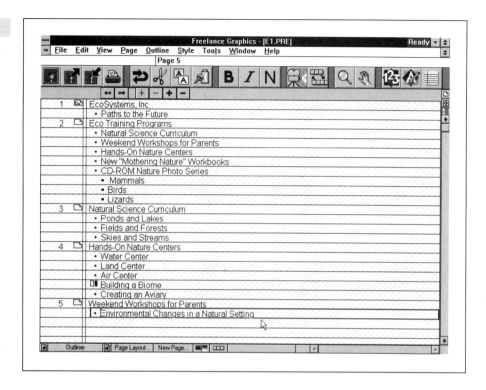

options for selecting more than one text line or paragraph:

- Position the mouse pointer on the first item you want to select and click the *left* mouse button. Then choose other items you want to select by pointing to them with the mouse button and clicking the *right* mouse button.

- Position the mouse in the upper left corner of the range of pages or text items you want to select. Press and hold the mouse button, while dragging the mouse down and to the right, until all necessary text items are included. A rectangle encloses the box, indicating the range you've selected. Release the mouse button.

Figure 7.11 shows how the Outliner looks when a range of text items has been selected.

FIGURE 7.11

Selecting a range of
bulleted items

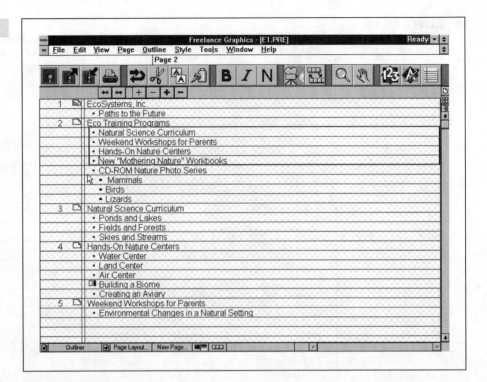

TIP   To cancel the selection, click anywhere outside the
selected area or press Esc.

Now that you've selected the range, you need to move it. And by now, the
process should be familiar. Position the mouse pointer at the left end of
the selected box. Press and hold the mouse button, and drag the box to
the desired location. When you release the mouse button, the lines you
selected are inserted at the new place in your outline.

TIP

Because the Outliner shows you only the text involved, it may be more difficult for you to envision the actual flow of the pages until you see them displayed one-by-one. Therefore, when you need to rearrange pages in a presentation, you may find it more helpful to use the Page Sorter view than the Outline view. To display the Page Sorter, click the Page Sorter icon above the Outliner icon in the right edge of the screen or open the View menu and choose Page Sorter.

Un-Moving Text

Lucky for us, almost nothing you do in Freelance Graphics is irreversible. Suppose, for example, that you were toying with the idea of moving a substantial chunk of your introductory page to a later page for a more thorough discussion. But after trying it, on-screen, you decide that you really like things better the way they were originally.

You could go through the process of selecting the text again and dragging it back to its earlier spot. Or, you could issue one simple little command: Undo Move.

As you learned in earlier chapters, the Undo command reverses the last action you took. (In some procedures, Undo may sequentially reverse up to the last ten actions.) To undo the move, simply open the Edit menu and choose Undo Move (see Figure 7.12). The text is immediately put back the way it was before the move procedure.

Using Outlines

Thus far, you've learned to enter and edit text in your Freelance Graphics outline view. This chapter concentrates on some special features available only in the Outliner.

FIGURE 7.12

Un-moving text

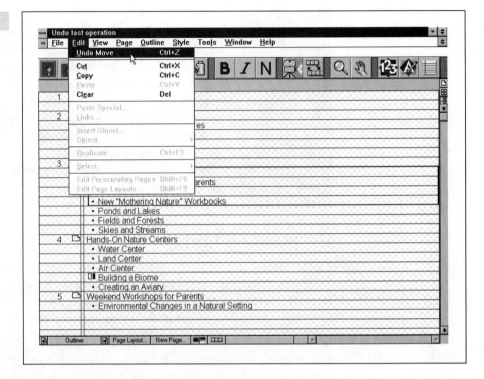

Collapsing an Outline

Many of the most popular word processing programs available today come equipped with a built-in outline feature. Why? Probably because this feature encourages you to think logically and keep your documents—or presentations—well-organized. And, if you are unfamiliar with creating text for presentations, you can "brainstorm" ideas, organize them into a logical outline, and then use the outline to write the presentation. Each step of the way you'll have something to refer to and you won't ever have to worry about being seized by writer's block.

One popular aspect of most outliners is their ability to collapse an outline. Simply put, collapsing an outline means hiding all the lower levels (second- or third-level bullets, for example) and showing only the primary sections. This can help you review, in broad-brush style, how you've organized the major sections of your presentation.

In Freelance Graphics for Windows Version 2.0, you can either collapse the outline on a page-by-page basis, or you can collapse the entire outline.

Collapsing a Page

To collapse a page, follow these steps:

1. Position the cursor in the page you want to collapse.

2. Click the light gray minus (–) icon.

The current page is collapsed, showing only the page title, as seen in Figure 7.13. A small plus (+) sign appears beside the page number, indicating that the outline has been collapsed at that point.

Collapsing a single page

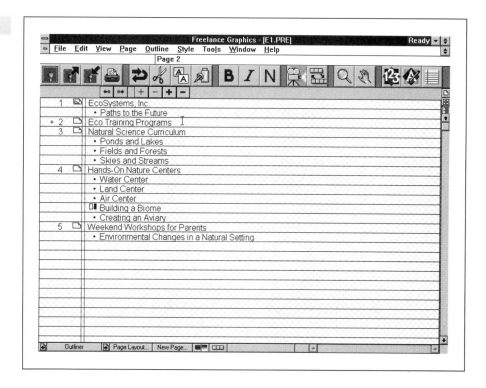

TIP

If you prefer, you can open the Outline menu and choose the Collapse command to collapse the current page.

Collapsing the Entire Outline

You can also collapse the entire outline and show only the page titles. To do this, use one of these methods:

- Click on the Collapse All button (the black – sign)
- Open the Outline menu and choose the Collapse All command.

The entire outline is reduced to the page titles. Each of the pages, as you can see in Figure 7.14, appears with a plus sign to the left of the page number, indicating that these pages have been collapsed.

FIGURE 7.14

The entire collapsed outline

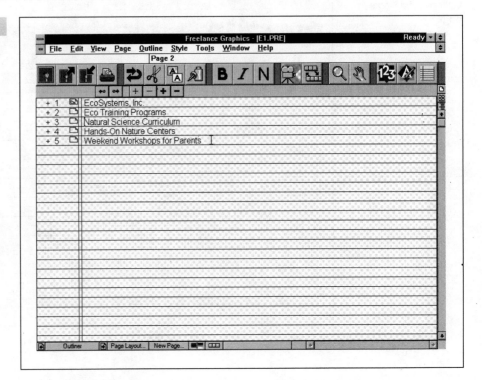

Expanding an Outline

Obviously, after collapsing it, we need some way to return the outline to its normal display. As with the collapse procedure, you can expand a single page or the entire outline.

Expanding a Single Page

To expand a single page, position the cursor in the line you want to use, and choose one of these methods:

- Click on the light gray plus symbol
- Open the Outline menu and choose the Expand command.

Freelance then expands the page at the cursor position. Figure 7.15 shows the outline with one page expanded.

FIGURE 7.15

The expanded page

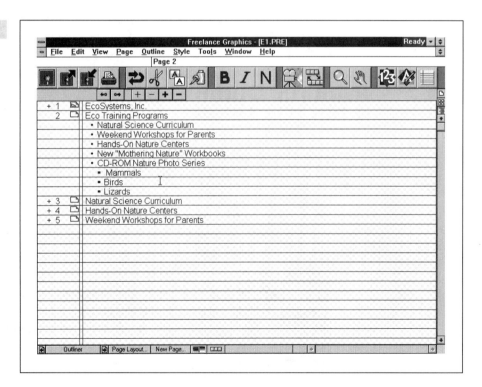

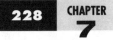

Expanding the Entire Page

This procedure is basically the exact opposite of the collapse process. To expand an entire outline, choose one of these actions:

- Click on the black plus (+) button in the line above the text area
- Open the Outline menu and choose Expand All.

The entire outline is returned to full display.

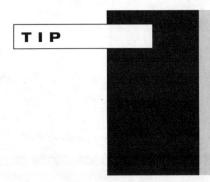

TIP

If you are working with a very large outline—one that spans several pages, you can use the collapse and expand procedures to quickly move to a specific place in the outline. Just collapse the outline, position the cursor in the page you want to see, and click the Expand Page button. Rather than paging through lines and lines of text, you can move right to the page you want with a minimum of hassle.

Printing Outlines

How many times have you come up with the basic idea for a presentation and then wished for some way to pass it around? Getting input and approval from superiors—or co-workers—can make the process of preparing a presentation a little less harrowing.

Now, with Version 2.0, you can print the outline and hand it out to twenty of your closest friends. And with the easy editing features of the Outliner, you can make any changes easily—right up until showtime.

WARNING

You can print only fully expanded outlines. So, if you've collapsed a portion of the outline—or even the entire thing—don't forget to expand it before starting the print process.

There are two ways to get to the Print File dialog box:

- Click the Print SmartIcon (the fourth icon from the left)
- Open the File menu and choose the Print command.

The Print File menu appears, as shown in Figure 7.16. In the top portion of the dialog box, you see the Print options, in which you choose the number of copies you want and the range you want to print. You can have Freelance print only the current page by clicking the Current page only box.

The Format section of the Print File dialog box contains a series of different radio button selections. Select the Outline radio button, located at the bottom of the Format section. Finally, click the Print button. Freelance Graphics then sends the outline to your printer.

FIGURE 7.16

The Print File dialog box

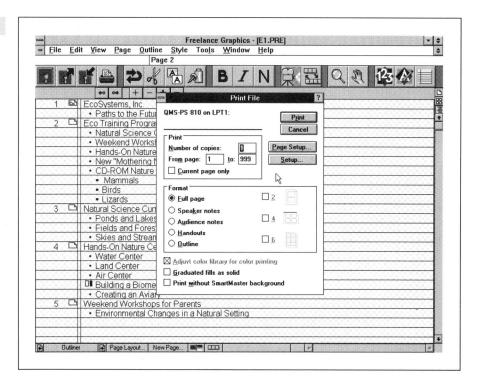

N O T E   Only one radio button can be selected at a time.

Using Outlines from Other Programs

Version 2.0 now supports outlines you create in other popular programs. For example, suppose that in addition to Freelance Graphics for Windows you also work in Ami Pro or Microsoft Word. Using outlines created in these programs involves copying them from the Windows clipboard and placing them in the Outliner.

When you want to copy an outline from the other application to the Freelance Outliner, follow these steps:

1. If you're working in Freelance Graphics, minimize the program to an icon by clicking on the minimize button in the top right corner of the screen. (The minimize button is the one pointing down.)

2. From the Program Manager, start the application program from which you're going to copy the outline (in this case, let's use Ami Pro).

3. Open the file containing the outline.

4. Copy the outline to the Windows clipboard.

5. Exit the application program and restore Freelance Graphics by double-clicking on the Freelance icon.

6. Position the cursor in the Outliner view at the point you want to paste the outline.

7. Open the Edit menu and choose the Paste command.

The outline is then pasted from the Windows clipboard into the current cursor position in Outliner view.

TIP You also can paste the contents of the clipboard at the current cursor position by pressing Ctrl-V or by clicking on the Paste SmartIcon.

In this chapter, you've learned how to perform a number of text entry, editing, and organization tasks in the Outliner. This chapter rounds out Part Two, bringing to a temporary conclusion our discussion of text in your presentations.

The next chapter begins Part Three with a look at creating and editing a basic chart.

PART THREE

●

Creating, Importing, and Linking Charts

Now that you know the basics of Freelance Graphics for Windows and have discovered various ways of entering, editing, and enhancing text, you're ready to move on to another Freelance feature: charts. Charts add to your presentations something words cannot—a quick-look method of explaining information visually. With a single glance, your audience can see sales trends or understand how overhead affects net income.

Part Three covers the basics of creating and working with Freelance charts. In Chapter 8, you'll learn to create and edit a simple chart. More specifically, you'll learn to find your way around the various chart types and work with the dialog boxes used in the charting process. Chapter 9 focuses on more advanced chart features by exploring the topics of importing chart data from other programs and linking chart data to other files.

EIGHT

Creating
and Editing
a Basic Chart

f a s t ~~TRACK~~

● **To select a chart type,** 253

> first click on the chart tool or click New Page and choose one of the chart page layouts from the displayed list. When the New Chart Gallery screen appears, click on the chart type you want, then click on one of the displayed styles. Finally, click OK.

● **To enter chart data,** 262

> position the mouse pointer in the first cell of the data-entry area. Click the mouse button. The cell is highlighted. Type the data as necessary. When you want to move to the next cell, press Enter. You can use Tab, the arrow keys, or Enter to move the highlight in the text-entry area.

● **To create an organization chart,** 268

> begin by selecting the New Page button at the bottom of the screen or by clicking the organization tool in the tools row. The Organization Gallery appears so you can choose the type of organization chart you want to create. Click on the chart type you want; then choose whether you want to add a drop shadow and specify whether you want Freelance to automatically resize text so all entries fit on one page. After you make your choices, click OK.

● **To create a table,**   **273**

start by clicking on the New Page button at the bottom of the page or click on the table button in the tools row (the button to the left of the organization tool). When the New Page dialog box appears (only when you're creating a new page), choose Table and click OK. The Table Gallery appears. Select the type of table you want to create and choose any additional settings that apply to your table type. Click OK. Freelance adds the table grid to the current page view. To enter table data, simply begin typing when the table is selected. A gray border appears around the table. You can use Tab, the arrow keys, and Enter to move from cell to cell within the table.

So far in the book, you've learned quite a bit about preparing Freelance presentations. You know how to choose a SmartMaster, enter and edit text, and work with the Outliner. This chapter builds on your previous experience by introducing charts—a simple way to add extra impact, making your presentation a memorable one.

An Overview of Freelance Charts

For any particular operation—whether you are entering, formatting, or enhancing text, or adding any number of special objects like symbols or charts—Freelance Graphics gives you a wide range of options from which to choose.

Charts are no exception. When you begin to add charts to your Freelance presentations, you'll find eighteen different chart types from which to choose. And, what's more, you can choose from a number of chart *styles* within each particular *type*.

But all I really want is a simple bar chart, you say. No problem. What kind of bar chart did you have in mind? Do you want regular bar, stacked bar, horizontal bar, or bar-line chart? 2D or 3D? With the legend on the bottom or the right? With grid or without?

As you can see, Freelance provides you with the flexibility to design any chart you can imagine. But, if you're not feeling too imaginative, you can let the SmartMasters create the chart for you. Just plug in your own data, and, voilá—a ready-made chart.

When Will You Use Charts?

Chances are, anytime you are making a presentation, a good chart can wake up your audience—just when their eyes were beginning to glaze over from too much text.

Let's face it. Bullets are helpful, but not very entertaining. In a presentation, page after page of bulleted information could put the viewer to sleep. But by using charts, in some cases, you can say the same thing in a more interesting way. If you're still not convinced, consider the following benefits charts offer:

- **Break up the monotony of text**. Charts can change the look and feel of your presentation by replacing words with powerful visual images. For example, you can *tell* your viewers that your business is doing better, making more profit than ever before. But when you *show* it to them with a chart, the message hits home a lot more clearly.

- **Help viewers understand trends and data relationships**. When you are comparing two or more items—whether they are products, salespeople, or companies—words may make it difficult to understand the relationships in the data you present. For example, suppose you work for Company A and, in a presentation to your sales managers, you want to illustrate how Company B's competing product is faring in the marketplace. If you simply stand up and recite information from bulleted lists, your audience may still have to struggle to see your point. If you show a simple chart, graphing your company's and your competitor's product, the differences will be immediately obvious.

- **Reinforce text items**. Charts can also reinforce ideas you've presented earlier. For example, suppose your presentation introduces a new line of products. After discussing sales of existing products, you could include a pie chart showing what percentage of total sales your new products represent. The pie chart reinforces what you've already said and helps set up information about the new products you plan to discuss.

Exploring Chart Types

In many cases, the charts you choose for your presentation will be a matter of taste. Do you like to use pie charts? Bar charts? Line charts? Other times, the type of chart you use will be mandated by the kinds of data you're displaying and the goal of your chart. For example, suppose you want to graph the opening sales of a particular product, closing sales, and average sales for each of four weeks. You couldn't do this with a pie chart. While using a bar chart might not be impossible, it certainly would be unwieldy. For this type of application, a high-low-close-open chart would provide you with the type of picture you want.

Freelance Graphics gives you eighteen different chart types from which to choose:

- Bar
- Stacked bar
- Horizontal bar
- Horizontal stacked bar
- Line
- Bar-line
- Single pie
- Multiple pies
- High-low-close-open
- Area
- XY (Scatter)
- Radar
- Number grid

- 3D bar

- 3D stacked bar

- 3D bar (XYZ)

- 3D pie

- 3D area/line

As you can see, many of these chart types are actually different kinds of the same chart. For example, stacked bar and horizontal bar are both *bar* charts, after all. Because many of the chart types are similar to one another but have slightly different characteristics, we'll limit our discussion to the following charts: bar, line, pie, area, XY, and radar charts.

Bar charts

Bar charts are great for comparing two or more data series. You might, for example, compare sales in four different regions to see how well each of them did in a recent sales competition. Or, you might contrast last year's projected income with actual income. You could show the productivity levels of several workgroups in your plant, the number of contacts made by various insurance agents, or the number of new businesses recruited in your Chamber of Commerce membership drive.

A bar chart is one of the easiest charts to read, as well. Consider the one shown in Figure 8.1. This chart compares the quarterly sales of four different products—videos, software, CDs, and workshops—produced by EcoSystems, Inc.

To read the bar chart, first look at the legend (each of the products is assigned its own color). Next, look at the y-axis (the vertical line along the left edge of the chart). You'll notice that the y-axis values are broken into increments of five hundred. We can see that the videos were most successful (in Quarter 2), selling almost 2,000 units. By comparison, Quarter 2 wasn't as good for the workshops, which brought in less than 250 participants.

FIGURE 8.1

A sample bar chart

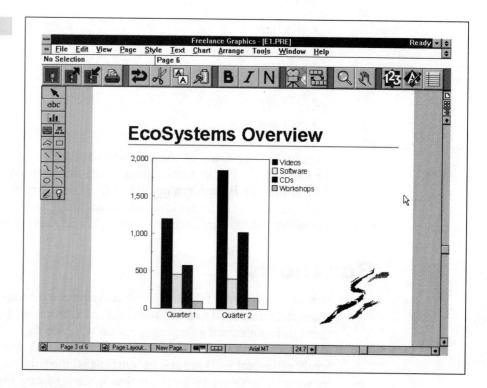

Line charts

Line charts are similar to bar charts except that line charts are generally used over a specified amount of time.

One advantage to using line charts is that the viewer's eye is naturally drawn along the line. So, drawing conclusions from the data—"The videos did quite well this year, didn't they?"—is easier. Instead of comparing tips of bars to y-axis values, the line chart draws your eye along the trend, helping you understand the chart's message. Figure 8.2 shows a sample line chart.

FIGURE 8.2

A sample line chart

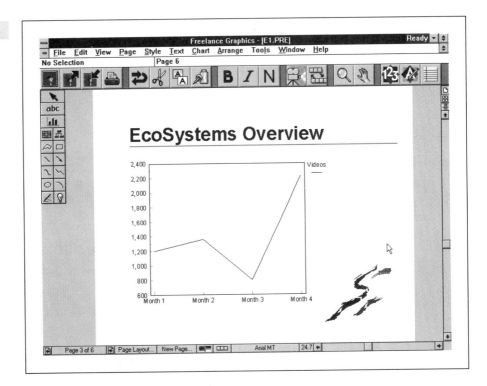

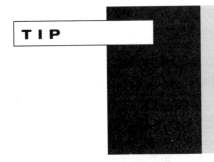

TIP

Using two different graph types—such as a bar chart and a line chart, producing a bar-line chart—in one combination graph can be very effective in a presentation. By using the bar-line combination chart to track, say projected vs. actual sales, you take away the possibility that viewers will confuse the two data series.

Pie charts

These unique charts show how individual data series relate to the whole. You might use a pie chart, for example, to show how each of the different products offered by your company contributes to gross income. You can tell which product is doing best by finding the largest piece of pie. Pie charts generally graph relative data, or percentages, rather than actual amounts. In other words, the pie slice that represents Videos in Figure 8.3 doesn't actually represent 1,200 units. Instead, it represents the portion of income brought in by video sales.

FIGURE 8.3

A sample pie chart

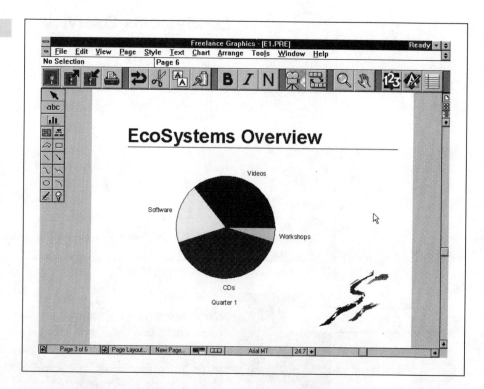

NOTE

Freelance Graphics for Windows lets you create a number of pie charts, including multiple-pie charts, 3D pie charts, and single pies. Pie charts also offer several other options, such as customized title placement, exploding slices, and a number of other preference settings.

Area charts

Area charts allow you to compare data items over a specified period of time. They also allow you to total the data you're representing. Consider, for a moment, the example in Figure 8.4. This simple area chart shows the results of Quarters 1 and 2 for the four sample products we've been tracking.

The darker section at the bottom of the chart represents sales for each item in Quarter 1; the lighter section at the top represents Quarter 2 sales. In addition to comparing these data items, you can easily see the six-month sales totals by comparing the top of the Quarter 2 sales with the values on the y-axis. Freelance automatically adds these data series together to give you yet another interpretation of your data.

FIGURE 8.4

A sample area chart

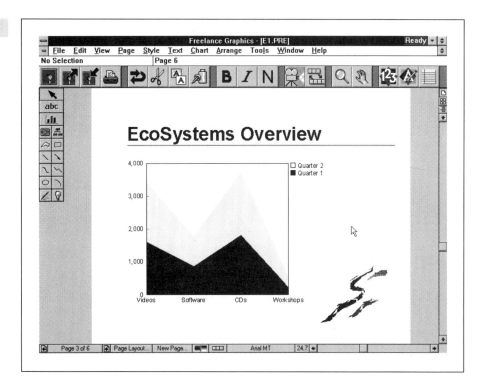

XY charts

XY charts, also called *scatter charts,* are a more specialized type of chart used to compare two different sets of data. Suppose, for example, that you are testing the sales price of EcoSystems' computer software. You suspect that when the price is reduced from $24.95 to $22.95, there will be a significant increase in sales that will more than justify the reduction. Is it possible that buyers feel that the software is worth the lower investment but that the higher cost is a turn-off? You can use an XY chart to see whether there is any connection.

An XY chart is more difficult to read than either the bar, line, or pie charts because you need a little training in order to understand what you're looking at. Values on both the y- and x-axis are numeric (rather than showing numeric values on the y-axis and text labels along the x-axis). Figure 8.5 shows an XY chart that demonstrates the effects of price reduction on software sales.

FIGURE 8.5

A sample XY chart

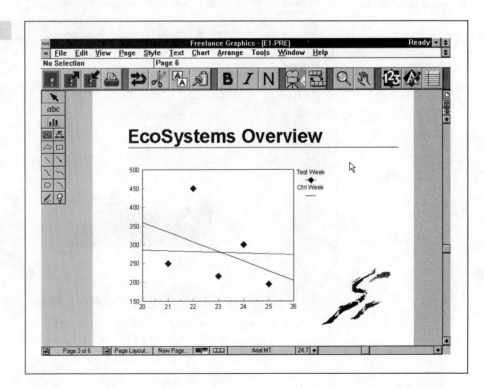

As you can see, the chart in Figure 8.5, without some explanation, doesn't make a whole lot of sense. Okay, so there are diamonds and two different lines, but what, exactly, do they represent? In this experiment, the range of prices stretch across the bottom of the chart as the x-axis values (ranging from 20 to 26). The y-axis values represent the number of units sold. The blue diamonds show the actual sales of the software during the week in which different prices were tested at different ranges. The blue horizontal line shows the trend that the test data revealed. The line stretching across the center of the chart, just below the 300 units mark, shows where the average sales in a non-test week would fall. So, for more complicated charting procedures—charts that need to show data regression and a more analytical representation of correlations—XY charts provide all the impact you need. For communicating a simpler message, using a bar, line, or pie chart would doubtlessly be less complicated.

High-low-close-open Chart

A high-low-close-open chart is another type of specialized chart that is often used in financial matters. This type of chart could track the fluctuation of stock prices over the course of a week. For each day, the chart could show the opening price, the high daily price, the low daily price, and the closing price of the stock. This type of chart can be used in other ways as well, such as to show the results of a sales competition between regions, the changing cost of daily health care in a retirement community, or weekly cost of long-distance telephone service among different divisions of a company.

Radar charts

This type of specialized chart is new with Version 2.0. A radar chart allows you to compare several independent elements of a data set. For example, Figure 8.6 shows a radar chart that shows the results of Quarter 1 and 2 sales for our four sample products. The Quarter 1 data series is represented by a blue line with diamond-shaped data points. The Quarter 2 data is represented by a lighter line.

FIGURE 8.6

A sample radar chart

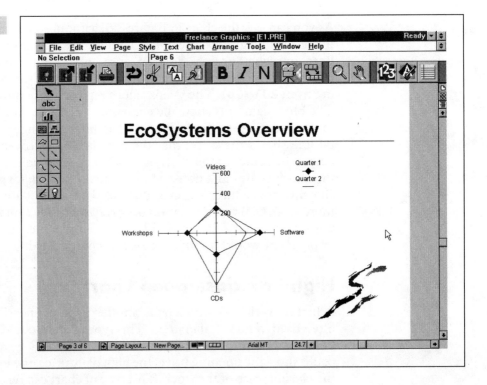

As you can see, each of the products has its own x-axis. The values on the axis (200, 400, and 600) represent the number of units sold. By comparing the data sets, we can see that in Quarter 1, the sales of software exceeded its Quarter 2 sales. We can also see that Quarter 2 sales of CDs blew the top off sales in Quarter 1.

Now that you understand the basic chart types available (and there are still other variations we have yet to explore), you're ready for some hands-on practice creating Freelance charts.

Adding a Chart

So, where do you want to place the chart you create? Should it appear on a separate page by itself, or do you want it on a page that already contains text? The answer to this question will determine how you will begin the process of adding charts. The following sections explain this procedure.

Starting a New Chart Page

Starting a chart page is no different from starting any other page in Free-lance Graphics. You can add a page in the middle of the presentation or at the end. Simply display the page after which you want to add the new page, and then use one of these two methods:

- Open the Page menu and select the New command
- Click the New Page button in the status bar at the bottom of the screen.

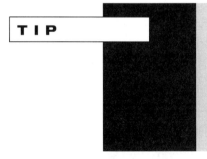

TIP

You can move from page to page in current page view by pressing PgUp or PgDn or by clicking on the arrows at either end of the page status box in the status line (at the bottom of the screen). The page status box shows the current page and total number of presentation pages (for example, *Page 2 of 6*).

The New Page dialog box appears in the center of your screen, as shown in Figure 8.7.

FIGURE 8.7

The New Page dialog box

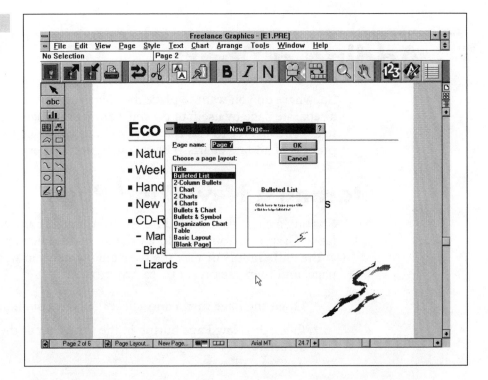

·Below the title bar, you see the *Page name:* text box. Depending on the number of pages you've already created for your publication, this box may show Page 2, 7, or any other number. Freelance uses this name to show the order in which the pages were *created*—not the order in which they *appear*. In other words, even though we're creating this seventh page for the presentation, it appears after page 2 (see the current page indicator in the bottom left corner of the status bar).

In the page layout portion of the dialog box, you see a number of different page options. As you learned in Chapter 3 when we first introduced SmartMasters, this is the dialog box you use to select the next page type for your presentation. When you are creating a chart page, you're most concerned, of course, with finding a chart format—1 Chart, 2 Charts, 4 Charts, or Bullets & Chart will do. If you prefer, you can highlight each of these chart types in turn and watch the preview box in the lower right corner of the dialog box.

For this example, click on 1 Chart and click OK. The new page is added after the current page (making the new page the third of seven, as shown in the page status box). As you can see from Figure 8.8, the new page is placed in typical SmartMaster format (the same SmartMaster background design is used for the new page that was used for all preceding pages). You're ready to enter a title and create the chart.

As you learned in Part Two, the easiest way to enter text in a SmartMaster page is to click on the Click here prompt. When the text box appears, enter text for the title (in this case, *EcoSystems, Inc.*). The text you type is placed in the same font, size, style, and color displayed by the SmartMaster prompt text. When you're finished entering text, click OK to close the text box and return to the page.

FIGURE 8.8

The new chart page

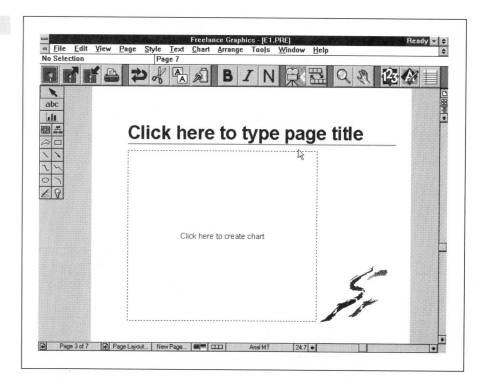

Now that the title is entered, you can start on the chart. The first step, as you can guess, is to click on the chart's Click here prompt. After a moment, the New Chart Gallery screen appears.

NOTE If you're creating a new chart page, you can skip to the "Selecting a Chart Type" section to find out how to use the New Chart Gallery screen.

Adding a Chart to an Existing Page

Freelance also gives you the option of adding a chart to a page that isn't preset for charts. In other words, you can add a chart basically anywhere you want.

To start the process of adding a chart on an existing page, follow these steps:

1. Display the page on which you want to add the chart.

2. Move the pointer over to the chart tool in the tool bar, along the left side of the screen. (The chart tool resembles a miniature bar chart, as shown in Figure 8.9).

3. Click the chart tool.

The New Chart Gallery screen appears, as shown in Figure 8.10. On this screen, you'll select the various chart types you create in Freelance Graphics. Working with the gallery is the subject of the next section.

FIGURE 8.9

Selecting the chart tool

Selecting a Chart Type

As you learned earlier in this chapter, the type of chart you create will have a lot to do with the type of information you're displaying.

Let's start with a simple bar chart. You may, however, prefer to look through the different options in the New Chart Gallery dialog box. Each time you click a different radio button, the chart examples along the right edge of the box (in the Chart Style options) change to reflect your choice.

When you know what chart type you want to use, click the radio button in front of that chart type. Next, move the mouse pointer over to the style samples and click on the chart style you like best. The styles show different selections of grids, sizes, and legend placement. After making your selections, click OK.

FIGURE 8.10

The New Chart
Gallery screen

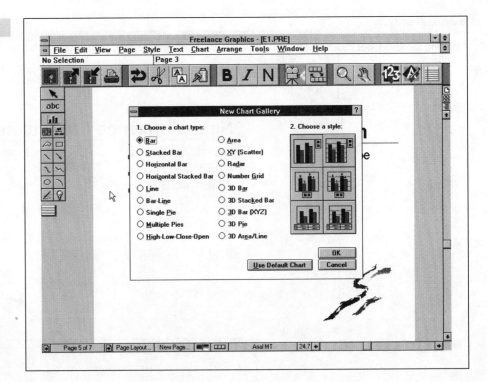

Understanding the Chart Data & Titles Screen

After you choose the chart type and style you want and click OK, the Chart Data & Titles screen appears. Depending on the chart type you are working with, this screen may appear differently. For example, the Chart Data & Titles dialog box shown in Figure 8.11 reflects our choice of a bar chart. Compare this with Figure 8.12, which shows the Chart Data & Titles dialog box for a pie chart.

FIGURE 8.11

The Chart Data &
Titles screen for a bar
chart

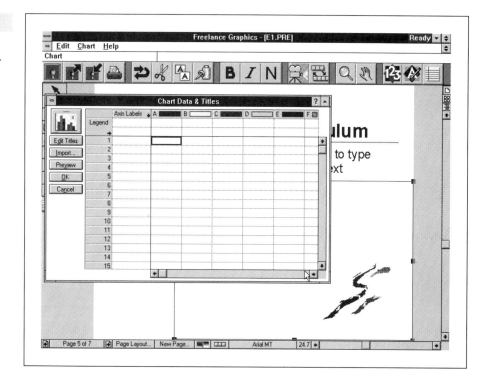

Simply put, you'll use the Chart Data & Titles screen to enter your chart's data and titles—no big surprise, I hope. Freelance Graphics takes care of the guesswork for you by providing you with clear instructions on what to place where (for example, notice the column for Slice Labels and Pie A in Figure 8.12).

Let's go back to the bar chart example. Our first task is to enter the labels for the data we plan to enter. Doing that will require a basic understanding of the way the Chart Data & Title screen places the information you enter. Figure 8.13 shows the Chart Data & Titles screen we'll be working with.

FIGURE 8.12

The Chart Data & Titles screen for a pie chart

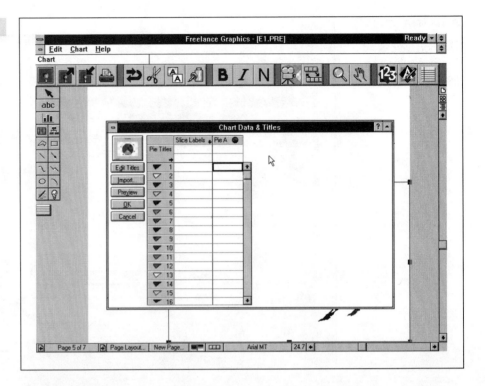

NOTE

In simplest terms, the x-axis is the horizontal edge along which your data is plotted. The y-axis is a vertical edge that traditionally stretches along the left edge of the chart. (In some charts the placement of the y-axis is different.) The x-axis shows what you're charting—things like Product A, B, and C or sales in January, February, and March. The y-axis shows the numeric increments by which the x-axis items are measured.

The Chart Data & Titles screen makes it easy for you by showing you where to place x-axis labels and labels for the legend. (The y-axis labels are figured automatically by Freelance Graphics.) The sections that follow show you how to enter labels, legend items, and chart data.

FIGURE 8.13

The Chart Data & Titles screen

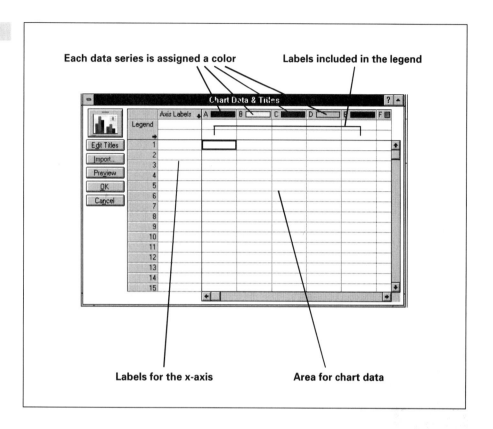

Each data series is assigned a color

Labels included in the legend

Labels for the x-axis

Area for chart data

Entering Chart Labels

Suppose, for this example, that we're tracking the first quarter sales of the top three products offered by EcoSystems, Inc. In order to do this, we need the following information:

- The names of the products
- The names of the months involved (January through March)
- The sales figures for each of those months for each product

That seems straightforward enough. But what goes where? Because this chart is showing the sales results over a period of time, the months need to be entered as the x-axis labels and each of the three products will appear as colored bars within each month. Then we can directly compare the sales in each month (see Figure 8.14).

If you organize the chart so that the products themselves are the x-axis values, you're left with a cluster of months for each x-axis item. (The months are displayed as the different colored bars.) As you can see from Figure 8.15, this type of graph works, but it involves more effort on the part of the viewer and is more confusing than it needs to be. If you were more interested in seeing how each of the products did in each of the three months (how Videos, for example, did in January, February, and March) rather than the overall comparison of the product sales (how Videos compared to the sales of the other two products in the first quarter), this type of chart may be sufficient.

FIGURE 8.14

Using the months as x-axis labels

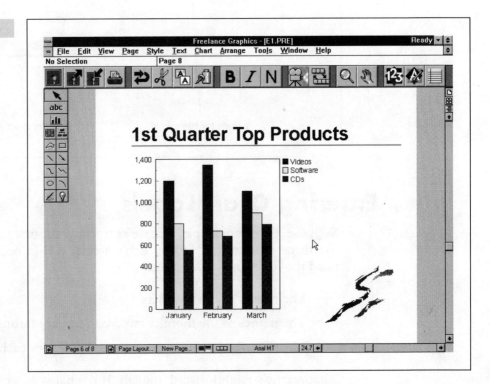

FIGURE 8.15

Products entered as
x-axis labels

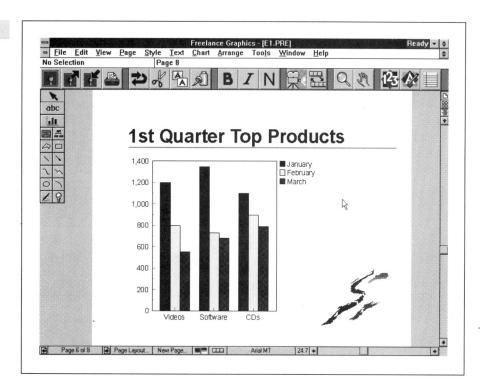

T I P

As a general rule, whenever your chart involves
graphing something over time, use the time values
as your x-axis labels.

To enter the data labels for the x-axis, follow these steps:

1. Move the mouse pointer to the first entry cell below the Legends
line in the Axis Labels column (beside the number 1).

2. Click the mouse button. A black rectangular highlight appears
around the cell.

3. Type January and press Enter. The highlight moves down one cell.

4. Type February and press Enter; then type March. The labels appear
as shown in Figure 8.16.

FIGURE 8.16

Entering x-axis labels

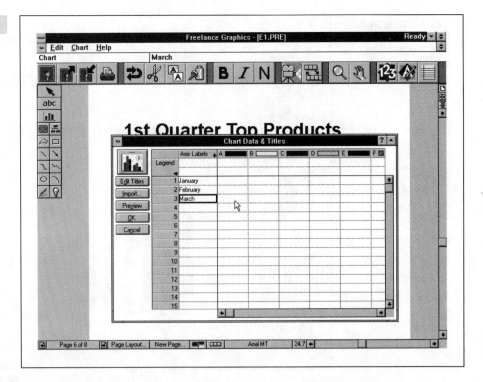

Entering Legend Items

The legend is the small table—also called a key—that tells your audience what the different colors (or lines, depending on your chart type) represent. The Chart Data & Titles screen provides a place for you to enter the legend items for your data.

The legend shows what you've used as your data series. For example, in creating the example shown in Figure 8.14, the products—Videos, Software, and CDs—were the items shown as colored bars; therefore, they were the entries in the legend. These entries, which are placed to the upper right of the chart or down below (depending on the chart style you've chosen), tell the viewer what the colored bars mean.

To enter legend items for your chart, follow these steps:

1. Position the pointer in one of the first two cells beneath column A. These cells are reserved for legend entries.

2. Click the mouse button. The black highlight surrounds the cell.

3. Type Videos (or an entry of your choosing) and press →. The highlight moves to the next cell to the right.

4. Type Software and press →. The highlight moves right.

5. Finally, type CDs. The legend entries should now appear as shown in Figure 8.17.

FIGURE 8.17

Entering the legend items

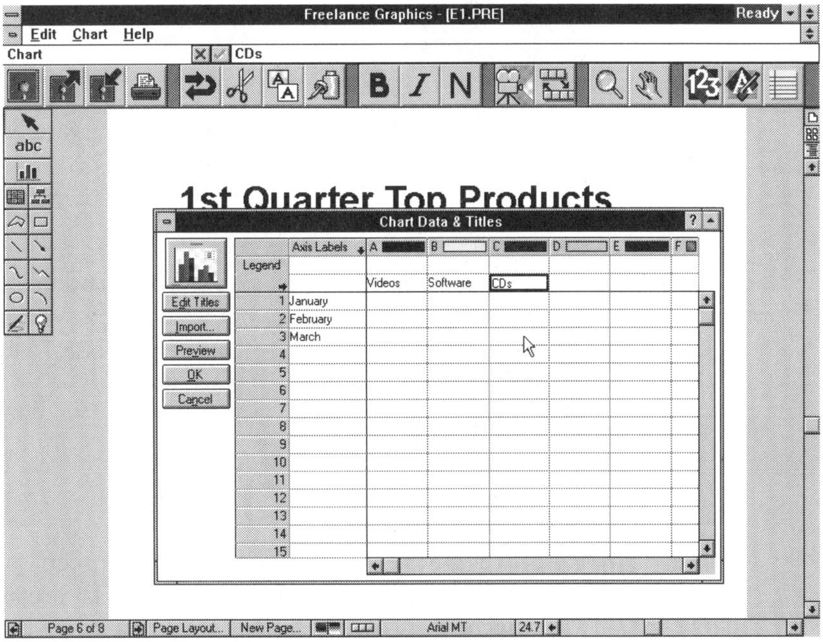

Entering Data

At this point, finishing off the chart requires little more except plugging in the data. Use the arrow keys or the mouse pointer to move the highlight to the cell in which you want to enter information; then type your data. When typing numeric amounts, commas and dollar signs are not necessary.

TIP   Freelance Graphics also accepts files you create in other popular programs—such as Lotus 1-2-3 for Windows—so you don't have to retype data you've already entered. The Import button on the Chart Data & Titles screen allows you to bring in files you've created elsewhere. To find out more about importing chart data, see Chapter 9.

Figure 8.18 shows the completed Chart Data & Titles screen for the bar chart under construction.

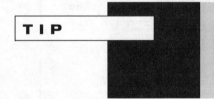

TIP   Only numbers are accepted in the data-entry portion of the screen. Reserve the Axis Labels and Legend sections of the Chart Data & Titles screen for your text information.

Previewing the Chart

From within the Chart Data & Titles screen, you can preview the chart without actually leaving the dialog box. To preview the chart, click on the Preview button to the left of the data-entry area. After a moment, the chart is shown—but wait—the Chart Data & Titles screen covers it right back up. You can click on the title bar of the Chart Data & Titles screen and move it to one side of the screen so you can get a look at the previewed chart, as shown in Figure 8.19.

FIGURE 8.18

The completed Chart
Data & Titles screen

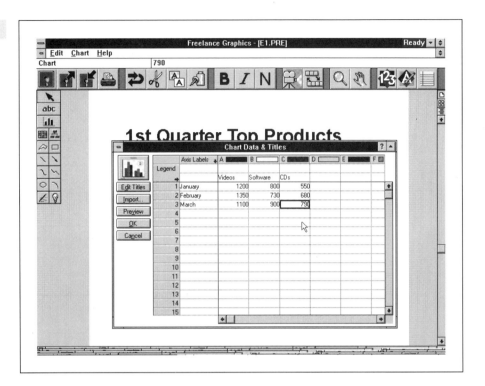

TIP

A better way to preview your charts is to click and
hold down the mouse button on the Preview option.
The Chart Data & Titles window won't come back
until you release the mouse.

The advantage of previewing the chart before actually accepting it by
clicking OK and returning to current page view is that, as long as the
Chart Data & Titles screen is displayed, you can still easily make modifications. When you're through previewing the chart, move the Chart Data &
Titles screen back into place and continue your work. At this point, you
may want to add titles or other notes (the subject of the next section).

FIGURE 8.19

Previewing the chart

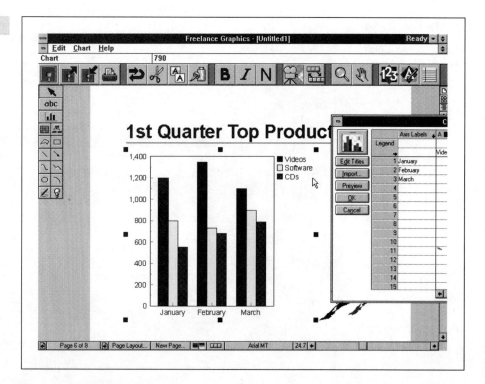

Adding Titles

You've already entered the basics of your chart. Now let's spruce things up a bit by adding titles or subtitles to your creation. The Edit Titles button on the left side of the Chart Data & Titles screen is provided for just this purpose.

To add titles, click the Edit Title button. The Edit Titles screen appears, as shown in Figure 8.20. The top section, Headings, provides you with three lines on which you can enter a heading for the chart. Remember, however, that the page title you entered at the Click here prompt provides the overall page title, so anything you enter in the Headings box will serve as a kind of subhead.

FIGURE 8.20

The Chart Data &
Titles dialog box

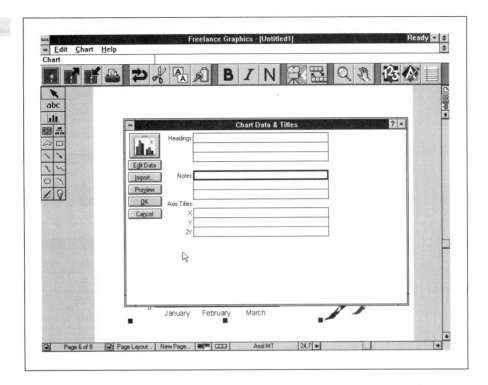

The Notes section provides you with three more lines of text in which you can enter a kind of footnote about the chart you've created. You might, for example, use the Notes section to name a source for your statistics, the date of a specific analysis, or the name of a sponsor.

The Axis Titles area of the screen allows you to enter labels for the axes of your chart. The first line, X, controls the label used as a title for the x-axis labels. The second line, Y, controls the title for the y-axis. The final line, 2Y, is for charts that have two y-axes (one on the left and one on the right).

To enter titles for your chart, follow these steps:

1. Position the mouse pointer in the first line of the Headings box.

2. Type EcoSystems, 1993 and press Tab three times (or click in the Notes box).

3. Type Moore Marketing and click in the Axis Titles area.

4. After X, type First Quarter '93 and press ↓.

5. After Y, type Sales in Units.

Figure 8.21 shows the completed Chart Data & Titles screen. When you're ready to return to current page view, click OK.

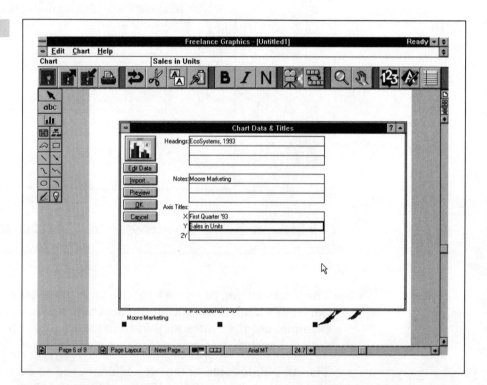

TIP

When you've finished entering titles for your chart, you don't have to go directly to current page view. You can return to the first page of the Chart Data & Titles form by clicking the Edit Data button to the left of the entry area. Also, if you prefer, you can click Preview to see how the chart looks before you return to the actual page.

Figure 8.22 shows the chart we've created up to this point. As you can see, things are looking a little cluttered. In an actual presentation, we might choose not to include the heading or axis labels. In Chapter 9, you'll learn to modify your chart by performing a number of editing tasks.

The next section explores creating organizational charts, another type of chart that is new with Version 2.0.

FIGURE 8.22

The completed chart

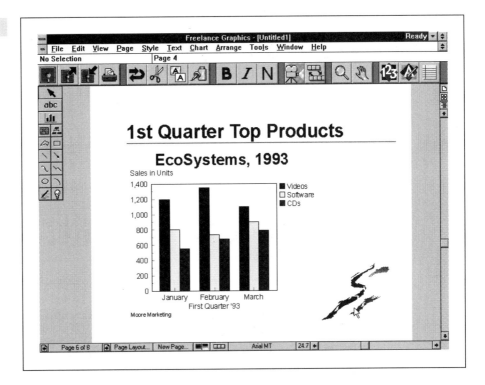

Creating Organizational Charts

What is an organizational chart and why do you need one? In some companies, the structure of departments isn't readily apparent from the title on an employee's desk. So, how do new employees know whom to go to and for what? Large companies often find organizational charts helpful in establishing clearly the power hierarchy within the corporation. But there are other uses, too:

- You can show the people involved in the different stages of a project
- You can define the steps involved in creating a new product—from concept to production
- You can establish roles for a fund-raiser or company benefit

In short, you can use an organization chart to organize data for basically any purpose, as long as you need to show a hierarchical progression (*this first, then that*).

You can create an organization chart two ways:

- Click on the organization tool (to the right below the chart tool)
- Start a new page by clicking the New Page button in the status bar and select Organization Chart from the page layout list. Then click OK.

The SmartMaster page with Click here prompt appears, as shown in Figure 8.23. To add the page title, click in the prompt at the top of the page. Enter the necessary heading in the displayed text box (we've entered *Software Development* as the title in this example). Click OK after you've entered the text.

FIGURE 8.23

The SmartMaster page
for organizational
charts

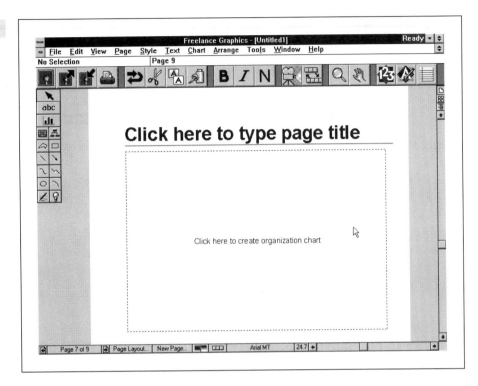

When you click on the chart area, the Organization Chart Gallery dialog box appears, as shown in Figure 8.24. You can make your style selection from the six displayed choices. If you want Freelance to automatically resize text as necessary to fit on one page, leave the checkbox checked. If not, click in the box to remove the X. Finally, select the way in which you want the lowest level of the chart to be displayed by clicking on the appropriate radio button at the bottom of the box. When you're finished making choices, click OK.

FIGURE 8.24

The Organization Chart Gallery

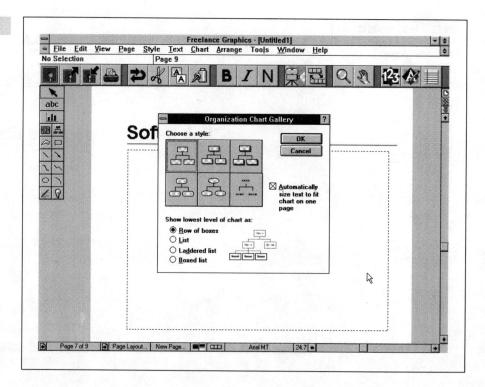

After you click OK, the Organization Chart Entry List appears, as shown in Figure 8.25. On this screen, enter all the names and titles for your organization chart. Freelance walks you through the process.

To add information to the organization chart, follow these steps:

1. Type the first name for the highest level entry and press Enter. The flashing cursor moves to the next line.

2. Type the person's title. Press Enter twice. When Freelance sees the second Enter keystroke, the program automatically displays the next entry information. The second entry is automatically placed as a subordinate to the first.

FIGURE 8.25

The Organization
Chart Entry List

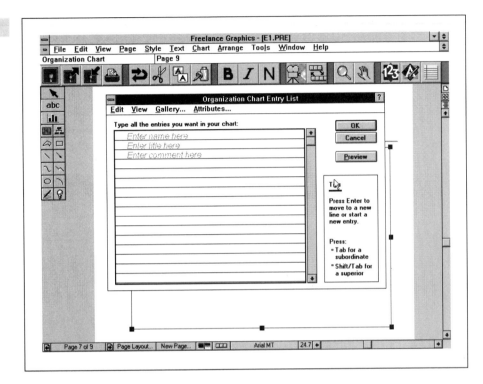

Continue entering information as necessary. Press Enter once to move to the next line or twice to begin a new entry. If you want to add a subordinate, press Tab to indent the text. If you want to add a superior level, press Shift-Tab. After you've finished entering information, click Preview to see how the chart looks before you return to the current page. Figure 8.26 shows the completed organizational chart.

FIGURE 8.26

The completed
organizational chart

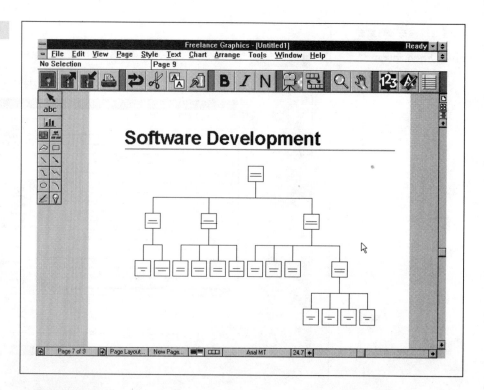

TIP

You edit the organizational chart in much the same way as you edit other chart types. In the Organization Chart Entry List, there are four menus you can use to fine-tune the look of your chart: Edit, View, Gallery, and Attributes. In the Edit menu, you can change the position of text entries. With View, you control how the names are displayed. Clicking Gallery displays the Organization Chart Gallery, and Attributes allows you to control the font, size, style, color, and alignment of selected text.

In the next section, you learn to create another of Freelance's unique formats—a table.

Creating a Table

Like the other chart types in Freelance Graphics, you can either add tables to a text page you're already using or creating a new page to hold the table.

If you start a table by clicking the New Page button at the bottom of the screen and choosing Table from the page layout list, a Click here prompt appears in the table box after you click the OK button and return to the current view. To start the table, click the Click here prompt. The Table Gallery appears, as shown in Figure 8.27.

If you start a table by clicking the table button (the button to the right of the organization chart button) in the tools row, the Table Gallery is immediately displayed.

FIGURE 8.27

The Table Gallery

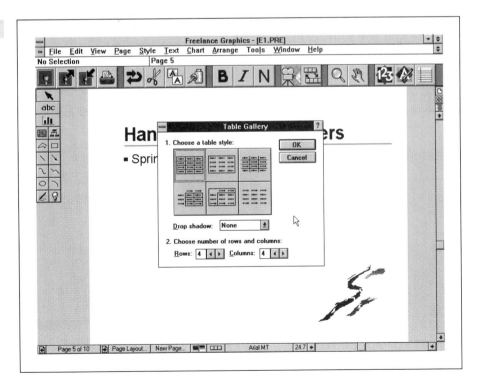

Choose the type of table you want to create. If you want to add a drop shadow to the table, click ↓ at the end of the Drop shadow box. A drop-down list of shadow options appears, allowing you to choose the position of the shadow. Next, select the number of rows and columns you want in the table. Click on the appropriate buttons to make the displayed number larger or smaller. When you're finished making choices, click OK.

Next, the grid for the table appears on the page (see Figure 8.28). To enter the values for the table, simply make sure the table is selected (the handles will appear around the outside edges of the table) and begin typing. A thick gray outline surrounds the table, and the text is entered in the first cell in the first column.

After you enter text in that cell, press Tab to move to the next cell or press ↓ to move to the cell below the current cell. Fill in information by typing text and pressing Tab or the arrow keys. You can add a second line in a

FIGURE 8.28

The table grid

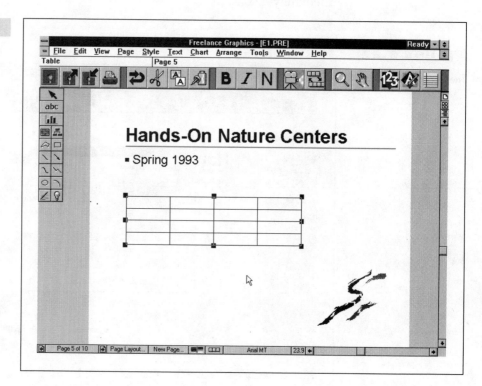

table cell by pressing Enter. Freelance automatically lengthens the cell to allow for the second line.

T I P

You can edit the information in a table much the same way as you edit and enhance regular chart data. The Chart menu contains commands that are available for controlling the text style, size, font, and color used to display text. You can also use the Table command in the Chart menu to insert and delete rows and columns.

 From a basic discussion of chart types to more specialized instruction on creating a simple chart and working with organizational charts and tables, this chapter has focused on creating simple charts. The next chapter builds on this foundation by showing you how to edit and enhance your charts and how to import data from other applications.

NINE

Editing, Enhancing, and Importing Charts

fast TRACK

● **To select a chart for editing,** 283

simply click on the chart with which you want to work. Small black squares—called *handles*—appear around the perimeter of the chart area, indicating that the chart is selected.

● **To change chart attributes,** 285

click on the chart you want to use. Then open the Chart menu and choose the Attributes command or double-click on the data series. The Bar Chart Attributes command appears. For each data set, you can select the color and pattern used to display data. You can also add a second y-axis to the chart, turn on 3D effects, and hide or display data sets. Make your selections and click OK.

● **To hide a data series,** 288

   display the Chart Attributes dialog box by opening the Chart
   menu and choosing the Attributes command. In the Data set
   box, click on the data set you want to hide. Then click the Hide
   this data set option checkbox. An X appears in the box. Click
   OK.

● **To display a hidden data series,** 288

   click on the chart you want to work with. Then open the Chart
   menu and choose Attributes. The Data set box shows which
   data sets have been hidden by marking them with a gray rectangle. To redisplay the data series, click on the grayed set you
   want to restore; then click on the Hide this data set option to
   remove the X.

THIS chapter continues the basic discussion of charts we began in Chapter 8. In this chapter, we'll go through the process of editing chart information and enhancing various elements of the chart—text, color, and individual chart characteristics. You'll learn to change the typeface, create a specialized legend, and change the labels along the x- and y-axes, among other things.

In this chapter, you'll also learn how to import chart data from other applications, thus saving yourself the time and trouble of retyping information you've already entered. Additionally, you'll find out about Freelance's capability to link files, so that a chart you create based on one file is automatically updated each time you make revisions to it.

But first, let's pick up where we left off—poised on the edge of editing our creation.

Editing Charts

Sometimes it's hard to tell how something will look before you actually create it. As your experience with charts grows, you'll be able to decide easily which charts should be used for what purposes and determine the best arrangement of labels and headings. At first, however, you'll probably go through the old trial-and-error method of learning how to best present your data.

Luckily, Freelance Graphics provides a number of ways in which you can modify what you've created. In fact, you can change virtually anything you've done—from entering text and data to assigning colors and patterns. This section introduces you to the ways to change your basic chart.

Understanding the Chart Menu

The first step in exploring our editing options is the Chart menu. To access it, all you need to do is select your chart (click on it so that the handles appear around the edges). Then open the Chart menu by clicking on the word Chart or by pressing Alt-C. The Chart menu opens, as shown in Figure 9.1.

As you can see, the Chart menu contains many different commands to make modifications to your chart. Table 9.1 provides an overview of the different commands on this menu.

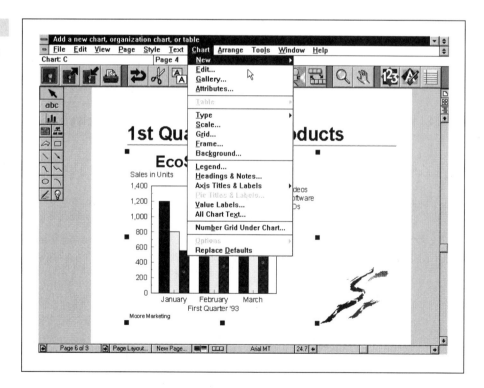

TABLE 9.1: Commands on the Chart menu

COMMAND	DESCRIPTION
New	Allows you to add a new chart, table, or organization chart
Edit	Displays the Chart Data & Titles dialog box so you can edit data you've entered
Gallery	Displays the New Chart Gallery dialog box so you can select a chart type and style
Attributes	Lets you select the color, pattern, and special effects of individual data series
Table	Available only when you're working on a table, this command lets you modify tables by adding or deleting rows, moving information, or resizing the table
Type	Allows you to choose a new chart type
Scale	Displays the Chart Scale dialog box so you can modify the increments used on the y-axis
Grid	Lets you fine-tune the x- and y-axes by controlling the way tickmarks are displayed and by adding or removing a background grid
Frame	Allows you to modify the frame used on your chart (the default is set to full frame)
Background	Lets you specify the color and line width of the background edge and inner area
Legend	Displays the Chart Legend dialog box so you can specify the font and style of text in the legend. You can also specify the color and line width of the edge and area of the legend box. Finally, you can select the location (Left, Right, Top, Bottom, Inside, or Outside) for the placement of the legend.
Headings & Notes	Allows you to choose the typeface and style used in the chart headings and notes. Additionally, you can choose the alignment of the text by selecting Left, Centered, or Right. You also can hide the headings altogether.

TABLE 9.1: Commands on the Chart menu (continued)

COMMAND	DESCRIPTION
Axis Titles & Labels	Lets you specify alignment, typeface, style, and color for information displayed along the x- and y-axes. Additionally, you can hide titles or labels.
Pie Titles & Labels	Lets you customize settings for titles and labels on your pie charts.
Value Labels	Controls the display of the value labels that appear on your chart, including the typeface, size, and color of text as well as the number of decimal places displayed.
All Chart Text	Allows you to select the various text sizes for information in your charts. You can also enter global settings for the typeface, color, and style used.
Number Grid Under Chart	Lets you add a number grid beneath the chart instead of using a legend.
Options	Allows you to enter chart options for some charts, including multiple pies, XY charts, or charts that use dates as labels.
Replace Defaults	Replaces the default settings used by the chart with the settings you have entered. (You can later reverse this by clicking the Use Default Chart button in the New Chart Gallery screen.)

Modifying Data Entries

The most basic of all editing tasks involves fixing errors that have accidentally crept into your work. Perhaps you transposed a few numbers or reversed two of the labels. To make these simple corrections, follow these steps:

1. Click on the chart you want to edit.

2. Open the Chart menu and select the Edit command. You've seen this screen before—this is the same Chart Data & Titles screen that you used to enter the data in the first place (see Figure 9.2).

3. Click on the cell you want to edit (whether that cell contains numeric or text data). The dark highlighting rectangle moves to that cell.

4. Retype the correct information. The information you type automatically overwrites the existing data in that cell.

TIP

To modify the heading, note, or x- or y-axis labels, click on the Edit Titles button to display the second screen of the Chart Data & Titles dialog box. Then click on the item you want to change and type the correct information. If, however, you *aren't* in the Chart Data & Titles dialog box, just double-click on the heading, note, or axis you want to modify and the appropriate editing box will appear.

FIGURE 9.2

Editing information on the Chart Data & Titles screen

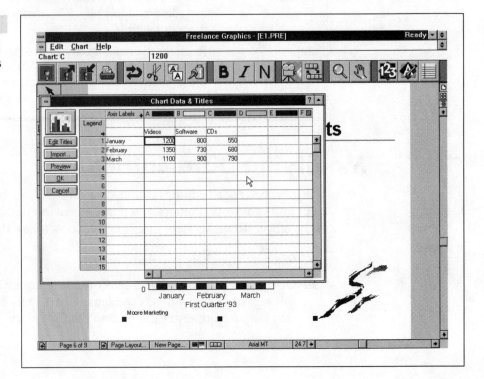

Changing Chart Attributes

Freelance offers you a staggering amount of options to help fine-tune your charts. Nevertheless, you don't *have* to use any of them—Freelance produces a perfectly acceptable chart for you as soon as you plug in the data. The rest is just icing.

But you may find that once you create the chart, there are a number of things you'd like to change. Maybe you wish you'd used different colors for the data sets. Or perhaps you'd like to change the width of the individual bars in your bar chart.

To change the look and feel of the data sets in your chart, use the Chart Attributes command in the Chart menu. When you click on this command, a Chart Attributes dialog box appears, as shown in Figure 9.3.

The attributes displayed depend on the type of chart you've created. For example, when you are editing a bar chart, the Bar Chart Attributes dialog

FIGURE 9.3

The Bar Chart
Attributes dialog box

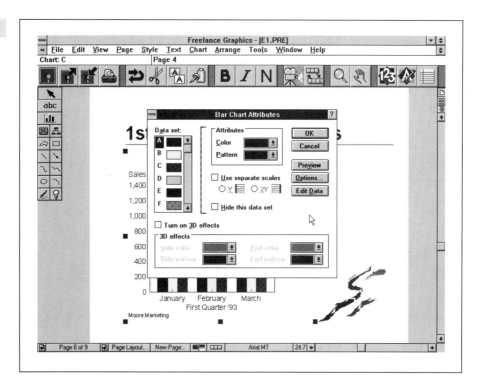

box is displayed. Similarly, when you are working with a line chart, the Line Chart Attributes dialog box is displayed.

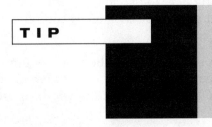

T I P

You can quickly display the Chart Attributes dialog box by double-clicking on a bar within the chart you want to modify. (*Note:* If you double-click on another area of the chart, the Chart Data & Titles screen appears.)

Changing Data Set Color

The first step in changing the attributes of a specific data set is to choose the data set with which you want to work. For example, set A is selected in Figure 9.3. To select a different data set, click on the one you want.

When you click on a different data set, the color shown in the Attributes box changes to reflect your choice. You can click on the ↓ at the end of the Color box to display a palette of available colors from which you can choose a new color for the data set (see Figure 9.4).

To select a different color for the data set, simply click on the one you want. You can choose a pattern from the Pattern box the same way—click on the ↓ and choose from the displayed choices.

Turning on 3D

You can turn a simple bar chart into a 3D chart with the simple click of a button. The Turn on 3D effects checkbox (located toward the bottom of the Chart Attributes dialog box) changes the flat bars into something more life-like. Once you select this option, you can choose some of the 3D special effects in the box at the bottom of the screen. The special effects work like this:

3D EFFECT	DESCRIPTION
Side color	Allows you to choose a color for the side of the 3D bar

FIGURE 9.4

Choose a different color for a data set

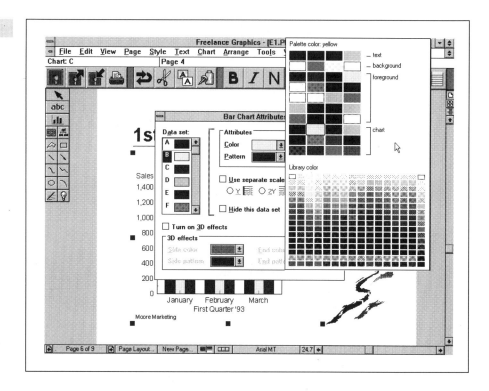

3D EFFECT	DESCRIPTION
Side pattern	Selects a pattern for the side of the 3D bar
End color	Specifies the color for the top of the 3D bar
End pattern	Lets you choose a color for the top of the 3D bar

Did you notice that there is no option for setting the color of the front of the bar? The initial color selected for the data set (in the Attributes Color setting) is the color used for the face of the bar. These other colors in 3D effects set the contrast between the front, side, and end of each bar.

Hiding and Displaying a Data Series

When you are producing a chart that shows the relationships of certain data elements, having the ability to hide a data series can be particularly helpful. For example, suppose you have graphed the results of a recent employee competition. In examining the data, you notice that by far the highest sales percentage was earned by a new employee whom *you* were training. To make the analysis more fair, you want to hide the data set that shows the trainee's sales results.

To hide a data set, simply click the Hide this data set checkbox. When you return to the chart (by using the Preview button or by clicking OK), the data will be removed from view.

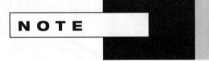

N O T E   Freelance Graphics does not delete hidden data—it merely suppresses it.

When you want to redisplay the hidden data, bring up the Chart Attributes dialog box once again. The data set you've hidden is marked with a gray box. Click on the data set, and the X in the Hide this data set checkbox becomes apparent. To display the data set, click in this checkbox to remove the X.

Setting Chart Options

On the right side of the Chart Attributes dialog box is the familiar row of command buttons. A new button, Options, takes you to another screen that allows you to further fine-tune your chart's appearance (see Figure 9.5).

Again, the options you see depend on the type of chart you have created. The options in the Bar Chart Options dialog box are specific to the bar chart, as you can see. The Bar options control the way 3D bars look, both in terms of width and angle. The first option, Width, controls how wide the bar is. If you choose 100 percent, the bars touch each other, with no white space in-between. (The default is 75 percent.) The second option, 3D effect, controls the amount of the bar that is used for the shadowed

FIGURE 9.5

The Bar Chart Options
dialog box

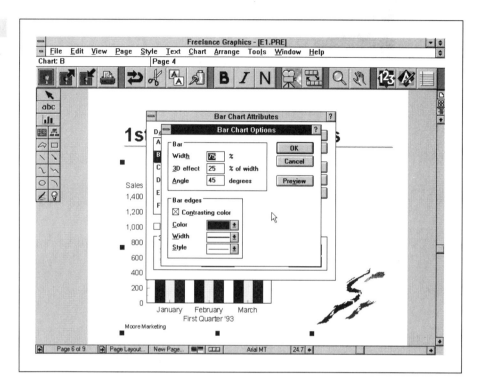

effect of 3D. Angle controls the angle at which the bar's 3D shadow is displayed (45 degrees is the default). You can move the bar's side and top view, for example, by typing any number from 0 to 360.

TIP

Although you can make changes in the Bar Options dialog box whether you have selected 3D display or not, you won't see the effects of your changes until you enable 3D in the Bar Chart Attributes dialog box.

The Bar edges settings allow you to make choices about the edges of the bars in your chart. You can make them a different color, a different width, or a different line style.

Changing Chart Type

At some point, you may want to completely change the entire look of your chart. Because so much of Freelance is automated and takes care of the details for you, you can change your chart from one type to another with a simple click of a button. Let's try it. To change the chart type, follow these steps:

1. Click on the chart you want to change.

2. Open the Chart menu and choose the Type command. A pop-up list of chart type options appears to the right of the menu (see Figure 9.6).

3. The current chart type is marked with a checkmark. To choose a different chart type, simply click on the type you want (in this case, we've chosen Single Pie).

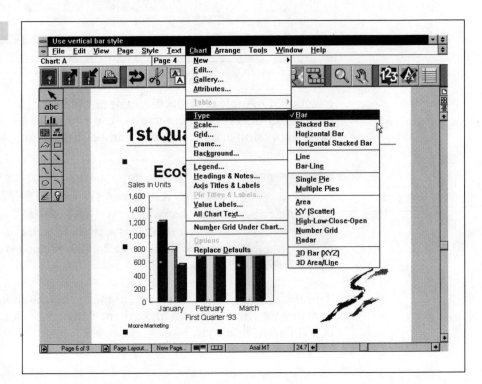

After you make your selection, you are returned to current page view and the new chart is displayed. In the example shown in Figure 9.7, a pie chart is created using the same data from the bar chart used earlier. Because each pie works with only one series of data, the pie chart shows only our first data set (set A) for each of the three months of the first quarter. Notice that the heading and note stayed with the modified chart.

TIP

If you select special effects—such as 3D—for the first chart, Freelance will apply the same settings to the new chart.

If you take a look at the Chart Attributes dialog box, you'll see something entirely different. Display the dialog box by double-clicking on one of the pie slices. The Pie Chart Attributes dialog box appears, as shown in Figure 9.8.

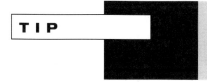

FIGURE 9.7

The chart changed into a pie chart

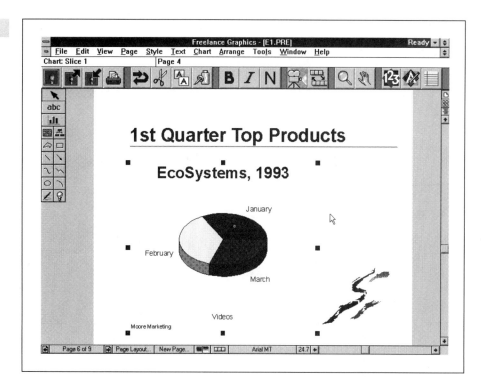

Many of the options are the same, but instead of working with bars, you're working with slices.

Now that you know the basics of editing chart data and settings, let's take a closer look at ways you can enhance the look of your charts.

Enhancing Charts

At first glance, the line between editing and enhancing may seem slim. Many of the operations you performed in the first part of this chapter—changing data set color, specifying 3D effects—could really fall into the

FIGURE 9.8

The Pie Chart Attributes dialog box

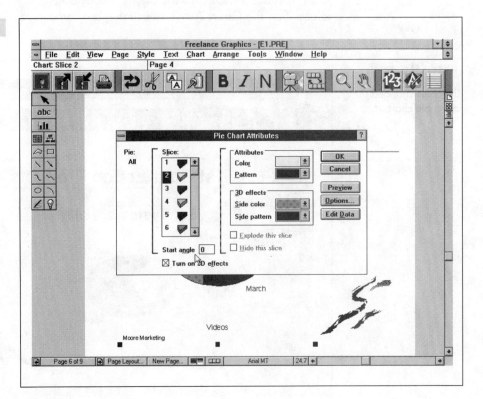

category of enhancements. In this section, however, we focus on some more specialized tasks—things like changing the typeface, style, color, and size of selected text, adding grids and frames, customizing the chart legend, and modifying axis titles and labels.

Making Text Changes

One of the first enhancements you might want to try is to change the way the text in your charts looks. Although Freelance Graphics uses Arial as the default font, you can choose from a wide range of additional fonts. (You may need to check your printer manual to find out which fonts are supported by your printer.)

Freelance Graphics gives you several options—you can choose several different text items individually, or elect to change all chart text at once. The following commands are available in the Chart menu in case you want to change the text attributes of individual items:

COMMAND	CHANGES TEXT SETTINGS FOR
Legend	The legend created with various chart types. Use this option to control colors, display placement, and background of the legend
Headings & Notes	Heading levels 1 through 3 and Note levels 1 through 3. You can specify the font, size, color, and style of text, along with the alignment. You can also hide or display headings and notes from this dialog box.
Axis Titles & Labels	Titles and labels that appear on charts that have an x-axis. If you are working on a chart that does not have an x-axis (such as a pie chart), this command is dimmed and you cannot select it.

COMMAND	CHANGES TEXT SETTINGS FOR
Pie Titles & Labels	The labels and titles that you've assigned to pie charts. When other types of charts are selected, this command is dimmed.
Value Labels	The labels displayed for the chart type you've created. You can specify the typeface, size, color, and style of values and percentages on the chart.
All Chart Text	Every text item on the selected chart. This dialog box enables you to specify the size for each of five text items, ranging from Tiny to Extra Large. You can choose typeface, color, and style in addition to size.

WARNING

Tiny and Extra Large are classifications of text sizes. Therefore, changing one of the categories could change *several*. For example, if Freelance classified four text items as Tiny and you change the Tiny size, all four items would change size.

Because all these commands work in basically the same way, we'll show you only how to change all text. Each individual setting is simply a variation of this procedure: select the item you want to change, click on the typeface, color, size, and style you want, and then click OK.

When you want to change all of the text in a selected chart, follow these steps:

1. Click on the chart you want to change.

2. Open the Chart menu and choose the All Chart Text command. The All Chart Text dialog box appears, as shown in Figure 9.9.

FIGURE 9.9

The All Chart Text
dialog box

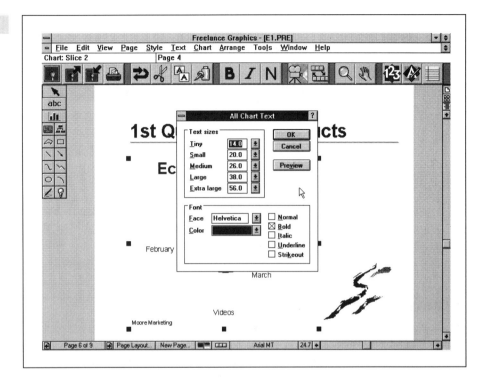

3. Click on the size you want to change. (Click ↓ to see a list of possible choices.)

4. Select the new size from the list (displayed when you click ↓) or position the cursor in the box and type the new size.

5. Change as many sizes as necessary.

6. Click the ↓ to the right of the Face box in the Font options portion of the screen. A drop-down list of possible typefaces appears, as shown in Figure 9.10.

7. Scroll through the list as necessary (click on the arrows in the scroll bar that appears to the right of the Face list). Highlight the typeface you want to use.

8. Click on the ↓ to the right of the Color box. The color palette appears. Make your selection by clicking on the color you want.

9. The final selection concerns the styles for your text. The series of checkboxes in the bottom right corner of the dialog box gives you the choices of Normal (no style), Bold, Italic, Underline, and Strikeout. Click on the style you want. (You can click more than one style, if you wish.)

10. When you've finished entering your choices, click OK. You are returned to current page view and all the text in the selected chart is changed to reflect your choices.

FIGURE 9.10

Selecting a typeface

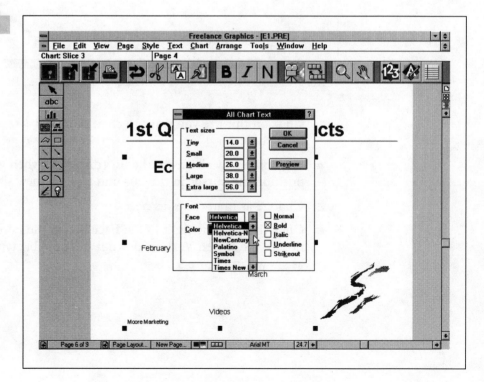

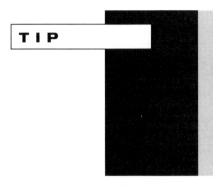

TIP

If you're not sure how your chart text will look after you modify the settings, press and hold the Preview button to see a quick version of your changed chart (when you release the Preview button, you are returned to the dialog box). If you like what you see, click OK to accept the changes. You can make other modifications in the All Chart Text dialog box or click Cancel to abandon your changes.

Working with Grids and Frames

Other special enhancements you may want to add include grids and frames. Neither of these enhancements apply to pie charts, so, using the procedure listed earlier, we've changed the example chart type back to a bar chart.

Grids

To add a grid to your chart, begin by selecting Grid from the Chart menu. The Chart Grid dialog box is displayed (see Figure 9.11).

You see several different options on the Chart Grid dialog box. On the left, you choose the type of axis you want to change. If you select X, the grid lines are added vertically, extending from the x-axis upward. If you choose Y, the grid lines are added horizontally, extending from the y-axis across the chart. Notice that these settings are radio buttons, meaning you can select only one at one time. If you have specified a chart with two y-axes (one on the left and one on the right), the option for 2Y is available.

The options in the center of the dialog box control the major grid and tick settings. What is a major grid? The chart has numeric increments (200, 400, 600) along the y-axis. When you first select Y and then click in the Display grid box in the Major grid section, grid lines are added to each of the major increments (the ones numbered along the y-axis). When you select Display grid in the Minor grid & ticks section, grid lines are placed halfway between the major increments, thus marking 300, 500, 700, and so on.

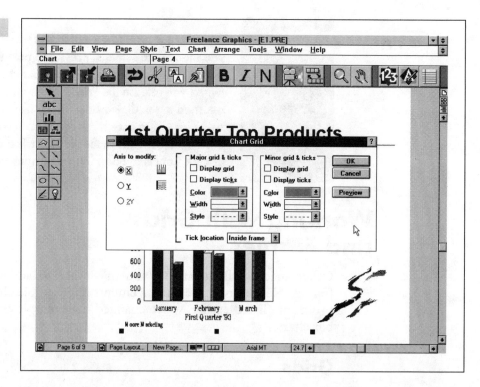

Ticks, also called *tickmarks*, are small dashes that appear only along the axis rather than extending all the way across the chart. If you'd rather use ticks than grid lines, click Display ticks in the options boxes. If you want ticks at only major increments, click only Display ticks in the Major grid & ticks box. If you want ticks to appear at both major and minor increments, click the Display ticks option in both boxes.

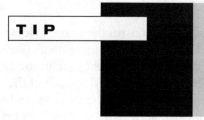

TIP

You can control where the ticks appear on the charts you create. After you've selected the Display ticks option, click on the ↓ beside the Tick location option. A drop-down list of locations appears. Make your selection and click Preview or OK.

When you've finished entering grid settings, click OK or Preview to see what your changes look like. Figure 9.12 shows how the sample chart looks after a grid has been added to the y-axis.

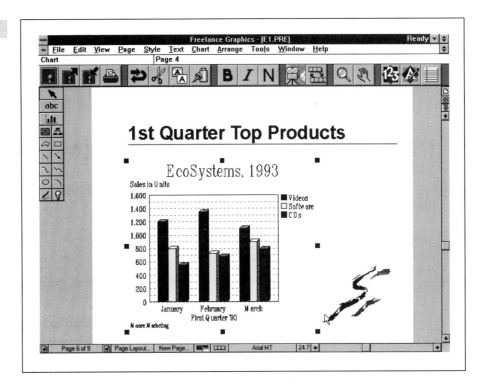

Frames

Adding a frame is just as easy. First, select the chart to which you want to add the frame. Then open the Chart menu and select the Frame command. The Chart Frame dialog box appears, as shown in Figure 9.13.

FIGURE 9.13

The Chart Frame
dialog box

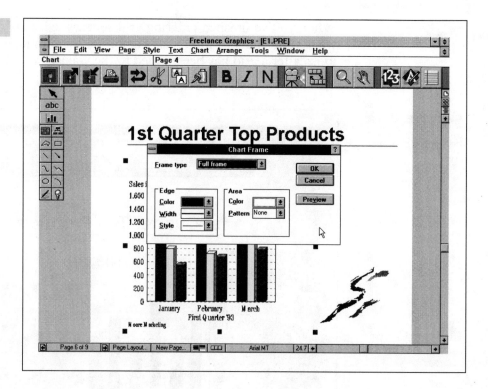

When you add a frame to your chart, you have three basic options to consider:

1. What kind of frame do you want to use? You have several choices.

- Full frame,
- A frame along the x-axis
- A frame along the y-axis
- A frame along both axes
- No frame

2. What color, line width, and style do you want the frame's edge to be?

3. What color or pattern do you want the inside area of the frame to show?

Answer each of these questions by filling in the Chart Frame dialog box. First select the type of frame you want from the following:

FRAME CHOICE	RESULT
Full frame (the default)	Encloses the entire chart in a frame
X	A frame is added only to the x-axis
Y	A frame is added only to the y-axis
None	Removes all frames

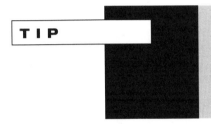

TIP

When you choose a color for the inside of a full frame (color is not available for X or Y frame types), remember also to choose a pattern. If pattern is set to None, Freelance won't display any color for the grid.

Backgrounds

Another option available to you—for all chart types—is to add a background. When you select Background from the Chart menu, the Chart Background dialog box appears. You can specify edge color and area fill color, choosing from a wide range of colors, patterns, and line styles for the background you create. You can also opt to add a drop-shadow to the background. The Display button, in the bottom right corner of the dialog box, turns the display of the background settings on or off. When you click OK, the area within the chart handles is filled with the background you specified.

Customizing the Legend

Thus far, we've made many different changes to the chart itself, but we haven't modified the legend. As you may know, the legend to a chart is like a key to a map. Viewers will look to the legend to get important information about which colors, shapes, or patterns are assigned to which data sets.

To customize the legend Freelance has created, first click on the chart you want to work with. Then, open the Chart menu and choose Legend. The Chart Legend dialog box appears, as shown in Figure 9.14.

The Chart Legend dialog box contains many options you'll use to control the display and placement of the legend. Your first choice involves deciding whether you want to display a legend at all. If you prefer, you can choose Use number grid under chart, which places the labels and values in a table rather than using a legend. Figure 9.15 shows the chart with a number grid instead of a legend.

Notice that the grid is placed below the chart but above any note text you have added.

FIGURE 9.14

The Chart Legend
dialog box

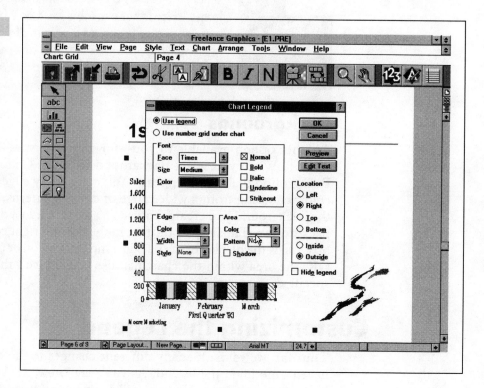

FIGURE 9.15

The chart with a
number grid

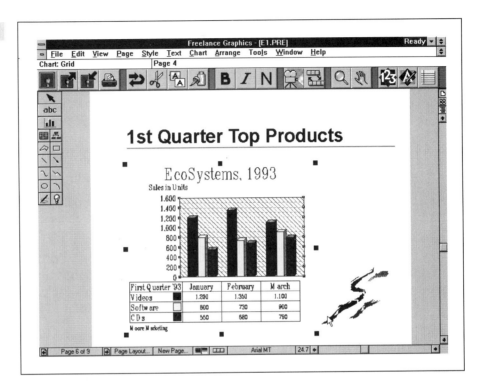

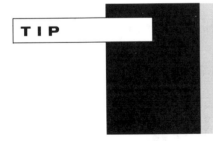

TIP

If you want to display a number grid under the chart, open the Chart menu and choose Number Grid Under Chart. A dialog box appears, in which you can choose the size of the grid, the total columns, the labels for the columns, the grid and frame settings, and label and data styles.

If you choose Use legend, you can work with the following options in the Chart Legend dialog box.

USE THIS OPTION	TO
Font	Choose the typeface, size, color, and style of text
Edge	Specify a border color, line width, and style for the line surrounding the legend
Area	Choose a color and pattern for the inside of the legend area as well as a drop-shadow for the outside
Location	Choose whether you want to place the legend to the left, right, top, or bottom of the chart. You can also select whether you want the legend displayed inside or outside the chart border
Hide	Suppress the display of the legend altogether (located in the lower-right corner of the dialog box).

Up to this point in the chapter, you've been learning how to edit and enhance your charts. The next section shows you how to import and link chart information.

Importing and Linking Charts

What does it mean to import chart data? Simply put, importing is nothing more than copying data from one file and using it in another. You might, for example, have created a 1-2-3 spreadsheet in which you've already entered some information that you now want to incorporate in a

Freelance chart. Rather than retype your data, you can import it into your chart.

Furthermore, suppose you're importing information from your 1-2-3 spreadsheet, and you realize that the spreadsheet will be updated this afternoon. Rather than put off creating the chart until then, you can do it now and link it to the 1-2-3 file containing the original data. Therefore, when you update your data this afternoon, thanks to the link you added between the 1-2-3 file and the Freelance chart, your chart will be automatically updated, as well.

Depending on the complexity of the charts you create, importing and linking may be features you rarely, if ever, will use. For that reason, the makers of Freelance felt it was even more important to make the process as simple as possible.

NOTE You can import files from Lotus 1-2-3, Symphony, Microsoft Excel, or dBASE and use ASCII and SYLK formats.

Here's how to import a chart:

1. Create the new chart or click on the chart you want to work with.

2. Open the Chart menu and choose Edit. The Chart Data & Titles screen appears, as shown in Figure 9.16.

3. Position the cursor in a blank cell (the cell to which you eventually want to add the imported data).

4. Click the Import button. The Import Data File dialog box appears, as shown in Figure 9.17.

5. Select the file name from the displayed list.

FIGURE 9.16

Starting the Import
process

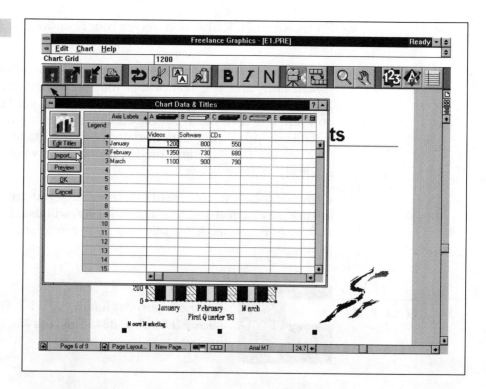

If you don't see the file name you want in the
displayed list, you may need to change the
Directories: or the *Drives:* settings. If you are
importing a 1-2-3 file, for example, the data file
you want is probably stored in your Lotus sub-
directory. To change directories, click on the directory you want. If the file name still is not displayed
in the box, click on the ↓ at the end of the *File
types:* line to see your choices for the types of files
supported by Freelance's import procedure.

FIGURE 9.17

Choosing the file to be imported

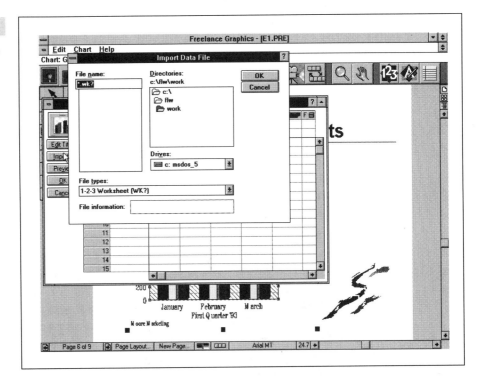

6. Click OK. Freelance then displays the Import Data dialog box, in which the selected file is displayed. Along the left side of this box, you see three checkboxes: Copy Legends, Copy Labels, and Copy Chart Data. (For this example, we'll copy only chart data. The other procedures are identical.)

7. Highlight the data you want to copy. (Remember how? Position the mouse in the upper left corner of the range you want to copy. Then press and hold the mouse button while dragging the mouse to the bottom right corner of the range. When you release the mouse button, the data is highlighted.)

8. Click in the Copy Chart Data box. An X appears in the box.

9. If you want to create a link between the data you're copying and the original file, position the mouse pointer in the Link selections check box and click the mouse button. An X appears in the box.

10. Click OK. You are returned to the Chart Data & Titles screen.

Your data is placed in the Chart Data & Titles dialog box and you can be manipulated in the usual ways. Whenever the original file is updated, the data in the Chart Data & Titles screen is changed to reflect the modifications. If you aren't working with Freelance when the original file is updated, the file will be updated as soon as you open the presentation file that contains the links.

T I P

Once you establish links with original data files, you have a choice for the way you update those links. You can have Freelance automatically update charts (this is the default mode) if you want to make sure you've got the most recent data in your chart. If you want to update less frequently, choose Manual update mode.

In this chapter, you learned a lot about editing and enhancing charts. You've seen the basic process for importing chart data from other supported applications. You also learned to change chart types, work with chart text, change labels and titles, and add grids and frames. This chapter completes your introduction to charts.

In the next chapter, you'll learn to add symbols to your presentation pages. You'll also find out how to import symbols from other applications and how to edit the symbols you create.

PART FOUR

●

Enhancing Your Presentation with Artwork

Now you know how to enter and edit text and add and enhance charts in Freelance Graphics for Windows. You've learned to rely on the Smart-Masters for your basic design, and you've learned to tweak the basic pages enough to make them your own. Part Four introduces you to a more specialized feature of Freelance Graphics: adding art.

Freelance Graphics for Windows comes equipped with over 50 different symbol files—each one containing numerous individual symbols (see Chapter 10). That's a lot of art at your disposal. In Chapter 11, we'll discuss how to use the drawing tools and commands to create your own artwork for your documents. You'll also learn how to bring into Freelance art files you create in a wide range of other applications. Finally, in Chapter 12, you'll learn to edit and arrange the art objects you create (the subject of Chapter 12). Whether you're a budding artist or someone who would prefer to leave art to everyone else, Freelance offers you a simple means of adding artistic touches to your presentations.

TEN

Working
with Symbols

fast TRACK

● **To place a symbol,**   319

click on the Symbol tool (in the bottom right corner of the tools row) or click on a Click here to add symbol prompt. The Add Symbol to Page dialog box appears. Make your selections and click OK. Freelance then places the symbol on the presentation page.

● **To choose a symbol file,**   323

display the Add Symbol to Page dialog box and scroll through the symbol files. As each new symbol file is highlighted, the display at the bottom of the dialog box changes to show the contents of those files.

● **To select an individual symbol,**   323

in the Add Symbol to Page dialog box, simply double-click on the symbol you want. The symbols displayed in the bottom of the dialog box change as you select different files. Some files include many different symbols; others, only a few. If your symbol file contains more files than can be displayed at one time, click on the arrows at either end of the scroll bar to see more. Double-click on the one you want. The symbol is then added to the presentation page.

● **To import a symbol**   **328**

from another Windows program, use the Edit menu's Copy
and Paste commands to copy the symbol from the other program and paste it into your Freelance presentation. If you're
using a non-Windows program, use the File menu's Import
command to bring the file into Freelance. When the Import
File dialog box appears, select the drive and directory in which
the file is stored. Then select the file name from the displayed
list. Finally, click OK.

● **To save a symbol,**   **328**

click on the art you want to save as a symbol. Open the Tools
menu and choose Add to Symbol Library. The Tools Add to
Symbol Library dialog box appears. Choose a symbol file to
which you want to add the selected symbol. Click OK. Freelance then saves the symbol to the file you specified and
returns you to the presentation page.

THIS chapter begins your introduction to Freelance art by helping you get acquainted with Freelance's library of ready-made symbols. You'll learn what symbols are, how to use them, and how to add your own art to the symbols files.

What Are Symbols?

Symbols are actually premade drawings you can use in your Freelance presentations. Freelance Graphics for Windows comes with over 50 symbol files, each containing from 1 to 54 individual symbols.

Since the symbols included with Freelance Graphics are professionally created, you can be assured that each one will retain its quality whenever you resize, stretch, or manipulate it in any way. Not all art files work this way, however. This type of art, known as *object-oriented* graphics, is based on grouping together a variety of different shapes. Each time an object is resized, it is redrawn to the right proportion with no loss of quality.

Another kind of art, known as *bit-mapped* graphics, is actually a pattern of dots displayed or printed in a certain sequence and color. Bit-mapped graphics, when resized, may be distorted and show the dots that comprise them. (Many popular graphics programs now have built-in smoothing features that take care of these "jaggies.") In addition to the object-oriented graphics in Freelance's graphics files, Freelance supports the use of graphics files in most popular graphics file formats. (More about this later.)

When Will You Use Symbols?

Symbols are an "optional necessity" in any good presentation. Sure, you have page after page of bulleted text, good-looking headings, and eye-catching charts. But symbols add a flavor that none of your other information items can give to the presentation. Symbols may or may not provide additional data for your viewers, but they *do* add some spark and may help provide an overall theme for your presentation.

Symbols can be functional. When you're discussing international sales, for example, many viewers in your audience may be very relieved to see a map of the region you're reviewing.

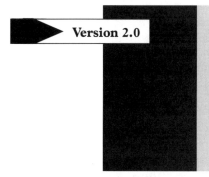

Version 2.0

In Version 2.0, you can now use symbols as bullets. To do so, double-click on the text box containing the text you want to use. In the Text Attribute dialog box, click the ↓ after the *Bullet:* setting. A pop-up list of bullet choices appears. Click Symbol in the bottom right corner. When the Choose Symbol for Bullet dialog box appears, scroll through the list of symbol files and choose the one you want to use.

Whether they are informational or simply entertaining, the symbols in your presentations can help you add your own personality to the work and vary the style of your presentation. Here are just a few of the many ways you might use symbols in your Freelance presentations:

- To add your company logo to the opening page
- To provide an illustration that supports the text
- To give readers' eyes a rest after several pages of text
- To make the presentation more entertaining for viewers

• To add personality to your presentations that words and charts cannot

Exploring Freelance Graphics Symbols

Freelance Graphics offers an incredible range of symbols in varying artistic styles. From serious business symbols to more light-hearted pieces of art, you'll probably find what you're looking for in one of the many symbol files. This section provides you with an overview of the different symbol files available in Freelance Graphics for Windows 2.0.

N O T E   Many companies sell packages of "clip art"—the more common name for Freelance's symbols—that can be used in a wide range of popular programs. If you are interested in purchasing more clip art symbols for use with Freelance, make sure the clip art files are saved in a format recognized by Freelance Graphics. (The list of supported file types is provided later in this chapter.)

For reference purposes, we've divided the different symbol files into several different categories: maps and countries, business symbols, functional symbols, animals and people, and miscellaneous.

In the maps and countries category, you'll find files that relate to a specific country or display a variety of maps. Business symbols include art commonly used for illustrating business presentations. Transportation symbols, financial symbols, and office buildings and supplies are just a few of the symbols in this category.

Functional symbols are art files you'll use as you create flowcharts, diagrams, and backgrounds for presentations. You may prefer to use functional symbols as bullets or buttons in your presentations.

Symbols for animals and people are grouped together in another category. You'll find only one file for animals (including seven wild animals) but several files for people—men, women, families, groups—giving you a range of choices for the people you display.

Finally, the miscellaneous group includes those symbols that didn't clearly fit in any other category. In this group, you'll find symbols related to time and weather, cartoons, and entertainment and environmental symbols. Table 10.1 provides an overview of the different symbol groups.

TABLE 10.1: Types of Symbol Files

CATEGORY	SYMBOL FILES
MAPS AND COUNTRIES	asia.sym
	asiamap.sym
	canada.sym
	canadamap.sym
	euromap.sym
	flags.sym
	france.sym
	germany.sym
	italy.sym
	spain.sym
	uk.sym
	usa.sym
	usamap.sym
	worldmap.sym
BUSINESS SYMBOLS	building.sym
	communic.sym
	compperi.sym
	computer.sym

TABLE 10.1: Types of Symbol Files (continued)

CATEGORY	SYMBOL FILES
BUSINESS SYMBOLS	finance.sym
	industry.sym
	medical.sym
	offobjct.sym
	science.sym
	transpor.sym
FUNCTIONAL SYMBOLS	shapes.sym
	arrows.sym
	backgrnd.sym
	bullets.sym
	buttons.sym
	commobjt.sym
	diagram.sym
	flowchrt.sym
	geoshape.sym
	grid.sym
	legends.sym
	presentn.sym
	textbox.sym
ANIMALS AND PEOPLE	animals.sym
	hands.sym
	men.sym
	people.sym
	women.sym

TABLE 10.1: Types of Symbol Files (continued)

CATEGORY	SYMBOL FILES
MISCELLANEOUS	0tutor.sym
	benelux.sym
	cartoons.sym
	entertai.sym
	environm.sym
	food.sym
	puzzle.sym
	sports.sym
	time.sym
	weather.sym

In the next section, you'll learn to place a symbol into your presentation.

Placing a Symbol

Before you can add symbols to your presentation, you must have a place to put them. You can start a new SmartMaster page that includes a Click here prompt for symbols by clicking on New Page at the bottom of the screen. When the Choose Page Layout dialog box appears, select the Bullets & Symbol layout option; then click OK (see Figure 10.1).

After you click OK, Freelance adds the page you selected. As you can see from Figure 10.2, the Click here to add symbol prompt appears on the left side of the screen. When you're ready to add the symbol, click in the symbol box. The Add Symbol to Page dialog box appears, as shown in Figure 10.3.

FIGURE 10.1

Selecting a new page
for a symbol

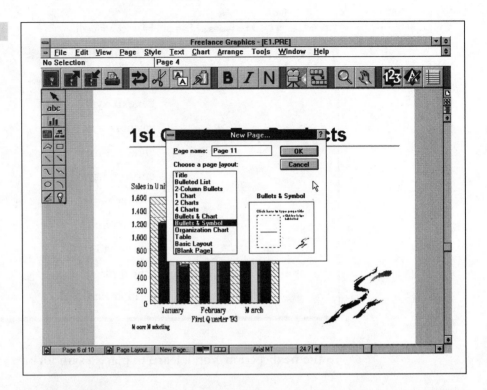

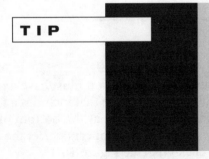

TIP

If you prefer, you can add a symbol directly to a page that doesn't have a Click here prompt. When you want to add a symbol to an existing page, simply click on the symbol button in the bottom right corner of the tools row (the button resembles a light bulb). After you click the button, the Add Symbol to Page dialog box appears.

The next section introduces you to the various features of the Add Symbols screen.

FIGURE 10.2

The new bullets and
symbol page

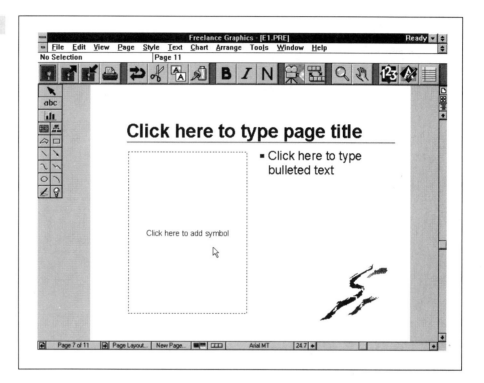

Understanding the Add
Symbols Screen

The Add Symbol to Page dialog box provides you with everything you
need to know about the contents of the various symbol files included with
Freelance Graphics. In the top left corner of the dialog box, you see the
list of symbol files. In the bottom of the dialog box, the individual symbols
included in the highlighted file are displayed.

Along the right side of the screen, you see the familiar OK and Cancel
command buttons. Another button (Directory) is also on the right side of
the box.

FIGURE 10.3

The Add Symbol to
Page dialog box

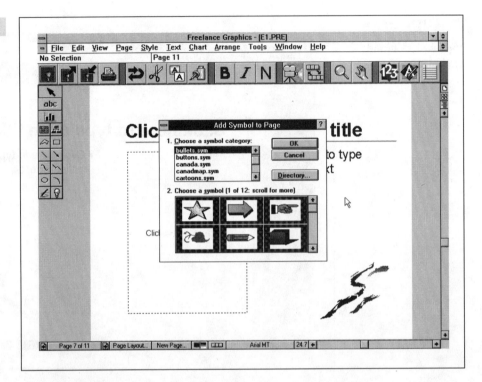

TIP

If you are using only Freelance symbol files, you
may not need to look in any directories other than
the one Freelance consults when displaying symbol
files. If, however, you display the Add Symbol to
Page dialog box and don't see the file you want in
the displayed list, click on the Directory button. The
Directory dialog box appears. You can then click on
the drive and directory settings you want and make
sure that the *File types:* option is set to the type of
file you're trying to find.

Selecting a Symbol File

To select a symbol file, simply position the mouse pointer on the file you want to see and click the mouse button. If you don't see the symbol file you want, click on the arrows at either end of the scroll bar (on the right side of the list) to display more. When you click on the file you want, the contents of that file are displayed in the symbol section in the bottom of the dialog box. For example, Figure 10.4 shows how the Add Symbol to Page dialog box appears when the *sports.sym* file is highlighted.

TIP

If you know the file you want to use, you can move there quickly by typing the first letter. For example, if you want to display the contents of *uk.sym*, type u and the highlight moves directly to the first file beginning with *u*.

Choosing the Individual Symbol

Within each symbol file, you need to select the specific option you want to add. After you highlight the file you want to see, various symbols appear in the bottom half of the dialog box. The number of symbols in that file is displayed beside the Choose a symbol prompt. If more than six symbols are included in the selected file, the message tells you to use the scroll bars to display more. To scroll through the various files, click on the arrows at the end of the scroll bar.

When you're ready to select the symbol you want, double-click on it. You are then returned to the current page and the symbol is placed in the Click here box.

FIGURE 10.4

Displaying the contents of the sports.sym file

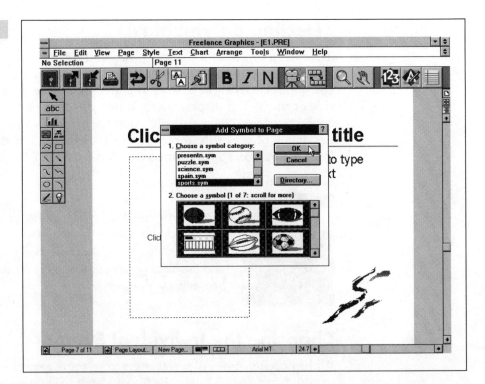

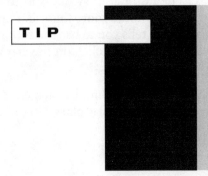

TIP

If you place a symbol in a Click here box with the same proportions, the symbol fills the box. (However, if the symbol must be resized in order to keep its proportions accurate, the entire width—or length—of the box is used.) If you are adding a symbol to a page without a Click here box, it is placed, in a smaller size, in the lower left portion of the page.

Figure 10.5 shows the page after a symbol has been added in the Click here box. Notice that the symbol has not been stretched vertically to fill the Click here box since doing so would distort the picture. Rather, the picture is resized to fill the width of the box and then scaled vertically to the correct proportion.

FIGURE 10.5

A symbol in the Click here box

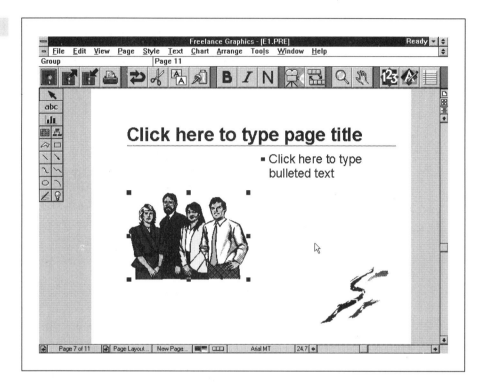

Now that you know how to place symbols, you may want to perform a few simple modifications. The following section explains how to resize the symbol you've just added.

Resizing a Symbol

If you've ever worked with any kind of graphics program, simple changes like resizing will be easy for you. Luckily, when initially placing a symbol, Freelance takes care of the scaling for you, so you don't have to calculate the angles at which you resize a symbol in order for it to look the way it is supposed to. To resize a symbol, follow these steps:

1. Click on the symbol you want to resize.

2. Move the mouse pointer to the edge of the symbol. The pointer changes to a double-headed arrow.

3. Press and hold the mouse button, while dragging the mouse in the direction you want to resize the symbol.

4. When the symbol is the size you want, release the mouse button. Freelance redraws the symbol to the size you've specified.

TIP

To keep the proportion of your symbol intact as you resize the picture, press Shift before you begin. Then position the mouse pointer on one of the corners of the symbol and, while keeping Shift pressed, drag the corner in the direction you want to resize the picture. When the symbol is the size you want, release the mouse button.

Moving Symbols

There will be times when you want to move the symbol you've added on the presentation page. To do so, just follow these simple steps:

1. Click on the symbol you want to move.

2. Position the mouse pointer in the center of the symbol. The pointer changes to a four-headed arrow.

3. Press and hold the mouse button while dragging the symbol's outline to the new location.

4. When the outline is in the place you want, release the mouse button. Freelance then moves the symbol to that point.

If you aren't happy with the way the symbol looks in its new location, open the Edit menu and choose Undo Move. (Or, press Ctrl-Z, if you prefer to bypass the menu selections.)

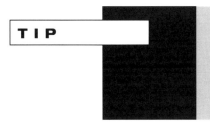

TIP

Because symbols are a type of graphics object, you can perform a number of art operations with them. They can be copied, cut, pasted, duplicated, flipped, and rotated. For more information on working with art objects, see Chapter 12.

Creating Your Own Symbols

As mentioned earlier, you also have the option of using in your presentations symbols you create yourself. In some cases, you may create the artwork in another Windows application—such as Windows Paint—and copy and paste it directly into your Freelance page. At other times, you may want to use tools included with Freelance Graphics to create your own symbol. Either way, you can then save the symbol to your own custom symbol library, which Freelance has already provided for you (*custom.sym*).

What Files Can You Use for Symbols?

Any graphics file you import from another program can be turned into a symbol. Freelance allows you to use graphics or clip art files from a variety of other programs—including Macintosh formats. Here is a list of file types supported by Freelance Graphics:

- .PCX files
- .TIF files
- .BMP files
- .EPS files

- .GIF files
- .TGA files
- .PCT files

Methods of Creating Symbols

There are two different ways to create symbols:

1. Import the art from another program
2. Use the Freelance drawing tools (in the tools row) to create your own.

Because Chapter 11 covers the drawing tools in detail, we'll save that discussion for the next chapter. If, however, you want to import the art, you have two methods from which to choose:

1. If the other program from which you're importing the art is a Windows application, you can copy the art to the Windows clipboard and then paste the art on the Freelance Graphics page.
2. If the other program is *not* a Windows application but saves files in one of the formats listed earlier, you can use the File menu's Import command to bring the file into Freelance Graphics. When the Import File dialog box appears (see Figure 10.6), select the drive and directory in which the file you want to import is stored. When you've entered the necessary settings, click OK. The art is then placed on the presentation page.

Saving the Art as a Symbol

Once you've got the art into Freelance Graphics, how do you turn it into a symbol? Here are the steps:

1. Click on the art so that the handles appear around the picture.
2. Open the Tools menu and select the Add to Symbol Library command. The Tools Add To Symbol Library dialog box appears, as shown in Figure 10.7.

FIGURE 10.6

The Import File
dialog box

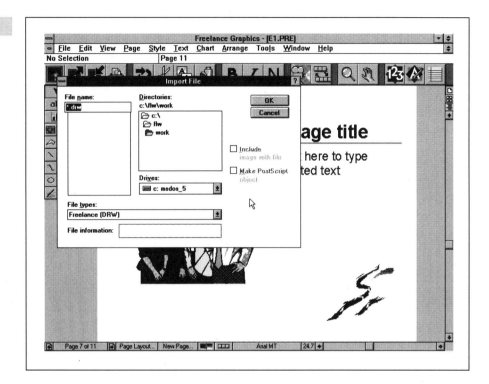

3. Select the drive and directory as necessary.

4. Enter the name of the file to which you want to add the symbol in the *File name:* box. (Click on the name of the file in the file list, if you prefer.) Freelance provides the *custom.sym* file to which you can add your own symbols, although you can add symbols to any file you wish.

5. Click OK.

Freelance then saves the file you've added to the symbol file you specified. When you later add a symbol to a Freelance page, the symbol will be displayed in the symbol selection box.

FIGURE 10.7

The Tools Add To
Symbol Library dialog
box

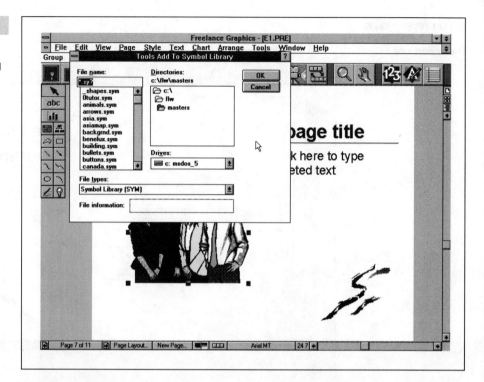

TIP

Since all symbol files are first and foremost graphics
files, you can perform a number of editing and
arranging tasks with all of them.

In this chapter, you've learned how to add symbols to your presentation
pages. Specifically, you found out how to use the Symbol tool and the
Click here box to bring a symbol into your page. You also learned to page
through the symbol files and to choose the symbols you want to work
with. Finally, you found out how to import or create your own symbols
and add the new symbols to a library.

The next chapter takes you more into the realm of custom-drawn art by
exploring all the drawing tools Freelance has to offer.

ELEVEN

Using Freelance Graphics' Drawing Tools

f a s t
TRACK

● **To change the unit of measurement on the ruler,** 340

open the View menu and choose Units & Grids. The Units box, at the top of the dialog box, shows the unit of measurement currently selected. Click on the measurement style you want. Click OK to return to the page.

● **To create a graphics SmartIcon set,** 342

open the Tools menu and choose SmartIcons. When the SmartIcons dialog box appears, drag the SmartIcons (one by one) from the column on the left (Available icons) to the column in the middle of the screen. After you've added all the icons you want, click on Save Set. A dialog box appears, asking you to enter a name and a filename. Enter the name (without the *.smi* extension) and click OK. When the SmartIcons box is redisplayed, click OK again to return to the page.

● **To add a drawing grid,** 347

begin by opening the View menu and choosing Units & Grids. The Units & Grids dialog box appears. In the Grids portion of the screen, click on Display grid. If you want Freelance to pull objects to the grid automatically, click Snap to grid. Click OK to return to the page. A grid of small dots is added to the display.

● **To use a drawing tool,** **351**

first click on the one you want to use. Then position the cross-hair pointer in the work area, and press and hold the mouse button while drawing with the tool. When the line or shape is the size you want, release the mouse button.

● **To add curved text,** **361**

begin with a simple text box. Click the text tool and draw the box on-screen. Then enter the text you want to use. Next, open the Text menu and choose Curved Text. The Curved Text dialog box appears. Select the layout in which you want the text to appear by clicking on the one you want (click ↓ to scroll through your choices, if necessary). Click OK to add the layout to your text or click Preview to view the change before accepting it.

UNDOUBTEDLY, there will be times when you'd like to use artwork that isn't available in the symbol files. Perhaps you've thought of an interesting way to illustrate your discussion. Maybe you need to add the company logo to your presentation pages.

Whatever your purpose, Freelance Graphics gives you a library of art tools with which you can create your own masterpieces. The tools are always visible along the left side of the work area (see Figure 11.1).

The art tools

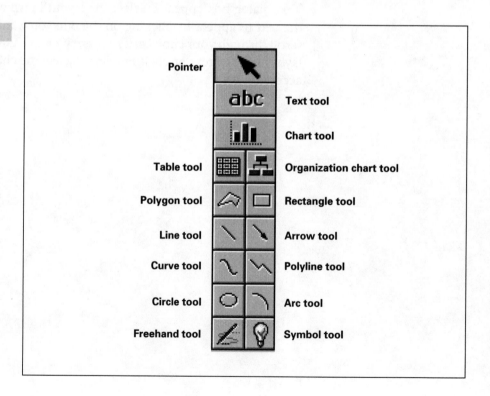

Each of the tools in the tools area serves a different function. The pointer tool, as you know, is used to select text, chart, or symbol objects on the presentation page. The text tool is used to add text in text boxes or graphics text as part of an illustration. The chart tool, of course, allows you to add a chart. The table and organizational chart tools bring up the necessary dialog boxes for you to create those elements.

But below these first five tools, you see some rather odd-looking shapes and lines. Those are your drawing tools. The freehand tool, located in the bottom left corner of the tools area, is new to Version 2.0. The last tool on the right is the symbol tool, which displays a dialog box enabling you to add a symbol to the presentation page.

Understanding Object-Oriented Drawing

Freelance Graphics for Windows, provides you with a high-quality, object-oriented drawing program which enables you to create illustrations by putting together a series of shapes, lines, and curves. You can then "lock" the pieces together—not unlike a puzzle—to produce the finished effect. This type of drawing, in which the individual pieces comprise an object that can then be resized, rotated, or modified, is known as *object-oriented drawing*. Because the object-oriented drawing is created from a set of mathematical calculations, the object can be resized from very small to very large (and vice versa) without any loss of clarity.

Other programs, such as Windows Paintbrush, offer a different kind of graphics technology. These programs are commonly called *paint programs* (as opposed to draw programs) and produce what's known as *bit-mapped graphics*. These graphics are actually formations of dots, called *pixels*, that make up the picture on the screen and in print. When you edit a bit-mapped graphic, you do so by erasing or changing the color of the individual dots in the picture. Bit-mapped graphics cannot be resized without a loss of quality and, in many cases, the edges are jagged and the dots are easily seen.

Before You Draw...

There's no law that says you have to spend a lot of time planning before you can design your own killer graphics. In fact, too much planning can take the fun out of sheer creation. And anyway, in the business world, there's not much time for fun or, for that matter, trial and error. If you're preparing to create a piece of art using the art tools, you may want to take a moment before you begin and weigh these considerations:

- Do you need the art you create to be positioned in a particular place on-screen?

- Is it important that the graphics have specific measurements?

- Would you prefer to have your frequently used commands represented as SmartIcons?

- Do you want the art you create to appear on every page of your presentation or only a selected page?

Before you do anything else, think about where you want to add your art. You have several options. If you want to add it to every page of your presentation, display a SmartMaster layout page (by opening the Page menu) and choose the Background command. If you want to add the art to a new page, click the New Page button at the bottom of the screen and select the new page from the Page Layout dialog box. (For the examples in this chapter, we've chosen Blank page.) If you want to add art to an existing page, display the page you want to work with before you start creating your work.

T I P

Remember that the Cut and Paste commands in the Edit menu apply to Freelance drawing, as well. You can create your object on virtually any page in the presentation, and then cut it to the clipboard. After you locate the page where you want to place the graphic, select Paste and position the art the way you want it. For those of us who prefer working with a clean slate, this option keeps the page less cluttered while those creative juices are flowing.

The following sections explain how you can control the precision and placement of the art you create and cut down on extraneous keystrokes by creating another SmartIcon palette for your graphics work.

Displaying and Hiding Rulers

The simplest way to measure things is, of course, with a ruler. Freelance actually has two rulers—one across the top of the work area and one along the far-left edge of the screen. This gives you the maximum amount of control over where you place an item, how large a specific object is drawn, and how much space is left between objects.

By default, Freelance does not display the graphics rulers. You use the View Preferences command to tell Freelance that you want the rulers displayed. Here's how:

1. Open the View menu.

2. Choose the View Preferences command. The View Preferences dialog box appears, as shown in Figure 11.2. In the Display options box, you see the option Drawing ruler.

3. Position the mouse pointer on the box preceding Drawing ruler and click the mouse button. An X appears in the box, indicating that you've selected it.

4. Click OK. You are returned to the page, and the rulers are placed along the top and left sides of the page (see Figure 11.3).

FIGURE 11.2

The View Preferences
dialog box

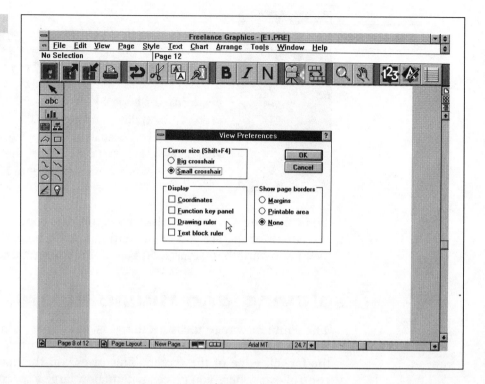

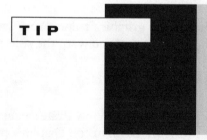

TIP

The measurements in the graphics ruler may not be
what you expected—perhaps you wanted inches,
but got, instead, millimeters. Change the unit of
measurement by selecting Units & Grids from the
View menu and clicking on the measurement type
you want.

When you want to hide the rulers, repeat the process of selecting View
Preferences from the View menu and disable the Graphics ruler option by
clicking on the box containing the X. When you return to the page, the
rulers will be removed.

FIGURE 11.3

The graphics rulers added to the page

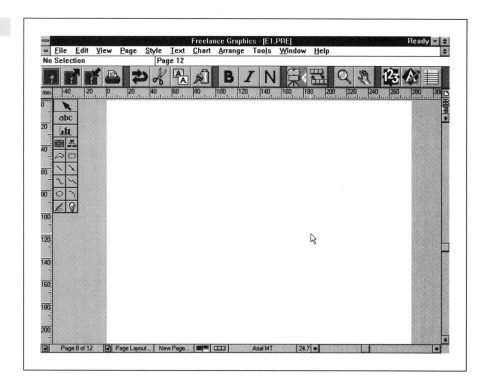

You can also use two SmartIcons—Show Drawing Ruler and Hide Drawing Ruler—to display and hide the rulers quickly. Before you can use these Smart-Icons, however, you must have first created another SmartIcon set that you can swap for the set currently displayed. The next section shows you how to create and use a graphics SmartIcon set.

Creating a Graphics SmartIcon Set

As you become more familiar with the commands used to create and work with graphics, you may get tired of the old open-the-menu-and-choose-the-command routine. Freelance provides another option. As you may remember from Chapter 3, Freelance includes many more SmartIcons than those displayed by default in the SmartIcon row above the work area. How you organize those SmartIcons is up to you. But you may find it helpful to have, for example, one general (default) set, one set with graphics commands, another with commands for charts, another for slide shows, etc. In this section, you'll learn to create a graphics set of your own that you can swap into the SmartIcon row as necessary.

First, open the Tools menu and choose the SmartIcons command. The SmartIcons dialog box appears, as shown in Figure 11.4. In the left

FIGURE 11.4

Choosing a different SmartIcon set

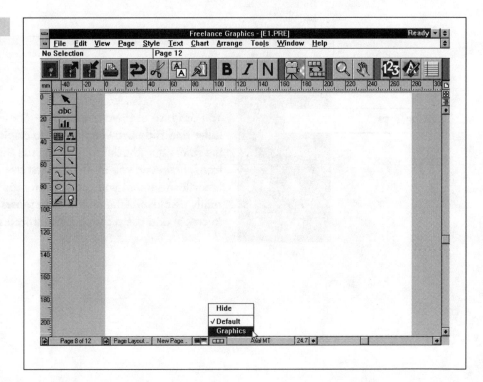

column of the box, you see the icons that are available for display. You can scroll through the available icons by clicking on the ↓ in the bottom of the scroll bar for that box.

The second column contains the default SmartIcons (the one you see in your SmartIcon row now). Also, at the top of the column, you see a box with the name Default in it. After you create and name other SmartIcon sets, the names of the new sets will be displayed in a drop-down list that appears when you click ↓.

Along the right edge of the box, you see the familiar command buttons as well as a few new ones:

> **The Position box** controls where on the screen the SmartIcon palette is placed.
>
> **Edit Icon** displays a dialog box that allows you to change the attributes of the selected icon.
>
> **Save Set** is the button you click after you've created the new set.
>
> **Delete Set** removes the selected set.
>
> **Icon Size** displays a dialog box in which you can change the displayed size of the icon you've selected.

To create the new set, simply scroll through the Available icons column until you find one you want to include. Position the mouse pointer on the icon and press and hold the mouse button while dragging the icon to the center column. Don't worry—you're not deleting the default set. The icons in the center column move down to make room for the newly added icon.

Continue adding icons (Table 11.1 lists some SmartIcons you might want to include in a graphics set) until you've added all necessary SmartIcons. Then click Save Set. A dialog box appears, asking you to provide a name and a filename for the set you've created. Type a name and a filename (but don't add the extension; Freelance will add .*smi* for you). Then click OK. The set is saved. Click OK on the SmartIcon dialog box to return to the presentation page.

TABLE 11.1: Possible Graphics SmartIcons

SMARTICON	NAME	DESCRIPTION
	Replicate	Makes a copy of the selected object and places the object on the page
	Select All	Selects all objects in a specified range
	Select Inside	Selects items within the specified object
	Curved Text	Allows you to curve selected graphics text
	Change Font	Enables you to change fonts easily (displays Font dialog box)
	Group	Locks objects together to form one item
	Ungroup	Separates individual elements in an object
	Bring to Front	When objects are layered, brings the selected object to the front of the stack
	Send to Back	When objects are layered, sends the selected object to the bottom of the stack
	Redraw	Each time you change an object, Freelance redraws the picture on the screen. You can turn off this redrawing feature by pressing Esc. Then, when you really do want to redraw the picture, click on the Redraw SmartIcon or press F9.

TABLE 11.1: Possible Graphics SmartIcons (continued)

SMARTICON	NAME	DESCRIPTION
	Rotate	Rotates the selected object 45 degrees
	Flip Left to Right	Flips the selected picture to the right
	Flip Top to Bottom	Flips the selected picture upside down
	Points Mode	Displays the points of the object for editing
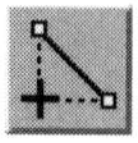	Add Point	Allows you to add a point on the object so that you can manipulate the drawing
	Cut to the Clipboard	Cuts the selected item to the clipboard
	Copy to the Clipboard	Copies the selected item to the clipboard
	Paste Clipboard Contents	Pastes the contents of the clipboard onto the presentation page
	Delete	Deletes the selected object
	Undo	Reverse last operation

When you're ready to use the new set you've created, you have two options: you can click in the SmartIcon exchange button in the SmartIcon palette (just below the Help menu), or you can click on the SmartIcon button at the bottom of the screen.

If you change the palette by clicking the SmartIcon exchange button, the other set is displayed automatically. If you click on the SmartIcon button at the bottom of the screen, a small menu appears from which you can select the name of the SmartIcon file you want to use (see Figure 11.4).

Figure 11.5 shows the blank page with the new SmartIcon set displayed. Throughout the remainder of this chapter and the next, we'll use this palette to illustrate various art operations in Freelance.

The next section shows you how to further prepare your screen for graphics work by adding a background grid.

FIGURE 11.5

The new SmartIcon palette

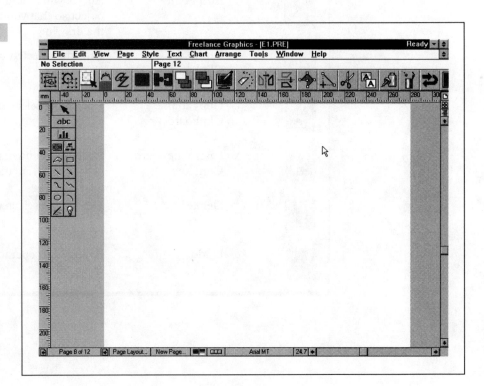

Using a Grid

As you may recall from an earlier chapter, we worked briefly with grids as they pertain to charts. Here, grids are important not for what they help us see (as was the case with charts) but for what they help us do. By adding a grid (which won't print, by the way) to your page, you can make sure you've evenly lined up elements of your page. You'll be using a tool that is more accurate than the eyeball for judging perspective and distance.

Suppose, for example, that you want to add an icon so it lines up with a page title. You could guesstimate the amount of space between the left margin and the beginning of the text and then take a shot at lining up the icon underneath. By doing this, however, you're setting yourself up to be just a hair or two off, which would make your presentation look much less professional. You also could use the rulers to line up the two items ("Let's see...the title starts at 40mm, so if I drag this down here..."). That's still a lot of work. But by using the grid, you can easily see how the items align. And by enabling the Snap To feature, which causes the items in your clutches to lock onto the grid (making small placement errors impossible), you can further control the accuracy of your work.

To add a grid, start by opening the View menu and choosing Units & Grids. The Units & Grids dialog box appears, as shown in Figure 11.6. (If you want to change the unit of measurement shown on the ruler, this is the place to do it.)

The Grids options, located at the bottom of the dialog box, contain the settings you're concerned with right now. The first option—Display grid—controls whether or not the grid appears on-screen. (Remember, the grid will not print.) The Snap to grid option controls whether you turn on the "magnetic" feature that causes the pointer (and the selected object) to stick to the grid. The Horizontal space and Vertical space options also give you the chance to control the grid spacing. (The default is 5 millimeters. If you have chosen a different unit of measurement, the equivalent of 5mm is used as the default—for example, .196 for inches.)

FIGURE 11.6

The Units & Grids
dialog box

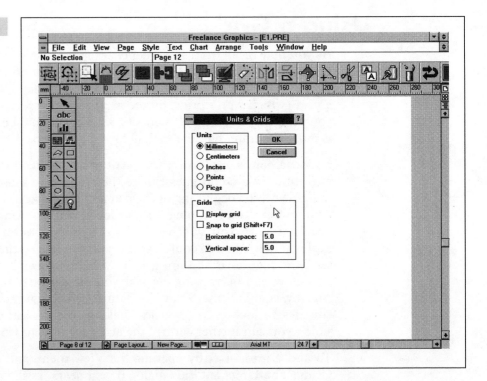

TIP

**You can turn the Snap To feature on and off easily
without leaving your work by pressing Shift-F7.**

To enable the options in the Units & Grids dialog box, click in the box
before the option. To change the spacing of the grid, click in the box following the setting you want to change and type the new value. When
you're happy with your changes, click OK to return to the page. Figure 11.7 shows the page after a grid has been added.

FIGURE 11.7

The page with a background grid added

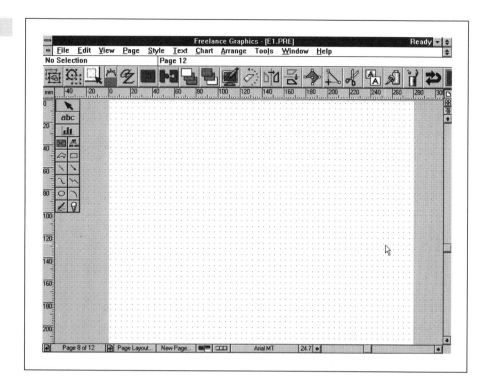

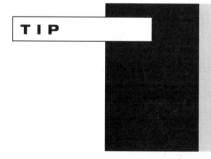

T I P

Coordinates is another option that's available to you if you're concerned about pinpoint accuracy in your Freelance artwork. Start by opening the View menu and choosing View Preferences. When the dialog box appears, click Coordinates. This causes the cursor coordinates to be displayed in the status line of the screen.

Now that you're equipped with rulers, new SmartIcons, and a grid, you're ready to start working with the various Freelance tools.

Working with the Drawing Tools

As you get to work with the drawing tools, take some time to experiment. Most of them will do exactly what you expect them to. Others may surprise you.

This section will help you find out how the tools function. Keep in mind, however, that you can change the attributes—such as line color, inside color, line width, pattern, and shadow—for each tool individually or for all tools in the tools area. Chapter 12 explains how to make these modifications.

TIP

You can display a description of a particular tool by holding down the right mouse button and floating the pointer over the tool palette.

Using the Shift Key with the Drawing Tools

The Shift key performs a number of different functions when you're using one of Freelance's drawing tools. The following list illustrates:

WHILE DOING THIS...	PRESSING SHIFT DOES THIS:
Drawing a line	Draws the line in a 45-degree angle
Using the circle tool	Creates a perfectly round circle (rather than an oval)
Drawing a rectangle	Makes a perfectly square box
Using the Polygon tool	Creates 45-degree angles

WHILE DOING THIS...	PRESSING SHIFT DOES THIS:
Using the arc tool	Draws the arc within a perfect square
Using the polyline tool	Creates lines at 45-degree angles

Drawing Lines and Arrows

The first step in drawing lines and arrows involves, of course, clicking on the tool you want. Let's try the line tool first:

1. Click on the tool to select it.

2. Position the pointer (which has changed to a crosshair) at the point on-screen where you want to begin the line.

3. Press and hold the mouse button, while dragging the line in any direction you want. When the line is the desired length, release the mouse button.

TIP

If you've enabled Snap To and forgotten about it, the line you draw will "jump" from one grid line to another. This can be extremely annoying if you aren't sure what's going on. To disable Snap To, press Shift-F7.

Well, there's the line (see Figure 11.8). Granted, it may not be a work of art, but still, it is a beginning. Notice that the handles surround the object you've created. Click anywhere outside the object to remove the handles.

Using the arrow tool is very similar to using the line tool, except that an arrowhead is placed at the end of the line you draw. Again, select the tool, press and hold the mouse button while dragging the line in the direction you want. When you release the mouse button, the arrow appears and handles surround the item. This type of line is great for annotating charts, adding callouts to illustrations, or for showing information in a flowchart.

FIGURE 11.8

Using the line tool

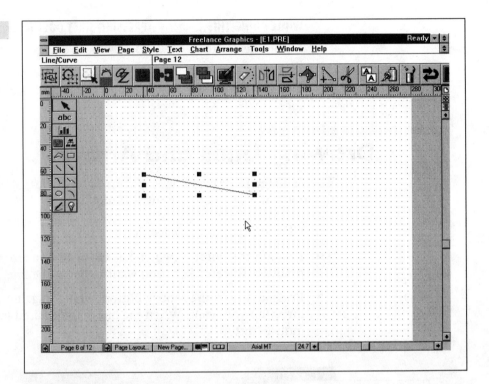

N O T E   Don't worry if you don't like the way the colors turn out—in Chapter 12, we'll show you how to change them.

Drawing Rectangles

A rectangle is another common object that comes in handy in day-to-day graphics use. Remember: you can use Shift to make the drawing a perfect square, if you like. Again, the process is simple—click on the rectangle tool and move the pointer to the place on-screen where you want to draw the shape. This time, press and hold the mouse button while dragging the pointer down and to the right. As you drag, a box appears. When the box is the size and shape you want, release the mouse button.

By default, Freelance selects the pointer tool each time you finish using a tool. For example, you've just used the rectangle tool. After you create the rectangle, the pointer becomes active. This is fine if you plan to draw only one rectangle, but what if you want to draw a series of rectangles? Each time, you have to click the rectangle tool before proceeding.

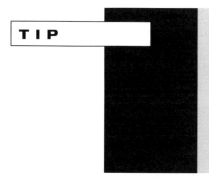

TIP

Freelance gives you the option of keeping the selected tool active until you select another tool. To do this, choose the User Setup command in the Tools menu. The User Setup dialog box appears. Click on the Keep tool active option in the Drawing tools area. Now, when you return to the presentation page and click on a tool, it remains active until you select another tool.

Drawing Polygons

A polygon is a distant relative of the rectangle (it's also a catch-all term for any odd-shaped multi-sided object), but is a little harder to draw. A polygon is an enclosed shape, meaning that when drawing one, you end up at the same spot you began.

To use the polygon tool, first click on it. Then move the pointer to the place on-screen where you want to begin drawing. Press and hold the mouse button while dragging the mouse in the direction you want. Click the mouse button to end the first line segment.

Now you have an several options: you can press the mouse button and drag the mouse in the direction you want the next line to go, or you can move the cross-hair pointer to that point and click the mouse button. Either way, Freelance fills in the line for you. Continue adding line segments until you've created the shape you've envisioned. Figure 11.9 shows the almost-completed polygon (we've got one line to go).

After you complete the shape, which usually requires a double-click of the mouse button, Freelance fills the shape with color and displays the handles surrounding it (see Figure 11.10).

FIGURE 11.9

Drawing a polygon

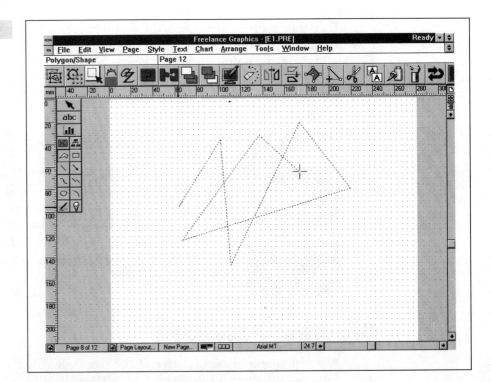

NOTE

Don't worry if the polygon is not exactly the shape or size you wanted—Chapter 12 explains how you can make changes to your artwork.

Drawing Curves

The curve tool is a backward-S looking symbol in the tools row. Unlike lines, arrows, rectangles, or polygons, the curve tool brings with it a new talent—Freelance understands at what point you want the line to curve and draws the curve to your exact specifications.

Let's try one:

1. First click on the curve tool.

FIGURE 11.10

The finished polygon

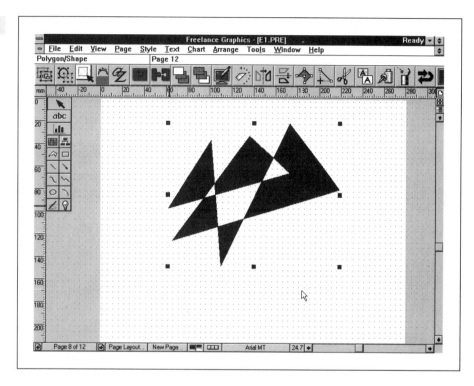

FIGURE 11.10

The finished polygon

2. Move the cross-hair pointer to the place on-screen where you want to begin drawing.

3. Press and hold the mouse button and drag the line in the direction you want. Looks like a regular line, doesn't it?

4. Click the mouse button to indicate the end of the first line (see Figure 11.11).

5. Now move the pointer to the place you want the line to end (such as up and to the left, as in this example). Freelance automatically makes the turn for you (see Figure 11.12). You can get as elaborate or as simple as you want with the curve tool. Figure 11.13 shows a more exaggerated version of curve tool use.

T I P

With both the polygon and the curve tools, it is possible to add lines you really don't want. To delete the last line segment, press the backspace key.

Drawing Circles and Arcs

The circle tool is about as familiar as Grandma's round cookie cutters. In fact, although different in shape, the circle tool works the same way as the rectangle tool.

1. Click on the tool, move the pointer to the work area.

2. Press the mouse button.

3. Drag the mouse down and to the right.

FIGURE 11.11

Drawing the first line segment with the curve tool

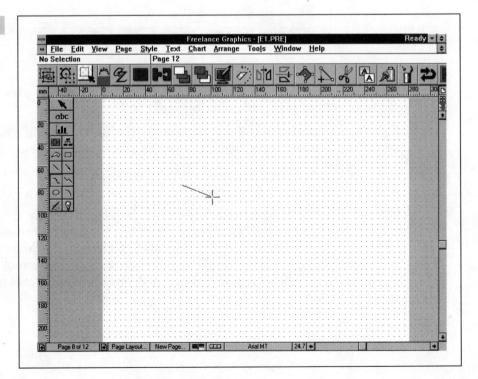

FIGURE 11.12

Adding the second
line segment

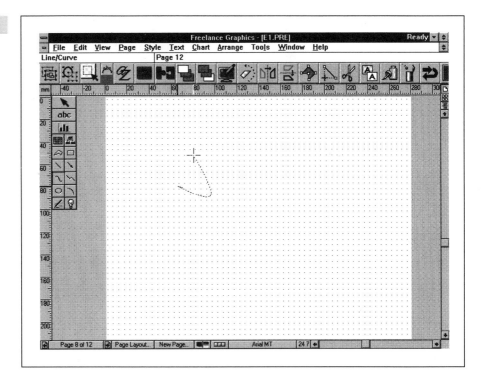

4. If you want a perfect circle rather than an oval, press Shift while you drag the mouse. When the circle is the size you want, release the mouse button.

Voilà. A circle.

The arc tool allows you to create curved lines (as opposed to curved shapes). To use the arc tool

1. Click on it.

2. Then position the mouse at the point on-screen where you want to begin drawing.

3. Press and hold the mouse button while dragging the mouse in the direction you want.

4. Release the mouse button, and...wait a minute. Looks like a line, doesn't it?

FIGURE 11.13

The finished object done using the curve tool

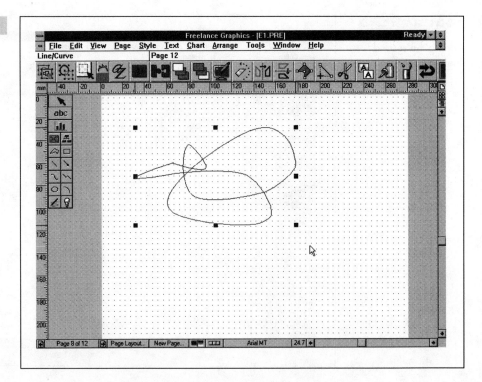

The curve tool initially draws a line. Freelance then waits for you to position the cross-hair pointer at the point you want the curve to meet. Sounds a little strange in English, so let's look at it on-screen. Figure 11.14 shows the line we just created. Notice the cursor position. Clicking the mouse with the cursor in this position tells Freelance to arc the line up to this point. Figure 11.15 shows the arc after the mouse button has been clicked.

Drawing Polyline Figures

Hmmm...after your polygon experience, you might be getting a little suspicious of anything that begins with the poly- prefix. What does the polyline tool do? Draw shapes with multiple lines, of course. Ready?

1. First click on the tool and position the mouse pointer.

FIGURE 11.14

The arc line segment
with placed cursor

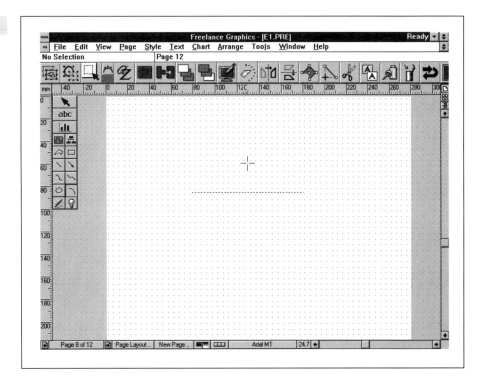

2. Press the mouse button and drag the mouse to create the first line segment.

3. Release the mouse button. Just as with the curve tool, the polyline tool adds another segment of line with each click of the mouse. You can delete the last line segment, if necessary, by pressing the backspace key.

4. When you're finished adding line segments, double-click the mouse button. Freelance turns the dotted line into a colored one and encloses the object in handles.

FIGURE 11.15

The completed arc

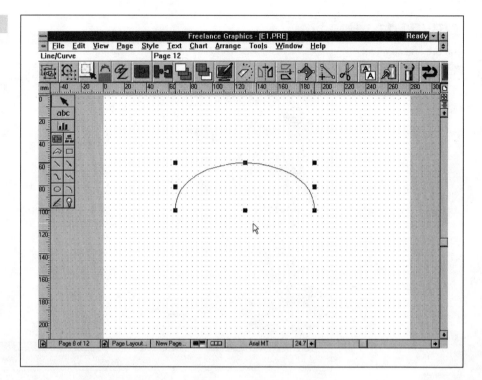

Drawing Freehand

Another art tool that's new with Version 2.0 is the freehand tool. This allows you to sketch your own images without relying on shapes and line segments to do it for you. The freehand tool turns the mouse into a pencil, more or less, leaving you free to create your own shapes and oddball artwork.

To use the freehand tool, follow these steps:

1. Click on it and move the pointer to the drawing area.

2. Now simply press and hold the mouse button, dragging the mouse in the direction you want to draw. *Do not* release the mouse button until you're done, however.

3. When you release the mouse button, Freelance assumes you are finished with the object and encloses it in handles.

Adding Graphics Text

You might expect to find a discussion of text in a chapter related to text issues. Some kinds of text, however, are more aesthetic than functional (graphics text is a good example). When you curve, rotate, or flip text, you're not looking for readability—you're thinking more about text in terms of art. For that reason, we've included these specialized text features in this section.

The ability to curve text is new with Version 2.0. Now you can wrap text in a number of different configurations, creating unique logos, adding a little personality to your page.

To add curved text, follow these steps:

1. First click on the text tool beneath the pointer tool in the tools area.

2. Draw a text box, and, when it appears, enter the text you want to curve. Figure 11.16 shows the text as entered in the text box.

3. Now, open the Text menu and choose Curved Text. The Curved Text dialog box appears, as shown in Figure 11.17. In this dialog box, you see a gallery of layouts from which you can choose the way you want to curve the text.

4. Scroll through the various choices by clicking on the ↓ at the bottom of the scroll bar. You can make your choice from among these amazing text layouts:

   - Upward and downward curves
   - Full circle
   - S curves
   - A "hill" curve
   - Two flattened ovals
   - Two thin ovals
   - Four vertical stretches

FIGURE 11.16

Entering text

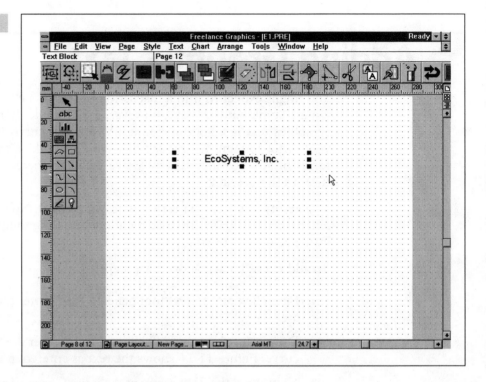

- Four rotated squares
- A sharp peak
- A triangle

5. Make your selection by clicking on the choice you want.

6. Preview the change by positioning the mouse pointer on the Preview button and holding the mouse button until the image appears.

7. When you release the Preview button, the Curved Text dialog box reappears.

8. Click OK to accept the changes or click Cancel to abandon changes. You are then returned to the page, and the text is curved in the fashion you selected.

FIGURE 11.17

The Curved Text
dialog box

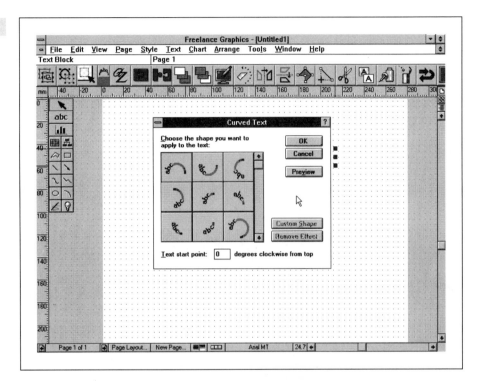

In this chapter, you've explored the various artistic tools Freelance provides to help you add personalized touches to your presentations. From an introductory discussion of graphics to a more individualized look at each of the drawing tools, this chapter has set the groundwork for any future masterpieces you might create. The next chapter builds on this theme by showing you how to edit and arrange the images you create.

TWELVE

Editing Art
Objects

f a s t **TRACK**

● **To change drawing attributes,**

double-click on the object you want to change and enter your new settings in the Style Attributes dialog box that appears. If you want to change the default attributes for certain shapes or for all of them, open the Style menu and choose Default Attributes. Make your changes and click on the Object Type to which you want to apply the settings. Click OK when you're ready to return to the presentation page.

● **To change line width and style,**

double-click on either the line you've just drawn or the line tool itself. When the Style Attributes dialog box appears, click on the options you want to change and enter your new selections. Click OK when finished.

● **To resize objects,**

click on the item you want to resize. Move the pointer to the edge of the item you want to move. When the pointer changes to a double-headed arrow, press the mouse button and drag the edge of the graphic to the new size you want. Release the mouse button.

● **To move an object back,**   387

> first select the item you want to change. Then open the Arrange menu, choose Priority, and select Fall Back One to move the object back one layer or Bottom to move the object to the lowest layer. (Or, if you prefer, you can press F8 to move the object one layer back.)

● **To move an object forward,**   387

> first select the object with which you want to work. Then open the Arrange menu and choose Priority. When the submenu appears, select Send Forward One if you want to move the item up one layer or choose Top if you want to bring the item to the topmost layer. (You can also press Shift-F8 to move the item forward if you prefer not to use the menu selections.)

● **To group and ungroup objects,**   391

> click on the objects you want to join as a group. Then open the Arrange menu and choose the Group command. To ungroup, click on the item you want to separate and select Ungroup from the Arrange menu.

FEW of us are able to create artwork exactly the way we want it every time. Chances are, especially if it's been a while since your last graphics endeavor, that you'll need to spend some time experimenting with Freelance's art features before you feel really comfortable. One of the great things about working with on-screen, electronic art, is that you'll never again have to ball up those pieces of paper and shoot at the wastepaper basket—Freelance will help you change the art you're working on until you're satisfied with the results.

This chapter concentrates on editing changes you might want to make to any pieces of art you create in Freelance Graphics for Windows. Remember: because Freelance Graphics offers object-oriented drawing features, each item you create—line, square, or undefined shape—is seen as an independent object. Most of the procedures in this chapter focus on working with these objects by changing their color, line width, layer position, and alignment.

What Kind of Editing Can You Do?

As you learned in the previous chapter, there is a specific kind of editing that can be done for object-oriented (also called *vector*) graphics. Unlike their bit-mapped counterparts, object-oriented graphics are items that are calculated each time they are moved, resized, or changed in any way. There are no individual lines or stray pixels to erase. The type of editing you'll perform on these graphics is much different from the type of editing you'd do in, say, Windows Paintbrush.

You'll be better able to keep things straight if you remember that each item you add to your art is kept on a layer of its own. Remember way back in Kindergarten, when your teacher had you experiment with shapes? Start with a circle, add two triangles, and you've got the head of a cat, right? Well, the circle is still under there, complete. The triangles, although they overshadow part of the circle, do not replace the unseen sections of the circle. And so it is with art objects in an object-oriented graphics program—each shape is intact, stored in memory.

Most object-oriented drawing programs—and Freelance is no exception—allow you to "join" the shapes in an element into one object. Suppose, for example, that we want to make the cat's head a single object, not two separate triangles and a circle. When the items are selected, you see several sets of handles—one set for each object (see Figure 12.1). When the items are grouped into one object, only one set appears (see Figure 12.2).

FIGURE 12.1

The items selected individually

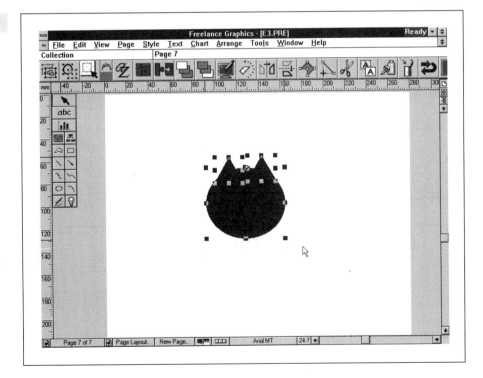

FIGURE 12.2

The items as they have
been grouped

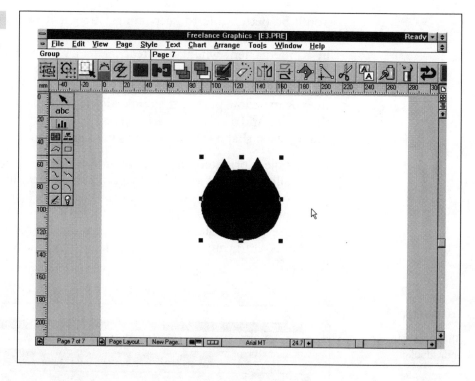

But grouping items into a single object doesn't have to be forever. You can use the Ungroup command or icon to separate items as necessary. The next section gets you started with the different types of options you can set for your graphics objects.

Selecting Objects

The first thing you need to do is let Freelance know which object you plan to modify. You do this by selecting the item(s) you want to use.

If you're selecting only one object, simply position the mouse pointer on it and click the mouse button. If you're selecting more than one object, you have two options:

- You can either

    1. Click on the first item.

    2. Press and hold the Shift key while clicking on subsequent items.

    3. When you're finished selecting objects, release the Shift key. All the objects you clicked appear with handles.

- Or, you can

    1. Make sure the pointer tool is selected.

    2. Then position the pointer tool in an area above and to the right of the objects you want to select.

    3. Press the mouse button and drag the mouse down and to the right, capturing all the objects in a selection rectangle.

    4. When all objects are included, release the mouse button. The individual objects appear with handles, showing that they have been selected. Figure 12.3 shows an example of this method of selecting multiple objects.

Once the object is selected, you are ready to perform any number of editing operations. The next section explores some of the standard settings you might want to change as you modify your Freelance graphics.

Changing Attributes

The word *attributes* might seem like an odd word to use when referring to drawing options. Freelance uses the word as a catch-all to mean any of the following:

- The color, width, and style of the line surrounding the outside of the shape

FIGURE 12.3

Selecting multiple objects with the pointer tool

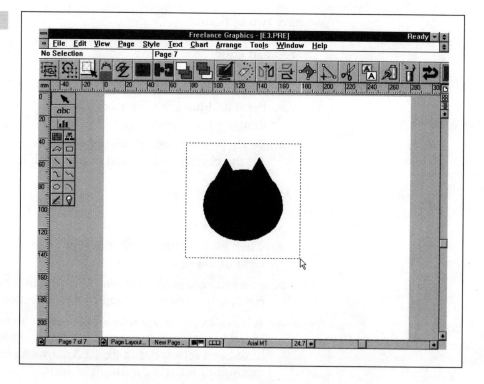

- The primary fill color used

- A secondary fill color (Freelance allows you to use color mixing by adding a second color for shading)

- A fill pattern to which the color you select is applied

- What variation of rectangle rounding you want to use (from None to High)

- Whether you want to use a shadow, and, if so, the position of the shadow (Bottom Right, Bottom Left, Top Right, Top Left)

Freelance gives you two options to change the attributes of the objects you create. You can change the settings you've selected for an object you've already made, or you can change the default attributes so any object you create from that point on will be displayed with the new attributes.

To change the attributes of objects you've already created, display the Style Attributes dialog box for that object by double-clicking on it. Similar options are also available in the Style Default Attributes dialog box that is displayed when you choose Default Attributes from the Style menu. Figure 12.4 shows the Style Default Attributes Rectangle dialog box. (If you choose a different object shape, such as a circle or polygon, a slightly different dialog box is displayed.)

NOTE   Changing settings by using the Style menu's Default Attributes command and entering new specifications in the Default Attributes dialog box won't change the currently selected object. These settings affect only objects you create after changing the defaults. If you want to change an object you've already created, double-click on the object to display the attributes box relative to that shape.

The following sections explain each of the options in this dialog box.

Changing Line Color, Width, and Style

The Edge settings, as you might expect, adjust the lines surrounding the shape you're working with. You can change the color of the line, select one of several thicknesses, or choose a different kind of line style for the outer edge.

To change the color of the line surrounding the shape, click on the ↓ beside the Color option. A color palette, similar to the one in Figure 12.5, is displayed. To select a different color, simply position the mouse pointer on the color you want and click the mouse button. The palette then closes and the hue shown in the Color box is changed to reflect your selection.

FIGURE 12.4

The Style Default
Attributes Rectangle
dialog box

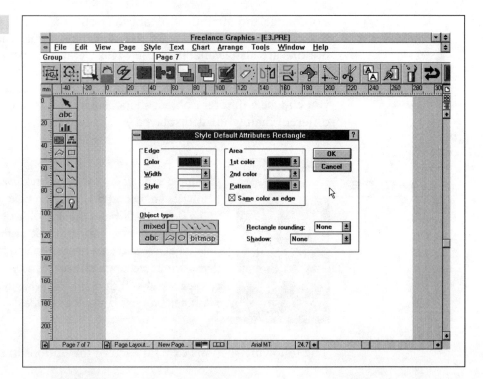

TIP

When you return to the Style Default Attributes dialog box, you'll notice that the Color option in both Edge and Area have been set to the new color you've chosen. If both have been changed, the *Same color as edge* option in the Area box is selected. (If the box is selected, it will show an X.) If you want the outer edge of the shape and the inside area to be two different colors, click on the box to disable the option. You can then set the Area color to any color you choose.

The Width setting controls the thickness of the line used to border the object. When you click on the ↓, you'll see a drop-down list of eight different line thicknesses—from very thin to very heavy. To select a new line width,

FIGURE 12.5

Selecting a new edge
color

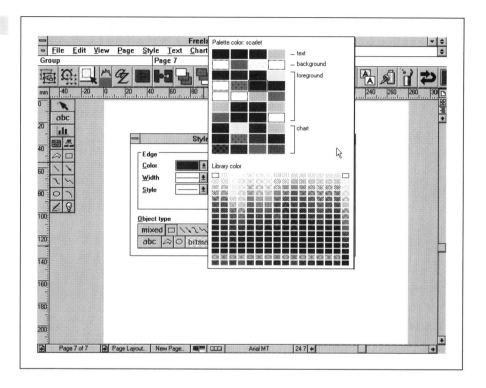

click on the one you want. The drop-down list is then closed.

The Style setting determines what type of line is used. You can select a solid line (that's the default) or choose from a variety of dashed lines. If you prefer, you can select None, turning off the line altogether.

Specifying Color and Pattern

The Area portion of the screen controls the color and pattern of the center of the object—the area within the border. Here's how to choose a color different than that specified for the edge:

1. Make sure the Same color as edge box is disabled.

2. Then, to change the color of the inside of the object, click the ↓ beside the 1st color box.

3. When the palette appears, click on the color you want to use.

The 2nd color setting controls a secondary color used for contrast and shading. The second color will be used only if you specify a pattern in the Pattern box.

To choose a pattern, click the Pattern box. A pop-up box showing you all available patterns appears (see Figure 12.6). Notice that a variety of shading patterns, as well as some simple line-art patterns, are included. In these patterns, the white sections indicate where your second color will be used while black shows where the first color is used.

Other options in the Style Default Attributes dialog box include the Object type settings, (shown as a series of buttons in the lower left corner of the dialog box). You can select the type to which you want these settings to apply by clicking on the appropriate button. For example, if you want the default settings to apply to every shape you create, click the Mixed

FIGURE 12.6

Selecting a pattern

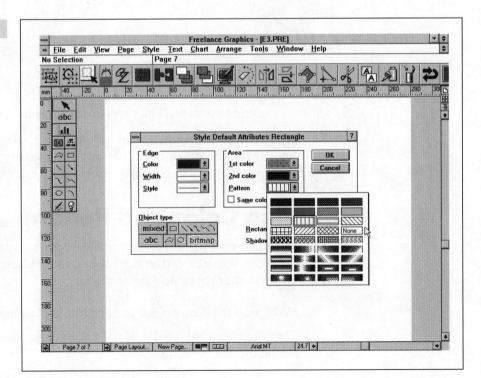

button. If you want the settings to apply to only rectangles, click the rectangle button. These settings are available only in the Default Attributes dialog box.

The rectangle rounding setting gives you the option of choosing how much rounding you want done on your rectangles. Click the ↓ to display a drop-down list. Then select from one of the following settings: None, Low, Med, or High. None, of course, doesn't round the rectangle at all, while each of the other settings increase the amount of rounding used.

The Shadow setting controls the placement of shadows behind the selected object. Choose from None, Bottom Right, Bottom Left, Top Right, or Top Left.

When you've finished entering settings, you can preview the changes by pressing and holding the Preview button. When you're satisfied with your changes, click OK to return to the presentation page.

Changing Screen Display

As you begin editing your objects, you may want to look at things from a different perspective. The View menu provides you with the necessary commands to change the display from magnified back to normal. As shown in Figure 12.7, Full Page is the currently selected display.

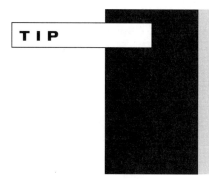

TIP

Two different SmartIcons exist to help you change the display quickly. To magnify a specific area, click on the Zoom Page icon (it resembles a magnifying glass). Then move the pointer to the area you want to magnify and drag a rectangle around the selected area. To return to normal page display, click on the View Full Page icon (it resembles a computer monitor).

FIGURE 12.7

The View menu options

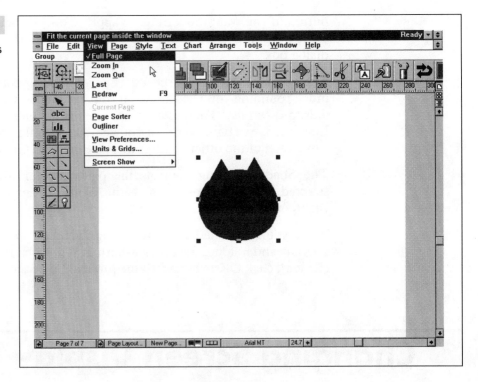

Zooming In and Out

To magnify the current page, simply select the Zoom In command from the View menu. The page display changes slightly—the object(s) on the page appear larger. Select Zoom In (up to eight times) until the object reaches maximum size. Figure 12.8 shows the screen after Zoom In has been selected several times.

FIGURE 12.8

Zooming in on the
page display

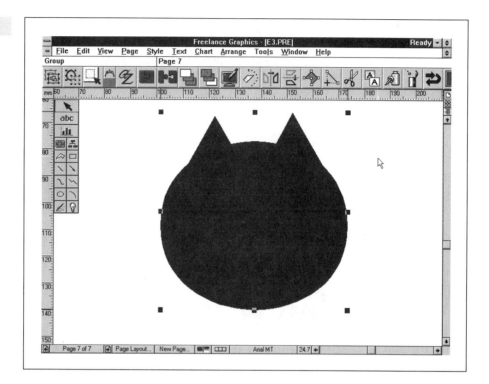

The Zoom In and Zoom Out commands in the View
menu aren't all-or-nothing commands; that is, you
don't select Zoom In once to zoom in to fully
magnified view and select Zoom Out once to return
to normal display. These commands work in small
increments, so each time you select the command,
the display is magnified or shrunk a bit more.

Returning to Normal View

Once you've magnified the view, you'll eventually want to return the page to normal view. To do so, you can either use the Full Page command in the View menu or select Zoom Out.

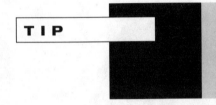

TIP

You can continue selecting Zoom Out—even beyond the point where your object returns to full page. You can reduce the size of the page in an effort, for example, to see how the object will look when printed.

Working with Objects

Once you've selected the object you want to work with and have displayed it the way you want, you're ready to try other kinds of editing. Specifically, you might want to move, resize, copy, paste, or delete objects. This section introduces you to these basic editing procedures.

Moving Objects

Here's how to move an object (or objects):

1. First select the item you want to move.

2. Move the pointer toward the center of the object until the pointer changes to a four-headed arrow.

3. Then press and hold the mouse button while dragging the object to the new location.

4. When you've placed the object where you want it, release the mouse button.

Resizing Objects

Resizing an object is another simple operation. Just follow these steps:

1. Click on the object you want to resize.

2. Move the pointer to the edge of the object. The pointer changes to a double-headed arrow.

3. Press and hold the mouse button and drag the mouse in the direction you want to resize—one way to increase, the other to decrease. A dotted outline shows you the current size as you're resizing the item (see Figure 12.9).

4. When the object is the size you want, release the mouse button.

FIGURE 12.9

Resizing an object

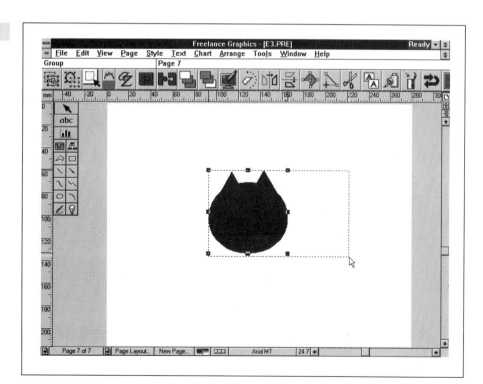

Copying and Pasting Objects

The Copy feature comes in handy when you're copying items from page to page. Copy, available in the Edit menu, makes a copy of whatever you've selected and places it on the Windows clipboard. The copy remains on the clipboard until you replace it with something else, perhaps by copying another item or using the Cut command.

TIP You can also copy an item to the clipboard by selecting the item and pressing Ctrl-C.

To copy an item to the clipboard, start by selecting the object. Then open the Edit menu and choose the Copy command. Although there is no visible change on-screen, Freelance has copied the item and placed the copy on the clipboard.

Suppose, for example, you want to make a copy of the cat's eye shown in Figure 12.10. Drag a rectangle around the area you want to copy (if the object is a single one, you can simply click on the item). Open the Edit menu and choose the Copy command. The eye is copied to the clipboard.

TIP You can paste an item from the clipboard by using the quick-key combination Ctrl-V.

Now you're ready to paste. Pasting an item from the clipboard is really just copying the item—once again—from the clipboard back to the page. A copy of the object remains on the clipboard. To paste the cat's eye onto the page, open the Edit menu and choose Paste. The object is placed on the page. You can now select the item and move it to the desired location on the screen (see Figure 12.11).

FIGURE 12.10

Making a copy of
an item

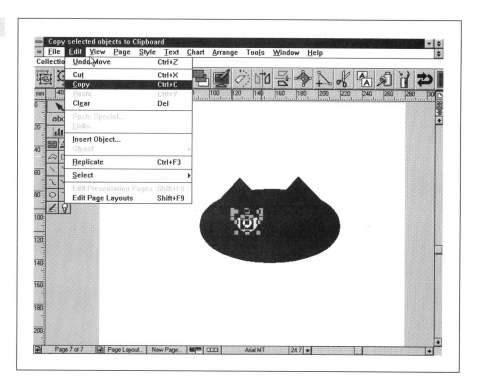

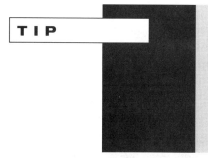

T I P

The Replicate command (in the Edit menu) allows you to make a duplicate of an item without having to copy it to the clipboard and paste it back on the page. Just click on the object you want, open the menu, and choose Replicate. The item is duplicated on the screen. Another way to access Replicate is to use the Ctrl-F3 quick-key.

Deleting Objects

You can delete an object easily by selecting it and then pressing Del or by opening the Edit menu and choosing Clear. The Clear command removes the item from the page. If you deleted something accidentally, you can use Undo to recover it.

FIGURE 12.11

The pasted item

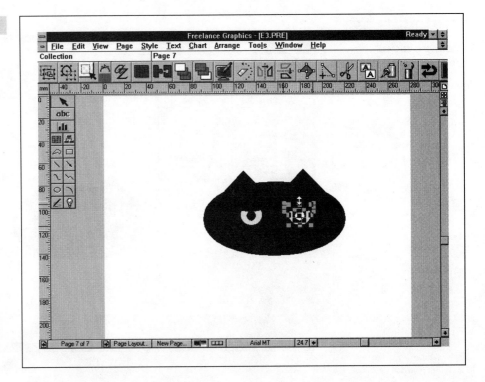

Another Edit menu command, Cut, enables you to remove the object from the page but place it on the clipboard temporarily. This feature can come in handy if you think you might want to remove an object but are unsure how the page will look without it. Later, you can use the Paste command or Undo to return the object to the page.

TIP

You can use Cut's quick key, Ctrl-X, to move an object to the clipboard without using the menu commands. If you want to use Undo, press Ctrl-Z to do it quickly.

Arranging Objects

As mentioned earlier, Freelance Graphics for Windows places each item you create on a different layer of the drawing. This allows you to create the effect you want by arranging and perhaps overlapping different objects. For example, the simple drawing in Figure 12.12 actually consists of twelve different objects: the background oval for the face, two triangles for ears, two more triangles for inner ears, two circles for the eyes, ovals above the eye for each eyelid, two black circles for pupils, and a triangle for a nose.

In this case, the background oval is placed behind the other objects. The ears are placed on top of the oval and the inner ears are on top of the ears.

FIGURE 12.12

This simple drawing consists of twelve items

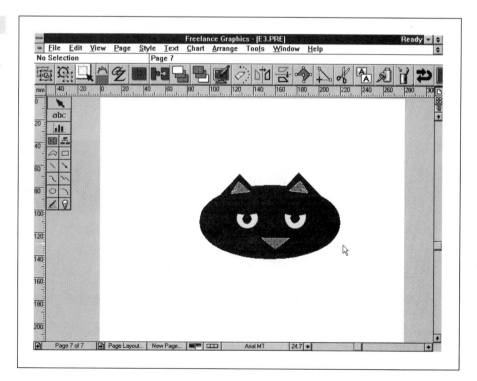

When you click on the inner triangle, it is selected first because it occupies the topmost position. The same scenario applies to the eyes: the background oval is the bottom, then the yellow eye, then the pupil, and finally the oval for the eyelid.

Freelance Graphics lets you change the order in which items are arranged. As you might expect, commands on the Arrange menu help you select an appropriate arrangement for the objects in your design.

To see what your arrangement options are, first click on the object you want to use. Then open the Arrange menu, and choose the Priority command. A pop-up box of options appears beside the menu, as shown in Figure 12.13.

FIGURE 12.13

Layering objects

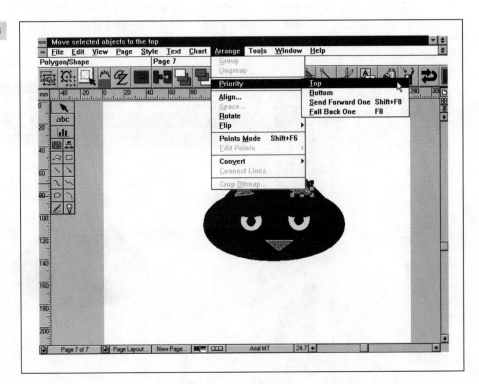

Here's what to expect from these commands:

COMMAND	ACTION PERFORMED
Top	Moves the selected item to the top of other objects
Bottom	Sends the selected item to the bottom of other objects
Send Forward One	Moves the item forward one object
Fall Back One	Moves the selected item back one item

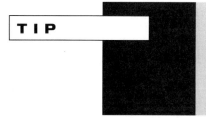

T I P

If you are changing an object's layering, and it suddenly disappears, don't panic—it's still there. To redisplay the item, open the Arrange menu, choose Priority, and select Top to return the object to the top of the heap.

Aligning Objects

You can control the way various objects in your page align by using the Arrange menu's Align command. To use this command, first select the objects you want to align. Then open the Arrange menu and choose Align. The Align Objects dialog box appears, as shown in Figure 12.14.

You can select different options and see how they look in the preview box in the upper left corner of the screen. You can align objects along the left, right, top, or bottom of the far left item.

FIGURE 12.14

The Align Objects
dialog box

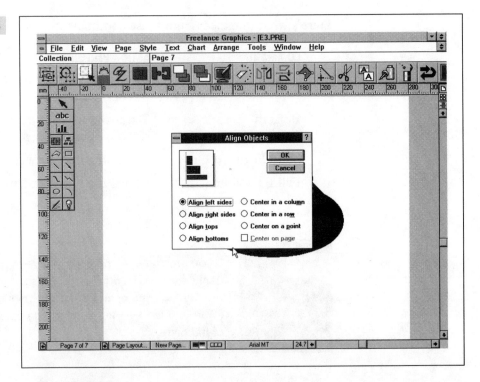

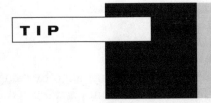

TIP

Use the alignment SmartIcons—three blue dots with
an arrow showing alignment—instead of opening
the Arrange menu and choosing the Align
command.

Flipping Objects

Ever flip over an object? Well, they can flip over you. Click on the one you
want and open the Arrange menu. When you select Flip, two options are
displayed: Left to Right, and Top to Bottom.

Left to Right turns the object, hinging it on its right edge, creating a mirror image of the object as it was originally shown. Top to Bottom flips the
object downward, again making a mirror image. If you don't like what you
see, select the command again to return the object to its normal state.

Rotating Objects

The Rotate command offers you another arrangement option. It's a little more complicated than the other arrangement options, but using Rotate is a piece of cake. Here's how:

1. Click on the object you want to rotate. (For this example, we've first used the Group command to turn all the individual objects into one.)

2. Open the Arrange menu and choose Rotate. The pointer changes to a different kind of tool, showing an X with a sliding rule.

3. Click on the edge of the item you want to rotate and hold the mouse button down.

4. Move the pointer in the direction you want to rotate the item. A dotted outline shows you the position of the object as you move the mouse (see Figure 12.15).

FIGURE 12.15

The rotation begins

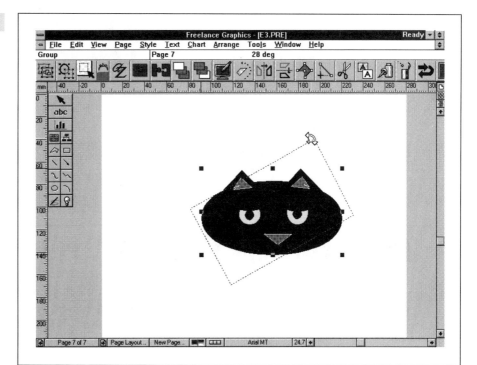

5. When the object is rotated to the desired angle, release the mouse button.

Figure 12.16 shows our cat after he's been rotated. If you want to undo the rotation, open the Edit menu and choose Undo.

FIGURE 12.16

Rotation complete

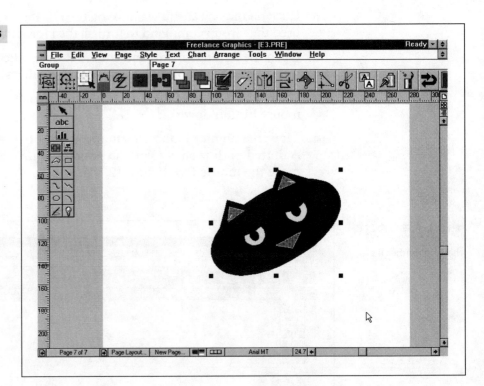

Modifying Objects

You might think that working with an object-oriented graphic, as opposed to working with a painted piece of art, is a disadvantage when you're trying to fine-tune the work you've done. For example, suppose that in drawing a body for our cat friend, we curve one line out a bit too far. It seems like it would be easy to simply erase the portion of that line that doesn't fit and pencil a better line back in, right?

But Freelance has a better idea: the Points Mode command. This command gives you fine control over the individual elements in the graphic—you can move line segments, drag curves in and out, and move portions of shapes around any way we like.

The Points Mode command (in the Arrange menu) and other commands that allow you to further work with the object you're creating are the subjects of the final section of this chapter.

Grouping and Ungrouping Objects

Earlier in the chapter, we talked briefly about "group" and "ungroup." As you learned, the art objects you create in Freelance Graphics may actually be a number of different objects combined into one. As you've already discovered, the cat's mug created earlier is really 12 separate shapes on several different layers.

Freelance provides you with the ability to gather all these elements into a group and create a single object. This is handy when you're cutting and pasting, resizing, or moving an object. Think about what a hassle it would be to select and move 12 different items. Even if you could select all of them at the same time, moving them would be a chore. But if you group them all into one, you have only a single item to worry about. And later, if you need to change the attributes of one of the original items, you can always use the Ungroup command to separate the items into their original pieces.

To group items, simply select the items you want to group, open the Arrange menu, and choose Group. The handles that had been surrounding each item change and only the handles for the single combined item now appear. You can now work with this item as though it were an individual object—copying, cutting, pasting, changing attributes, and layering as necessary.

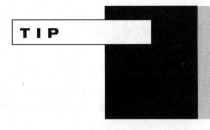

T I P

If you prefer, you can use the Group SmartIcon instead of the menu selections. First select the items you want to group, then click on the SmartIcon that resembles two joined puzzle pieces. The items are then grouped into one object.

When you want to ungroup items, simply click on the item and select Ungroup from the Arrange menu. The items are immediately separated into their individual elements. If you prefer, you can use the Ungroup Smart-Icon, which resembles two separated puzzle pieces, to ungroup the item.

Adding and Deleting Object Points

Although it doesn't look like it at first, the items you create are actually a series of small points that can be modified, moved, added to, or deleted from. Consider the cat, which is taking on a rather Ren-&-Stimpy-ish look (see Figure 12.17).

Suppose we're not real sure about the outer curve of his left shoulder (if you can call it a *shoulder*). We can modify that curve by using points mode.

To turn on points mode, open the Arrange menu and choose—you guessed it—Points Mode. (You can press Shift-F6, if you prefer to bypass the menu selections.) The pointer arrow changes slightly; now you see a small circle (a point) in the head of the arrow. In the upper left corner of the screen, the message *Edit Pts* appears, reminding you that you are in points mode. Move the pointer to the part of the item you want to change and click the mouse button.

FIGURE 12.17

Our poor cat

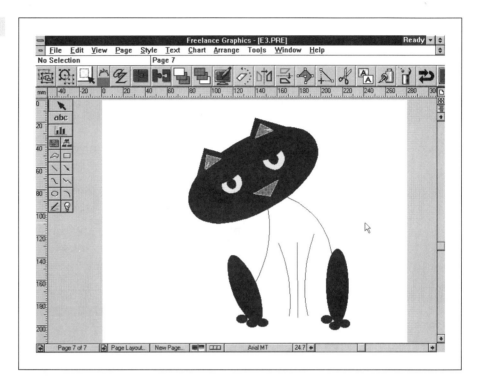

WARNING You can't edit the points on an enclosed shape such as a rectangle or circle. If you need to add or delete points on one of these shapes, click on the item, open the Arrange menu, and choose Convert. When the pop-up box appears, choose To Lines. This changes the shape to lines, which can then be modified in points mode.

You're now ready to edit the points along the line. You can add your own points, or you can delete points that are already there. Either of these actions requires the selection of the Edit Points command, available in the Arrange menu. When you choose that command, a pop-up box appears showing you additional options (see Figure 12.18).

Here's how to add a point:

1. Choose the Add Point command or press Ins. The pointer changes to show an X in the arrow head.

2. Position the pointer at the place you want to add the point and click the mouse button. A small black handle appears on the line.

3. Click on the point and move it in any direction necessary to fine-tune your art. Figure 12.19 shows the added point being modified.

FIGURE 12.18

Edit points options

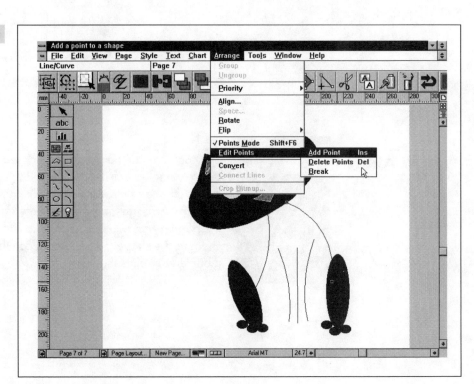

When you want to delete a point, select the point to be deleted (assuming, of course, you're still in points mode) and either select Delete Points from the Edit Points pop-up box or press Del. The point is immediately deleted.

TIP   Break, another command on the Edit Points submenu, actually divides the currently selected object into two objects at the point you indicate a break. If you break an item apart and then think better of it, use Undo to rejoin the items you divided.

FIGURE 12.19

Moving the added point

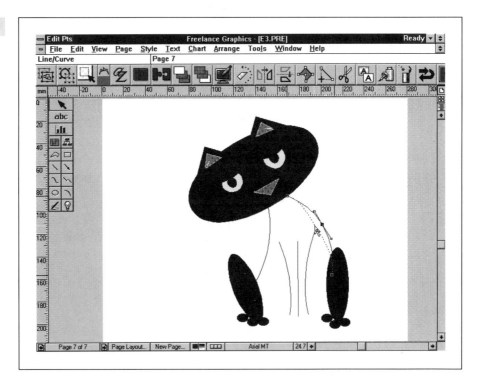

Connecting Lines and Making Polygons

The final editing issue we'll discuss in this chapter involves opening and closing objects. When you have a series of lines that are supposed to make up a picture (as in the case of the cat's body in Figure 12.19), you need some way of making them into a shape to which you can add internal color. This cat, for example, would look pretty silly if everything except his body and his front legs had color.

To take care of this problem, Freelance lets us turn lines into shapes and shapes into lines, if necessary. These means come to us in the form of the Arrange menu's Connect Lines and Convert commands.

To connect the lines you've drawn, follow these steps:

1. Select all the lines you want to connect. (Click on the first, then press and hold the Shift key while clicking on subsequent lines.)

2. Open the Arrange menu and choose Connect Lines.

Freelance turns the individual lines into one joined line, still in the shape you created. But what *really* happened? You were kind of expected to see a color fill up the white area, weren't you?

This is where the second command, Convert, comes in. Remember, Freelance can't "fill" lines—they're simply a single strip of color. If you want to fill an area, you must turn it into a polygon.

Open the Arrange menu and choose Convert. A pop-up submenu appears, with the options To Lines and To Polygons (see Figure 12.20). The first option, To Lines, is dimmed, meaning that you cannot select it. (You'll use that option when you want to turn a polygon back into a line.) Click on To Polygons.

FIGURE 12.20

Choosing a Convert
submenu option

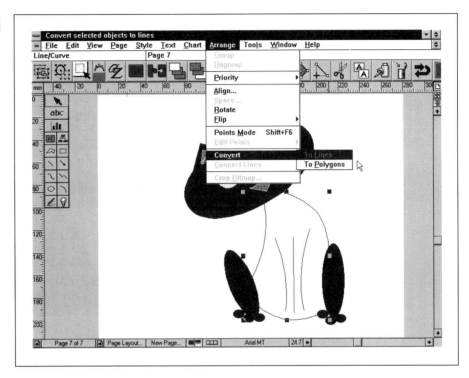

Now the area is filled, but it looks white with a red outline (the colors may
be different on your monitor, depending on the colors you've previously
selected). And the front legs are blocked out.

Remember how to change the color of a polygon? Double-click on the
shape to display the Style Attributes dialog box and change the color if
necessary. Figure 12.21 shows the cat after we've filled the polygon,
changed the color of the front leg lines (so they would appear contrasted
against the fill color), and added the all-important tail.

FIGURE 12.21

The finished cat

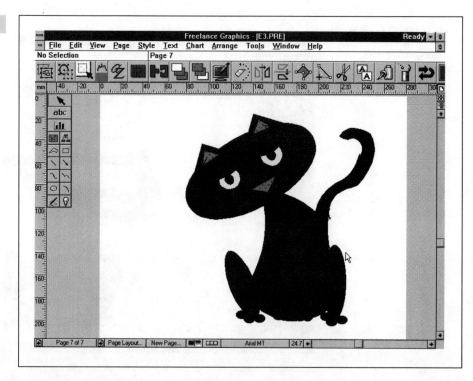

In this chapter, you've learned quite a bit about editing the art objects you create in Freelance Graphics for Windows. Whether your art needs are simple or complex, you'll find working with the various art options in Freelance easy to figure out and use. The next chapter explores working with and designing your own color palettes.

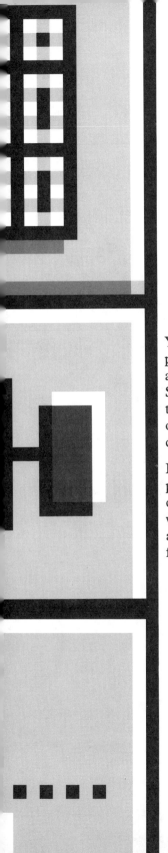

PART FIVE

●

Finishing Your Presentation

You're now entering the home stretch of your Freelance Graphics experience. Thus far, you've done pretty much everything you need to do—at least once—in preparing your presentation file. You've chosen a SmartMaster, entered text, edited and formatted text, added charts, customized charts, and worked with your own art creations. This final part of the book helps you put the finishing touches on the presentation you create.

In Chapter 13, you'll learn to control the color selections used in your presentations. Chapter 14 will take you through the process of double-checking the flow of the presentation to make sure everything is the way you want it. Chapter 15 explains the ins and outs of printing the presentation, and Chapter 16 finishes off the book by exploring Freelance's ScreenShow features.

THIRTEEN

Choosing Colors

fast TRACK

● **To change text color,** 404

> double-click on the text box containing the text you want to change (or click on the box and press F2). When the Text Attributes dialog box appears, click on the ↓ beside the Text color or Bullet color options. The color palette is displayed. Click on a different color from either the displayed palette or from the color library. Click OK.

● **To select a different color palette,** 410

> first open the Style menu and select the Choose Palette command. The Choose Palette dialog box appears. If the color palette you want is in another directory, click the Directory button to see your choices. Otherwise, select the color palette you want from the displayed list. Click OK.

● **To swap a color in the color palette,** 412

> open the Style menu and choose Edit Palette. When the Edit Palette dialog box is displayed, click on the color you want to replace and then click the Modify color button. The color library appears. Click on the color you want to use instead of the first color, then click OK. That color is used in place of the first color throughout your presentation.

● **To modify a color in the Edit Library box,**   **414**

   open the Style menu and choose Edit Palette. When the Edit
   Palette dialog box appears, click on the Edit Library button on
   the right side of the box. The Edit Library dialog box appears.
   Click on a color closest to the color you want to create. Then
   use the sliders for Red, Green, and Blue to mix the color combinations and create the new color. Finally, enter a new name
   for the color. Click OK.

● **To switch to a black and white palette,**   **415**

   use one of two methods: open the Style menu and choose Use
   Black & White Palette, or click on the Color/B&W button at
   the bottom of the screen. The screen is immediately displayed
   in black and white. When you want to return to a color display,
   click on the button a second time or open the Style menu and
   choose Use Color Palette. You can also use Alt+F9 to toggle
   between color and black-and-white.

IT'S nice to know that Freelance is flexible when it comes to choosing colors. Not all programs are this benevolent. Many display things in color but don't give you the option to change which colors are used to display which items. Freelance leaves everything up to you—although in some cases, you're better off leaving the color coordination scheme to the experts (like those people who decided which palette to use with which SmartMaster).

In this chapter you'll look at the various choices you have in color selection. You've already used color to some extent—for choosing text color, for changing the color of polygons and other shapes. Here, however, we'll look in more detail at the color palette and show you what options you have in deciding on the range of colors used for your presentations.

Understanding Color Choices

You may remember seeing the Color box pop up in several dialog boxes throughout the course of your Freelance experience. The first time it happened was when we were entering text. Remember?

Figure 13.1 shows the dialog box displayed when a section of text has been double-clicked. The Paragraph Styles dialog box appears. Here you see two choices: Text color and Bullet color. Selecting either one of these options (by clicking the ↓) displays the color palette shown in Figure 13.2.

FIGURE 13.1

Setting text color

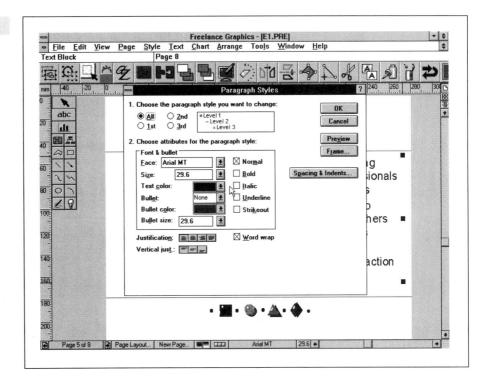

In Chapter 12 you learned that changing the color of an object is simple as well. To change the color of an art object, double-click on the shape, and the Style Attributes dialog box appears (see Figure 13.3). Depending on whether you've selected an enclosed shape (like a polygon or circle) or a line, you may have more than one color option. The dialog box shown in Figure 13.3 offers you three color choices: one for the outer edge of the picture, and two for the inner fill area of the picture. Again, clicking the ↓ for either of these color settings displays the default color palette.

Where do these color palettes come from? Who chooses them? As you can see, quite a range of colors is available—40 in the current palette, and 256 in the color library, to be exact. How did they get there and who says they are the best choices for your presentation?

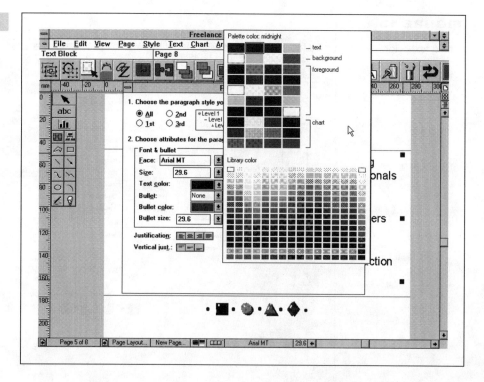

Different color palettes are selected for each SmartMaster set. The colors
have been selected to provide the maximum contrast and compatibility
for the various colors used in each presentation. For example, the background of one SmartMaster might be dark blue, which would require a
large range of lighter colors (so they will appear clearly against the background), while another SmartMaster with a white background would require a totally different set of colors. Because SmartMasters often contain
other images, such as boxes, buttons, or other pieces of art, the colors
chosen coordinate with the art in the presentation file.

Does this mean you can't change the colors in your presentation? Of
course not. With Freelance, you can do basically anything you want. Keep
in mind, however, that some SmartMasters are safer to change than
others. When you're changing the color scheme of a presentation, be sure

FIGURE 13.3

FIGURE 13.3

The color options in
the Style Attributes
dialog box

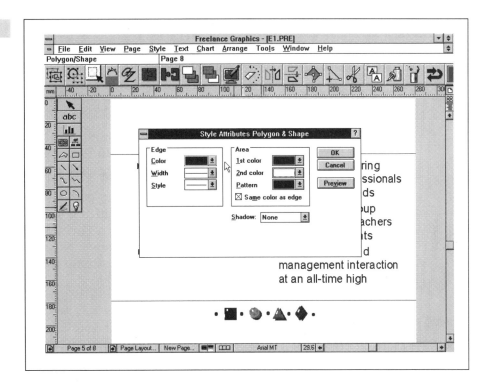

to look through everything—all art and text elements—before making
substantial changes. That way, you won't be surprised when a tree shows
up purple or a yellow frog jumps across your screen.

T I P

If you plan to mix and match colors, it's always a
good idea to first save a backup of the file—just in
case you're not happy with the results of your
experiment. To save the file, press Ctrl-S. When
Freelance asks you whether you want to replace the
existing file or keep a backup copy of the one
you're working on, click Backup.

The Basics of Color Palettes

So, no matter how you slice it, you wind up with a color palette that looks like the one in the dialog box shown in Figure 13.4. You'll see several interesting—but perhaps a bit confusing—things about this dialog box.

Various labels are attached to different parts of the palette. The first four colors, rather boring, show that two different blacks, a blue, and a gray are all text colors. The next four colors—white, gray, vanilla, and dark orange—are shown as background colors. Now we get to the more interesting range, with a variety of hues shown for foreground colors. And last,

FIGURE 13.4

Exploring the color
dialog box

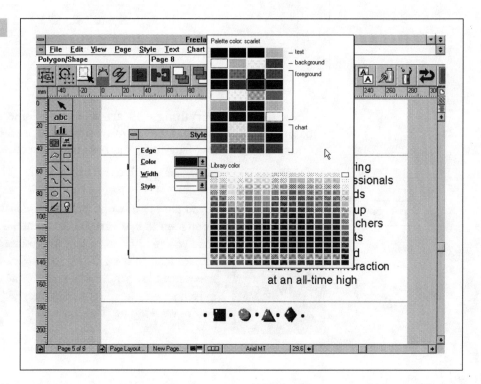

at the bottom of the first block of colors, are the chart colors. Does this mean you can only choose from those four boring colors for text, or from those odd, dull colors for backgrounds? Not a chance.

Freelance, again, will allow you to do anything you like. Choose green for text, or orange, or cyan. Create a rainbow if you like. But in this color palette, Freelance shows you what *it* thinks is the best choice of colors for this particular SmartMaster set. We have to admit, the combinations usually work. Maroon or dark blue will work better on a gray background than on an orange one. If you open another presentation file based on another SmartMaster, you may see that the suggested colors are totally different.

T I P

Before you make sweeping changes to the background color or text color of your presentation, think about things from the viewer's eye. Is the color contrast you're considering enough of a difference to allow people sitting in the back of the room to read your text without straining? Do the colors convey the tone you want for your presentations, or will you need to hand out sunglasses at the door? Fight the temptation to go overboard with color and use it sparingly and somewhat conservatively—at least for your first few presentations.

At the bottom of the color palette is the color library. This incredible palette offers 256 choices in various mixes and shades. In addition to choosing any of the colors in the color palette above the color library, Freelance will let you choose a color for text or an object from the library. When you do so, that color remains with that object (or text section), no matter which color template you choose in the future.

Choosing a Different Color Palette

So, you've decided that you want to try your luck with a different color palette. How do you do it?

Open the Style menu and choose the Choose Palette command. The Choose Palette dialog box appears, showing you a list of palette options and the displayed colors of the selected palette (see Figure 13.5).

FIGURE 13.5

Choosing a different color palette

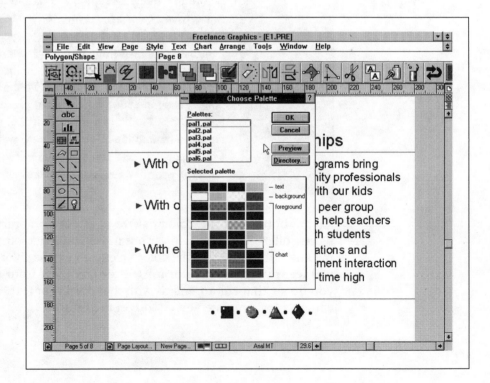

As you can see, each of the palette files ends with *.pal*. This is the extension used to distinguish color palettes from black-and-white palettes, which end with *.bw*. (Although to choose a black and white palette, you would use another option on the Style menu.)

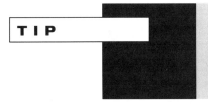

If you don't see the palette you want to work with, click the Directory button to display a dialog box in which you can select the directory of the file you're looking for.

Click on the palette you want to see and watch what happens to the selected palette area. As you can see, some of these are warm colors, some cool, some businesslike, some not-so-businesslike. When you've found the color palette that suits you and your presentation, press and hold the Preview button to see how the current page will look when the new palette is applied. If you like what you see, click OK. If not, click Cancel or choose a different palette.

Substituting Colors in the Current Palette

In some cases, you aren't as much interested in substituting a whole new palette as in adding a single color to the existing palette. When you want to add a new color in the 40-color palette, that means one has to go.

When you want to add a new color to the color palette, open the Style menu and choose Edit Palette. The Edit Palette dialog box, shown in Figure 13.6, appears.

FIGURE 13.6

The Edit Palette dialog box

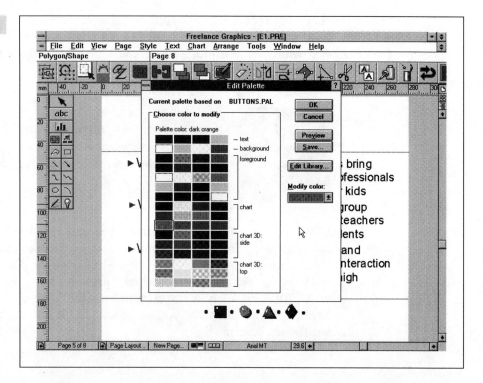

Again, an almost overwhelming number of choices are available. Simply click on the color in the current palette you want to replace, and then click on the Modify color ↓. The color library appears to the right of the Edit Palette dialog box. Click on the color you want to use to replace the color you selected in the Edit Palette dialog box. When you click OK, Freelance searches your presentation for the first color and replaces it with the second.

TIP

The modified palette is saved with the presentation, so the next time you open the file, the same colors will be used.

Creating a Custom Palette

Creating your own custom palette is no different than replacing a single color—times forty.

1. Open the Style menu and choose Edit Palette.

2. Then make the color exchanges you want.

3. If you want to save the palette so you can use it with other presentations as well, click the Save button in the Edit Palette dialog box. The Save As screen appears, giving you the opportunity to type a name for the custom palette (see Figure 13.7). (Remember to end a color palette with PAL and a black and white palette with BW.)

4. Type the file name and click OK.

FIGURE 13.7

Entering a name for the custom palette

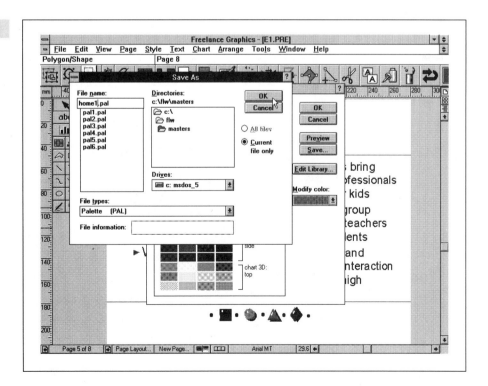

The custom palette is then saved in a stand-alone file so you can apply it to future presentation files as necessary.

Editing Colors

There may be times when you're looking for just the right color, but it doesn't appear in either the selected palette or in the color library. What can you do? Create your own.

Begin by opening the Style menu and choosing Edit Palette. When the Edit Palette dialog box appears, click the Edit Library button. The Edit Library dialog box appears, as shown in Figure 13.8.

FIGURE 13.8

The Edit Library
dialog box

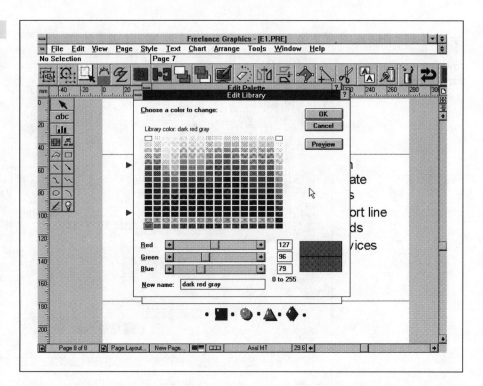

Here's how to create a new color:

1. First click on the color in the library that is close to the color you want.

2. Now move the mouse pointer down to the sliders for Red, Green, and Blue in the bottom left of the dialog box.

3. Click on the arrows at either end (or drag the elevator box) to add more or less of each color. The numeric values to the right of the slide rules show you the amount of that specific color used in your custom color. On the far right, you see two rectangular blocks. The color on top shows the color you started with; the color on the bottom shows the new color you're creating.

4. When you're happy with the color you've created, click in the New name box and enter a new name for the color.

5. Finally, you can press and hold Preview to see how the color will affect the current page of your presentation.

6. If you're happy with what you see, click OK to return to the presentation page and accept the new color.

Working with a Black and White Palette

With Version 2.0 of Freelance Graphics, you can now choose a black and white palette for presentation display with a single click of the mouse.

You might wonder why, when Freelance offers such an incredible color selection, you would ever want to choose black and white. First of all, unless you have a color printer, you're going to be printing in black and white anyway. For this reason, seeing how your presentation will look before you actually print it is a good idea. That way, you'll know what to expect and you can change some of the grayscales used, if necessary, to provide more contrast between elements in your presentation.

You have two options to choose a black and white palette:

- Open the Style menu and choose Use Black & White Palette. Then choose a palette (with the extension BW) from the displayed list.

- Click the Color/B&W box at the bottom of the screen (to the right of the New Page button).

The palette is immediately applied to the presentation and colors are changed to various shades of gray. If you want to return to the color palette you were using, simply click on the Color/B&W box a second time.

In this chapter you've learned how to work with color in your presentations. From a basic review of text and object color changes, you've also learned how to add colors to a selected palette, create a custom palette, use a black and white palette, and modify existing colors. The next chapter helps you analyze the work you've done so far and prepare your presentation for final production.

FOURTEEN

Fine-Tuning
the Presentation

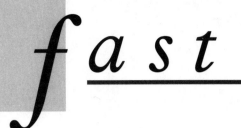
_f a s t_ **TRACK**

● **To return to current page view,**   **427**

> either open the View menu and choose Current Page or click on the current page button on the right side of the screen.

● **To preview your presentation,**   **427**

> move through the pages sequentially, looking through your audience's eyes. Determine whether your text, charts, and graphics are effective. Make sure you haven't used too much text. Make any last-minute changes as necessary.

IN the previous chapter, you learned how to customize the available color palette selections for both text and graphics work. In this chapter, we'll start by taking a step backwards and surveying what we've done so far. Does everything in your presentation work the way you envisioned it? Are the text and charts balanced? Will your presentation keep your audience awake? Is there room for improvement?

This chapter encourages you to slow down the race toward production and decide whether your presentation meets its goals. Checklists and reminders help you ensure that your presentation hits the mark when you're finally ready to present it to real people.

Checking the Presentation

The first step in evaluating your presentation involves displaying all the pages so you can see them easily. In this section, you'll learn to use the Page Sorter view to display all your presentation pages, and to move them around easily. You'll also use a checklist to evaluate the flow of your presentation.

Using Page Sorter View

As you recall, Freelance provides several different views so that you can easily get different perspectives on your presentation. The current page view, for example, is obviously best for checking up-close work like spelling, alignment, and spacing. What might the Page Sorter be good for?

The Page Sorter displays all your pages as thumbnails—or miniature replicas—of the various pages in your presentation. There are many advantages to displaying your presentation this way. You can:

- Check for consistency in placement of charts and/or artwork
- Check for variations in color and style of charts
- Ensure there's not too much text in too small a space
- See whether the layout of the pages is varied enough to keep your viewers interested
- Check for consistency of titles and subtitles
- Make sure all bullets are the same shape, color, and size.

To display the presentation in Page Sorter view, you can either open the Page menu and choose Page Sorter or click the Page Sorter icon (just above the Outliner icon) in the right side of the screen. The Page Sorter view then appears, displaying all the presentation pages in a miniature form (see Figure 14.1).

Notice that one of the pages—page 8—is displayed with a dark rectangle surrounding it. This indicates the page that was current before you selected Page Sorter view. Each page shows the background elements, the text items, any art items, and charts as they would appear on the full-sized page. Beneath the pages, the page number and its title are displayed.

Moving Pages

As you're surveying your work, you may find that a different organization would work better. For example, suppose you have three pages of bulleted lists, followed by two pages with charts. You could move one of the charts up so that the bulleted pages are broken up by the chart page.

To move a page in Page Sorter view, follow these steps:

1. Position the mouse pointer on the page you want to move. The gray rectangle surrounds the selected page.

FIGURE 14.1

Displaying the
presentation in Page
Sorter view

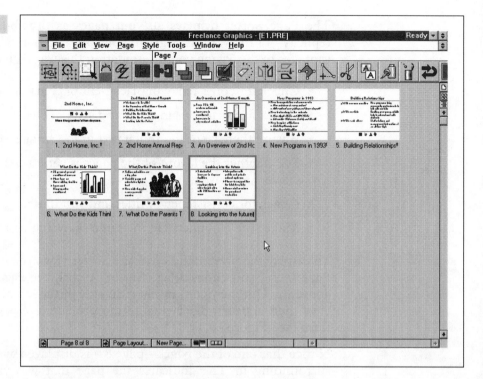

2. Press and hold the mouse button, while dragging the page to the
   new desired location. A dotted outline stays with the pointer as
   you move it across the screen.

3. Release the mouse button. The page is moved to the new location.

Figure 14.2 shows page 6 being moved to the place currently occupied by
page 5. Notice the dotted outline of the page as it is being moved.

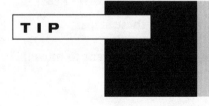

TIP

If you move the page and then change your mind—
you liked it better before you moved it—open the
Edit menu and choose Undo Move Page. The page
is automatically moved back to its original position.

FIGURE 14.2

Moving a page in
Page Sorter view

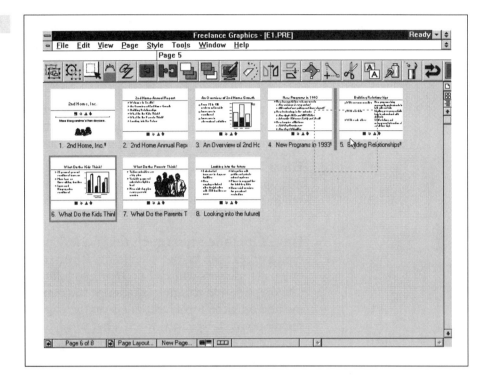

Editing Pages

In the Page Sorter view, you can also perform routine editing operations.
By using the commands in the Edit menu, you can Cut, Copy, or Clear a
page. You can also change page layouts, insert pages, add speaker notes,
change the color palette, and spell check the document.

To use any of these commands, simply select the page you want to work
with and select the necessary command from the Edit, Page, Style, or
Tools menus.

Presentation Flow Checklist

As you're looking over the layout of the pages in Page Sorter view, ask yourself these questions:

Does my presentation have a consistent look and feel? Your presentation should have similar features throughout—the Smart-Master you've chosen will usually take care of this.

Have I used enough charts and graphics? Nobody wants to sit through page after page of text. Every other page—or every second page—should provide some kind of art to give the viewer's eye a rest.

Have I included too much text on any page? Again, an overabundance of text can be overwhelming. If you try to cram too much onto one page, viewers will give up trying to follow you. (For example, the text on page 4 in this presentation is too dense.) You may want to include only the top-level bullets on the page and change the subordinate points to speaker notes. That way, you'll still be sure to say them, even if the viewers will never see them.

Are the colors consistent? When we first discover Freelance's open-minded attitude toward color selection, the temptation to over-colorize our presentations may be very great. Remember that the SmartMaster you originally chose already included all the colors you needed. But perhaps you customized the palette to include more specialized colors. In that case, it's possible to inadvertently mix and match too many different colors, and end up detracting from your overall presentation. As a general rule, choose a few colors but maintain a consistent theme: all rules the same color, all bullets the same color, and the same colors in charts and art files.

Did I vary the chart types used? Even though you may break up your text pages with charts, your presentation won't be very entertaining if you used nothing but pie or bar charts. Think carefully about which chart will best present your data, and then vary the kind you use. If you have charts that call for the same treatment of data, you can use the same type but vary the style. For example, if you really need to use several bar charts, you can make some of them horizontal, some vertical, and others stacked, etc.

Returning to Current Page View

When you're finished with Page Sorter view, you can easily return to the presentation view by following these steps:

1. Click on the page you want to return to.

2. Click the current page icon on the right side of the screen (or open the View menu and choose Current Page).

You are then returned to presentation page view. The page selected in Page Sorter is shown as the current page.

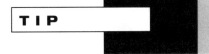

TIP You can return to the current page quickly by double-clicking on the page you want to view.

Checking Presentation Content

The content of your presentation is as important—if not more so—than the overall presentation flow. When you're considering the contents, think about how you've stated things, where you've placed artwork, and how you've worded headings and titles. Consider how your audience will react and try to anticipate questions, and avoid any ambiguities your words or charts may introduce.

Start at the beginning of the presentation and move through the pages one by one. Imagine yourself in your own audience, watching the presentation for the first time. The following section lists some questions you may want to consider as you review your presentation.

A Presentation Checklist

You might think about your responses to the following questions:

Was I as concise as possible? Presentations are supposed to be a quick-look, hit-em-fast type of communication. Viewers have less control over what they experience than they would, say, if they were reading the actual text you're using. Use the presentation pages as notes and expand your discussion as necessary. Use short phrases if possible, and rely on text labels to reinforce your graphics.

Do the headings include too much information? Again, headings that are too long detract from the meaning. Try to limit your heading to three to five words. Use plenty of white space around your headings so viewers can easily read them. Put only the major point in a heading and divide subordinate points into bulleted items.

Did I include in bullets text items that really should be speaker notes? Fight the temptation to put everything on the presentation page. Use speaker notes to cover information that would be too overwhelming for the page. Keep bulleted items brief and use enough white space so viewers can see where one item ends and the next begins.

Is my choice of graphics logical? If you designed your own artwork, make sure it applies to the theme of your discussion. Logos, certainly, should be considered, as should other art elements closely tied to your presentation. Sticking a picture of a cow in a presentation about life insurance won't make much sense. Make sure your graphics have a reason to be there.

Do my charts enhance the text in the presentation or do they confuse things? The same rule that applies to charts also applies to text: sticking too many elements in a chart will make the chart more confusing. Keep things as simple as possible while still getting your basic point across. Remember to reinforce, in words, information found in your charts.

Have I been consistent with the tense in the presentation?
You should begin all bulleted items with similar elements. For example, consider the page shown in Figure 14.3. Notice that the bulleted items are all different: one starts with a verb, one with a noun, and the last item uses the future tense ("will ease"). This type of inconsistency detracts from viewer understanding, even though many people won't be sure exactly why. The page is significantly improved when all items begin with a subject and are shown in the present tense (see Figure 14.4).

FIGURE 14.3

A page with tense inconsistencies

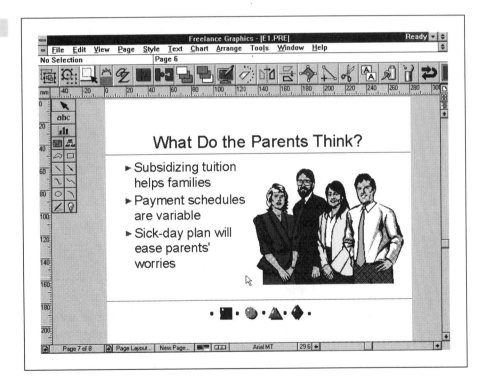

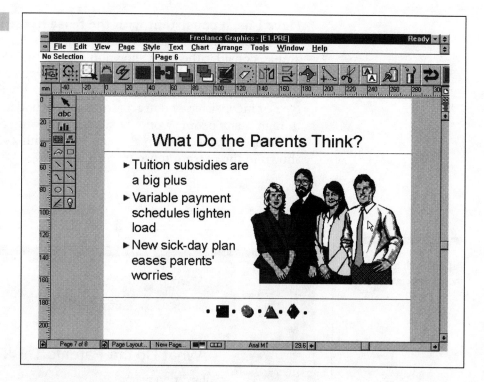

Last-Minute Editing

Remember that you can easily correct anything in your presentation right up until showtime. Here are some tips to help you remember different editing procedures:

EDITING OPERATION	DO THIS:
Change text style	Highlight the area you want to change, open the Text menu, and choose the style you want
Change text font	Highlight the text, open the Text menu, and click on Font. Make your selections from the displayed list.

EDITING OPERATION	DO THIS:
Change paragraph style	Double-click on the text box containing the style you want to modify, fill in the Paragraph Style dialog box, and click OK when finished
Change text color	Double-click on the text box, select Text color in the Paragraph Style dialog box, choose a color from the displayed color palette, and click OK
Start the spelling checker	Open the Tools menu, choose Spell Check, make selections as necessary, click OK
Change chart type	Click on the chart to select it. Open the Chart menu and choose the Type command. Select the type of chart you want from the displayed list.
To add a table	Click on the table tool (beneath the chart tool in the tools row) or open the Chart menu and choose Table. Enter information in the table box, and click OK.

In this chapter, you've taken a few minutes to consider the overall direction of your presentation. Does it accomplish what you hoped it would? If not, you can still make a few last changes before you print, which is the subject of the next chapter.

FIFTEEN

Printing the Presentation

f a s t TRACK

● **To add headers and footers,** 437

first open the File menu and choose Page Setup. The File Page Setup dialog box appears. Type a header (up to 512 characters), using the vertical bar (|) character to control spacing. To add a footer, press Tab or click in the *Footer:* line; then type the footer (also up to 512 characters).

● **To choose orientation,** 440

display the File Page Setup dialog box. In the Orientation area, select Portrait, System, or Landscape (the default). If you change the setting from Landscape to another setting, the page area on-screen changes to show your choice after you click OK.

● **To get a quick print,**   **441**

press Ctrl-P to display the Print File menu and click the format you want. Then, to print as quickly as possible, click Graduated fills as solids and Print without SmartMaster background. Finally, click Print.

● **To work with printing options,**   **443**

press Ctrl-P to display the Print File dialog box. Make your specifications for the print range and number of copies. Then choose the format from the Format area. Finally, further fine-tune your print operation by clicking the Setup button and entering any necessary specifications for your printer.

DEPENDING on how you plan to give your presentation, this may be the moment you've been waiting for. Throughout this book, you've planned, created, and organized a bunch of original, yet loose thoughts into an effective presentation. Now you're ready to print the presentation—something you can finally get your hands on.

There are actually several things to consider as you begin printing. You may want to add headers and footers, or change the orientation of the page. You might want to print to a printer other than the one you usually use, or you might want to print in color. This chapter helps you target your output so that you get it right the first time.

Remember that the majority of presentations provide viewers with something to take home after the meeting. For this reason, having a printout of some form—whether you use full-screen pages, handouts, audience notes, or speaker notes—is important if you want viewers to remember what was said. This chapter includes tips on printing all these items and helps you get out of trouble spots if the print routine doesn't work the way it should.

Controlling Page Settings

But, first things first. Before jumping right in and printing the presentation, let's consider a few of the things we've left out. Would headers and footers help your viewers remember the presentation? Probably—especially if they've had to sit through a lot of information in a short period of time.

Imagine that you've been attending a weekend conference for family therapists. You've been to six different presentations in two days. Your notes in your old, beat-up brown notebook have been jumbled around. How will you be able to figure out which notes go with which presentation? When you get back to your office and try to review the presentations you attended at this conference, how will you remember which ones offered which services? A clear header or footer showing the sponsor's name and the date of the presentation would help you quickly and easily make this distinction.

In this section, you'll use the Page Setup dialog box to add headers and footers, control page orientation, and review the margins set for the printed page.

TIP

There is more than one way to get to the Page Setup dialog box. You can open the File menu and choose Page Setup, or you can select the Print command from the File menu. The Page Setup button in the Print dialog box also gives you these same options.

Adding a Header and Footer

Not all presentations benefit from having headers and footers. And even those that *do*, don't necessarily need *both*. Generally, headers and footers provide important information about the presentation or the presentation-giver, such as the name, company, or private affiliation of the group. Freelance Graphics allows you to create headers and footers that are up to 512 characters long and can span several lines. You can also select the alignment and automatically add other information such as page numbers and dates.

NOTE Only 10-point Arial can be used to create headers and footers.

Aligning Headers and Footers

Freelance gives you a number of options for the way in which you display the text in the header or footer. When you type the information in the Header line of the File Page Setup box (which we'll do in a minute), the header is by default left-aligned, meaning the text is printed aligned with the left margin of the page.

If you want to center the header at the top of the page, type the vertical bar character (|) before the header text. For example, the following example will print a left-aligned header at the top of the page:

2nd Home, Inc., May 1993

The following line will cause the text to be centered:

|2nd Home, Inc., May 1993

You can right-align the header or footer by entering *two* bar characters before the text.

Freelance allows you to break the header up into three different elements, each with a different alignment. Sound confusing? It's not. For example, suppose you want to use one of the headers shown above, but you want to include a page number. The left-aligned header would look like this:

2nd Home, Inc., May 1993, Page #

Freelance would print this header, as shown, beginning at the left margin of the page. You can use the vertical bar characters to divide the elements, applying 2nd Home, Inc. to the left alignment, centering *May 1993*, and right-aligning *Page #*. The header would look like this:

2nd Home, Inc.|May 1993|Page #

You can also move part of the header to the next line, if you wish, by using the tilde character ~. In this example, if we wanted to move *May 1993* to the second line but still right-align the page number, we would enter the header as follows:

2nd Home, Inc.~May 1993||Page #

N O T E

Remember that headers and footers do not show up on-screen—they only appear when you print.

Including Dates and Page Numbers

Freelance makes it easy for you to add the date or automatic page numbering to your headers and footers. Two special characters—@ and #—control the display of these information items.

When you want to add a date, type @ at any point in the header or footer. For example, typing 2nd Home, Inc., @ automatically enters the date after the beginning portion of the header. The format in which Freelance displays the date depends on the format you've chosen in Windows.

When you want to add a page number, simply type # at the point where you want the page number to be printed. When you want to print, Freelance will automatically substitute that character for the sequential page numbers as they are called for in your presentation.

Entering Header or Footer Text

To add a header or footer to your presentation, follow these steps:

1. Open the File menu.

2. Choose Page Setup. The File Page Setup dialog box appears, as shown in Figure 15.1.

3. Type the header in the Header: line. (Remember to use the vertical bar character to control alignment, # to add a page number, or @ to add the date.)

4. Click in the *Footer:* box and type the footer, if necessary.

Choosing Page Orientation

The next area in the File Page Setup dialog box is the Orientation area. Orientation is the way in which the page is turned for printing. Most standard business documents—such as memos and reports—are printed in standard 8½-by-11, *portrait*, orientation. Charts, slides, and other kinds of visual aids are often printed in landscape orientation, which is 11-by-8½. Landscape is the default setting chosen by Freelance Graphics.

N O T E Once you select an orientation, your entire presentation must be printed in that orientation. Freelance (and your printer, for that matter) doesn't have the capability to change orientation in the middle of a print routine.

FIGURE 15.1

The File Page Setup dialog box

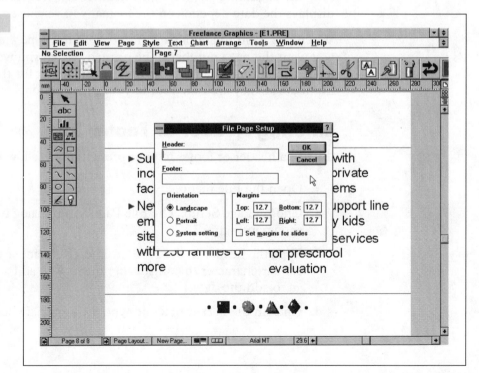

If you choose System Setting rather than Portrait or Landscape orientation, Freelance will use the orientation setting you specified for Windows. When you choose Portrait or Landscape, Freelance carries out those orientations, overriding Windows.

If you change to Portrait orientation, Freelance will work for several seconds and then recompose the display area of the screen, showing you the current page in portrait display.

Reviewing Margins

You've seen margins before—they control the amount of space reserved beyond the work area of the presentation page. The settings displayed in the margin boxes are measurements controlled by the unit of measurement you chose in the Units & Grids dialog box. (For example, the number 12.7 in Figure 15.1 is in millimeters.)

If you are planning to prepare slides, select the Set margins for slides option. This controls the aspect ratio so the page is fitted for 35mm slides.

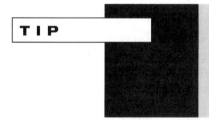

TIP

To see the margins you've assigned to the page, open the View menu, choose the View Preferences command, and click the Margins button in the Show page borders area of the View Preferences dialog box. Then click OK.

Exploring Print Options

When you are ready to print, there's not much left to do except start the printing process. The entire process, from start to finish, takes only a minute—all you have to do is select the Print command from the File menu, fill in the Print File dialog box, and click Print.

First, however, let's make sure you're ready to print to the right printer.

Choosing Your Printer

In today's business environment, it's not unusual to prepare a file on one computer and print it on another. For example, in your office, you may share a laser printer with several other people. Before you print your Freelance Graphics presentation, make sure you're set to print to the right printer.

NOTE

Before Freelance Graphics can recognize the printer you're using, Windows must have access to the printer driver for your printer type. For more information on installing printers in Windows, consult your Windows help system.

Before you print, open the File menu and choose Printer Setup. The Printer Setup dialog box appears. The first option, Optimize for screen show, is used only when your presentation requires you to output the pages to the screen. The second option, Printers, is the one you should select. In the Printers box, the printers currently installed are displayed. As you can see from Figure 15.2, only two printers are installed on this system: a Panasonic dot-matrix printer and a QMS PostScript laser printer. Your screen may show different printers. Select the printer you want to use by clicking on the printer name.

You've already seen the Set Margins for Slides option in the File Page Setup dialog box. For now, leave it unchecked. The Setup button on the right side of the box displays additional information about the printer you've selected. For example, you can control orientation, paper source, font information, graphics resolution, and a number of other options by attaching this information to the printer driver Freelance uses. We won't be concerned with changing settings in this way. We can, however, get everything we need done from within regular Freelance channels.

When you're finished choosing the printer type, click the OK button or press Enter. You are returned to the presentation page, ready to start printing.

FIGURE 15.2

The Printer Setup
dialog box

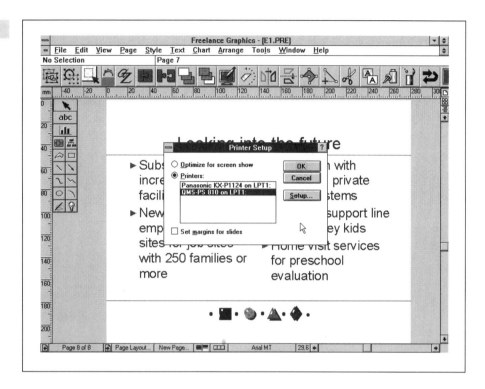

Specifying Print Copies and Range

When you're ready to print, open the Print File menu by selecting the File menu and choosing Print or by pressing Ctrl-P. The Print File dialog box appears, as shown in Figure 15.3. At the top of the Print File box, you see the printer you've selected.

Below the printer choice, you see the Print area. This is where you'll choose the number of copies you want to print and the range of pages for printing. The Number of copies option is already highlighted. To change the setting, simply type the number of copies you want.

FIGURE 15.3

The Print File dialog box

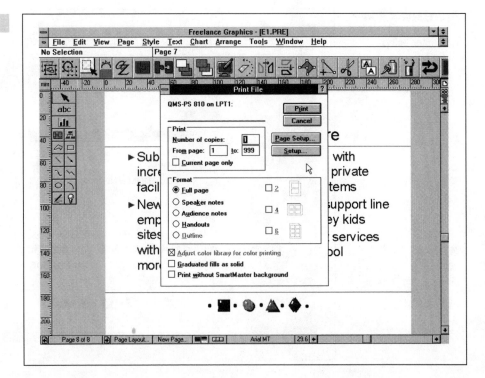

The From page option allows you to indicate the range of pages you want to print. These page numbers are inclusive—meaning that if you specify a page range of 3 to 15, Freelance will start printing with page 3 and end with page 15. If you prefer, you can elect to print just the current page by clicking the Current page only box.

Choosing Print Format

The Format area is an important part of the Print File dialog box. In this area, you choose how you want the presentation printed. Do you want each presentation page placed on a single page, full-size, or do you want the pages presented as handouts with several pages on each handout page?

When you select Full Page, the presentation page is centered on the page. If you select Speaker notes, the presentation page appears in the upper portion of the screen and the speaker notes are printed in the lower half. When you select Audience notes, the presentation page appears in the top half of the page and blank lines are printed in the bottom half so that viewers can write in their own notes. Finally, when you select the Handouts option, the graphical items on the right side of the box are darkened. You can now choose the format of the handout you want to print. As you can see, you can choose from 2, 4, or 6 pages per handout (see Figure 15.4).

N O T E   The Outline print format is unavailable when the pages are displayed in presentation view. If you want to print the outline of your presentation, first make sure none of the levels are collapsed, and then print from Outline view. When you display the Print File dialog box from within the Outliner, you'll be able to choose the Outline format option.

Understanding Color Considerations

If you are working with a color printer, Freelance Graphics will enable the Adjust color library for color printing option for you. If you have selected a standard black-and-white printer (such as our QMS or Panasonic) this option will be disabled.

For color printing, Freelance lets you fine-tune the colors you'll use in your final printouts. Because colors you see on-screen are not always true to what you see in print, having this option is a great benefit. That way, you can modify colors as necessary to get the effects you desire.

FIGURE 15.4

Choosing a handout
layout

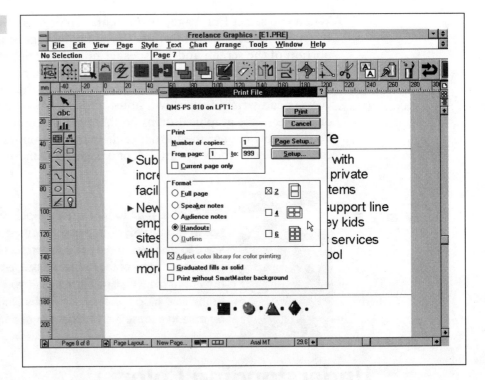

Setting Paper Size and Source

Also in the Print File dialog box, are two option buttons—Page Setup and Setup. The Page Setup options we've already seen—they control the headers, footers, orientation, and margins for the page. When you click the Setup button, a dialog box with the name of your printer is displayed. Figure 15.5 shows the dialog box displayed for the QMS PS 810 printer.

In this dialog box, you can control where the paper comes from (some printers have more than one paper source), the size of the paper (again, high-end printers support different paper sizes), orientation, and the number of copies. To see the Paper Source options for your particular printer, click the ↓. A drop-down list appears.

FIGURE 15.5

The printer driver
setup box

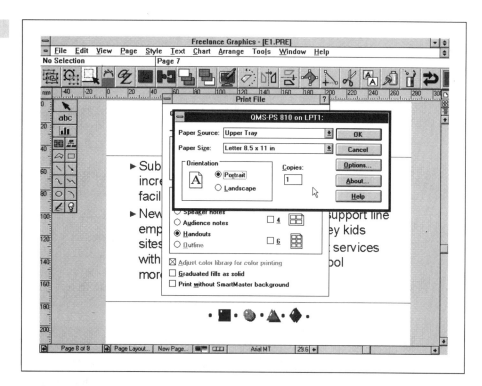

T I P

Other screens with options related to your printer
choice can be displayed if you click the Options
button. These options allow you to choose whether or
not you want to print to the printer or to a file, to print
with margins, to change scaling options, and to send
an identifying header with each print routine. Still
another screen of options, available at the click of the
Advanced button, enables you to control any TrueType
fonts you use, the graphics resolution used, and the
amount of memory reserved for graphics use.

Ready, Set, Print

The last two options in the Print File box concern how quickly you want the item to print. If you're printing a draft of your presentation and not the "real thing," you can speed up printing by clicking the Graduated fills as solid box and the Print without SmartMaster background. Each of these options allow Freelance to print the page more quickly because the details that must be communicated to the printer—such as the shading mix of colors or the formats of the chosen SmartMaster—take a substantial amount of printer memory and transmission time. For the final version of your presentation, of course, you would want to disable these options.

When you're ready to print, click the Print button to begin sending the file to the printer. A Printing Status dialog box appears, telling you that your file is being sent to the printer of your choice. If you're printing more than one page, the page status changes to tell you which page is currently being sent. If you want to abandon the print routine at any time, click Cancel.

NOTE Just like the watched pot that never boils, a stared-at printer never produces anything. Depending on the speed of your computer system and your printer, printing a simple page of bulleted text may take around 2 minutes, while a more complicated page with charts or graphics may take 4 or 5.

Evaluating the Printout

Well, what do you think? Does it look the way you expected it to? As you review your printed presentation, ask yourself these questions:

Is the page effective from a distance? Place the page on your desk (perhaps propped up against your computer) and take a few steps back. Can you tell what's going on? Is there too much text?

Did I use the right colors? If you printed in color (or even if colored screens were converted to black and white output), make sure that the colors you've chosen are not too light. Yellow text will print as very light gray, for example, so against a white background, this isn't the best possible choice. Think about contrast and the colors easiest on the eyes of your audience.

Is the page cluttered? Remember that white space is as important as the text and graphics on your page. Use white space to help draw the reader's eye to a certain area on the page.

Would my printed presentation be more functional if I left room for notes? You can easily add note lines by displaying the Print File dialog box and selecting the Audience notes layout.

Does the orientation I've chosen work for my presentation, or should I try a different setting? Sometimes a simple change from portrait to landscape can provide you with all the additional room you need to free your presentation from a cluttered look.

If you'd like to see your presentation in a different format, Freelance makes it easy for you to go back and do things again. Just open the Print File dialog box (by pressing Ctrl-P), make your changes, and click Print.

Troubleshooting Tips

Unfortunately—and this is especially true with computers—things don't always go the way you want them to. What if your file didn't print properly (or at all)? Before you pull your hair out, here are a few things you should check:

- Is the printer plugged in and turned on?
- Is there paper in the printer?

- Is the printer cable attached securely to the correct port in the back of your system? (The port to which the print is attached is shown in the top of the Print File dialog box. The port on the back of your computer may be labelled. If not, look for the port that matches the connector on the end of your printer cable.)

- If your printer emulates another printer, do you need to set a switch before that emulation can take place? For example, the QMS has the ability to "act like" an HP LaserJet or an Apple LaserWriter. Changing the printer to these modes, however, requires the push of a button on the back of the printer. Check your printer manual to see whether your printer supports emulation modes and find out whether there are any changes you need to make.

In this chapter you've learned a lot about the various print options and page settings in Freelance Graphics. You've finally got something to look at—besides the screen display—that proves you've mastered the presentation graphics learning curve. The next (and final) chapter gives you an alternative to printing your presentation: the screen show utility.

SIXTEEN

Producing a
Screen Show

f a s t TRACK

● **To optimize the display area,**   **457**

open the File menu and choose Printer Setup. Click the Optimize for screen show radio button.

● **To run a simple screen show,**   **458**

display the View menu and select Screen Show. Then choose Run from the submenu (or you can press Alt-F10).

● **To add special effects,**   **460**

display the Edit Screen Show dialog box by opening the View menu and choosing Screen Show. Then select Edit Effects. Select the page to which you want to add effects by clicking on the arrows at either end of the page status line. Then click on the effect you want. If you want the special effect to be used throughout the screen show, click the Apply effect to all pages checkbox.

● **To control screen show timing,** 465

open the View menu and choose Screen Show. When the sub-menu appears, select Edit Effects. When the Edit Screen Show dialog box appears, decide whether you want Manual or Automatic timing by clicking on the appropriate radio button in the Advance screen show area. If you choose Automatic, enter the number of seconds you want between page display in the Display page for box. If you want to apply the same length of time to all pages, click the Apply time to all pages checkbox.

● **To add screen show buttons,** 469

first click on the item you want to turn into a button (it can be a text box, a symbol, a chart, or some other page item). Then open the View menu, choose Screen Show, and select Create/Edit Button from the submenu. The Create/Edit Screen Show Button dialog box appears; select the necessary options and click OK.

IN the previous chapter, you learned to send your presentation to the printer. Printouts are nice, and handouts are helpful, but a really cool screen show will leave an impression on your audience that a printout simply cannot.

With Version 2.0, Freelance Graphics for Windows now incorporates multimedia capabilities in addition to a full library of special effects, fades, and wipes that allow you to control the on-screen presentation like a real video producer might.

With the screen show feature, you can display your presentation—page by page. But that's not all. You can add special transitional effects (ooh and ahh features) that add life and personality to your presentation. You can use a VCR-like control panel, complete with screen show buttons, to move forward or backwards through the pages in your presentation. You can also use the screen show to launch other applications that will complement your show and make the most of your system's multimedia capabilities.

What Is a Screen Show?

In its simplest state, a screen show is an on-screen presentation of pages. From the first page through the last, a screen show displays the pages you've created, complete with text, art, symbols, charts, and anything else you've added during the creation process.

What you do with those pages—and how you enhance the display process—is up to you. The numerous features in the screen show portion of Freelance Graphics make it easy for you to get creative with the display and the tone of your presentation.

Optimizing the Screen

One of the commands you saw in the previous chapter—Optimize for screen show—allows you to maximize the screen viewing area for screen show presentations.

Here's how it works:

1. Open the File menu.

2. Choose the Printer Setup command. The Printer Setup dialog box appears, as shown in Figure 16.1.

3. Click the Optimize for screen show option.

4. Click OK.

FIGURE 16.1

The Printer Setup
dialog box

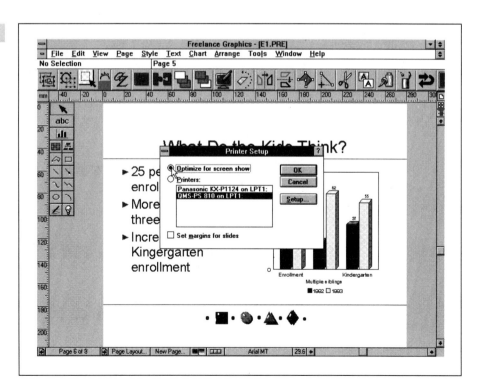

Freelance automatically resizes the margins and changes the display ratio of the screens, maximizing the screen display. When you select the Print command from the File menu, the Print File dialog box appears as usual, except that ScreenShow is shown in place of the printer name to which you're printing. Additionally, the Adjust color library for color printing option is darkened, so you can use it, if necessary, to fine-tune any colors you're using before you start the screen show.

Starting a Screen Show

When you're ready to start, open the View menu and choose the Screen Show command. A pop-up list of additional options is displayed (see Figure 16.2). You then have the following options:

FIGURE 16.2

The ScreenShow submenu

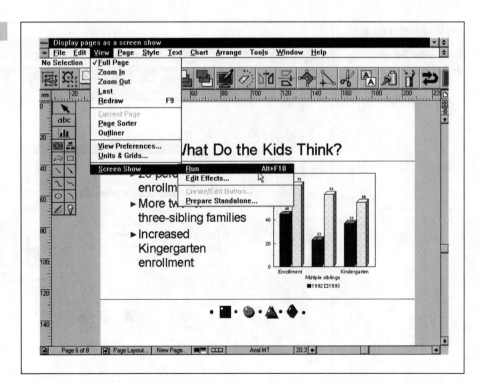

- You can select Run to start the screen show

- You can select Edit Effects to display the Edit Screen Show dialog box and add special effects

- You can choose Prepare Standalone to create a presentation that will be run from the DOS command without using Windows or Freelance Graphics. (You won't be able to use special effects or multimedia capabilities with this option.)

To start the screen show, select Run. If you have not yet displayed the Screen Show submenu, press Alt-F10 to start the show. Note that, at this point, all default values are used and no special effects have been added. We'll do that in the next section.

TIP

If you select Run from the screen show submenu, you may get an error telling you that there is not enough memory available for your presentation to run in screen show format. If this happens, click OK, save the file, close Freelance, and close any other open Windows applications or TSR (terminate-and-stay-resident) programs you may be running. Then restart Freelance and see whether you are able to display that screen show.

Moving through a Simple Screen Show

Earlier in this chapter, you learned that you can add a control panel that includes screen show buttons you can use to navigate through the screen show. But what if you've just started a plain vanilla presentation—with no special effects or screen show buttons—and you need to get through the pages? Here's how:

- If you're using the mouse, click the left mouse button anywhere on the page to advance to the next slide or the right mouse button to move to the previous page

• If you're using the keyboard, press PgDn or Enter to display the next page or PgUp to display the previous page.

Adding Special Screen Show Effects

Freelance offers a number of special screen show effects that can dramatically enhance the professional tone of your presentation. If you want to use slick presentation effects to change from one screen to another, Freelance has a library of special enhancements that let you add your own personal touch to the way the pages are displayed.

Here's how to display your options for special effects:

1. Open the View menu and choose Screen Show. The pop-up sub-menu appears.

2. Choose Edit Effects. The Edit Screen Show dialog box appears, as shown in Figure 16.3.

This dialog box contains a lot of information. The top left corner controls the page to which you apply the special effect you select. The center top area provides you with a list of special effects from which you can choose. The checkbox beneath the special effects box controls whether the effect is applied to all pages or to only the current page. Timing controls appear beneath the checkbox, enabling you to set the presentation on an automatic timer either globally or for individual pages.

The Advance screen show area (in the bottom left corner of the screen) controls whether subsequent screens are displayed automatically or whether the display waits for a specific action (such as the click of a button).

FIGURE 16.3

The Edit Screen Show
dialog box

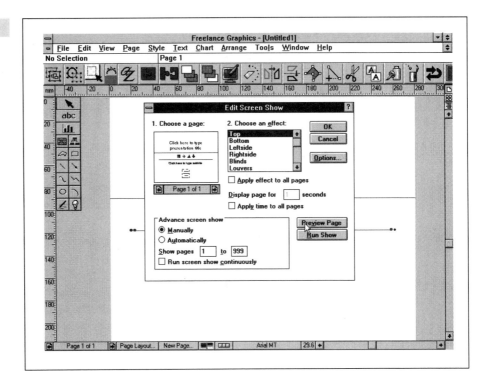

Finally, the command buttons in the Edit Screen Show dialog box perform the following actions:

BUTTON	PERFORMS THIS ACTION
Options	Displays the Screen Show Options dialog box, enabling you to set on-screen drawing, control panel, and navigation settings
Preview Page	When you press and hold the button, displays the current page with any applied special effects
Run Show	Begins the screen show

Choosing Pages

The first set of options in the Edit Screen Show dialog box determines the pages to which you apply the special effects. Use the arrow keys at either end of the page status bar to scroll through the pages. When you've displayed the one you want, move the pointer to the Choose an effect area.

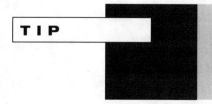

TIP

You can also select pages by clicking on the bar between the scroll arrows. This allows you to pick the page from a list (a convenient feature for longer shows).

Choosing an Effect

Freelance Graphics screen show capabilities provide you with 32 special transitional effects—things like fades, wipes, and scrolls—that whisk the old page off the screen and replace it with the new one. To choose an effect, use the arrows in the scroll bar to page through the available choices. When you see one you want to try, click on it to highlight it. Table 16.1 explains the actions of the various special effects.

After you preview the special effects option, you may want to return to the Edit Screen Show dialog box and make other changes. Simply press Esc, and the List Pages dialog box is displayed. Click Quit Show and you are returned to the Edit Screen Show dialog box.

TIP

You can apply a particular special effect to all pages, if you choose. To do this, click on Apply effect to all pages, underneath the effects box.

TABLE 16.1: Screen Show Special Effects

EFFECT	DESCRIPTION
Top	Displays page by beginning at the top and spreading the page down
Bottom	Spreads the page from bottom to top
Leftside	Spreads the page from left to right
Rightside	Spreads the page from right to left
Blinds	Horizontal effect of blinds being closed
Louvers	Vertical effect of louver blinds closing
Checkboard	Divides the screen into a checkerboard and fills in the page
Center	Spreads the page from the center outward
Box In	Starts from the outer border of the screen and spreads the page inward
Box Out	Starts from a small inside box and spreads the page outward toward the edges of the screen
Zigzag	Begins in the top center of the page and spreads the page in a zigzag pattern out toward the edges and back in toward the center
Hsplit In	Spreads page horizontally from top and bottom toward the middle
Hsplit Out	Starts in the middle and spreads page horizontally to top and bottom edges
Vsplit In	Spreads page vertically from left and right edges toward the middle
Vsplit Out	Starts at the center of the page and spreads the page vertically toward the left and right edges
Replace	Replaces screen with the next page by replacing it from top to bottom with new image
Fade	Brings in next screen by "dotting" it over the preceding page

TABLE 16.1: Screen Show Special Effects (continued)

EFFECT	DESCRIPTION
Diagonal Left	Spreads page (with a jagged edge) from top left corner to bottom right
Diagonal Right	Spreads page from top right corner to bottom left
Pan Left	Moves entire page in from left edge
Pan Right	Moves entire page in from right edge
Scroll Top	Scrolls the page from the top of the screen
Scroll Bottom	Scrolls the page from the bottom of the screen
Draw	Draws the page in layers, from the top down (background color; then background image; then text; then additional symbols)
Rain	Starts with "droplets" of water on the screen and then "runs" downward to reveal the complete page (really cool effect!)
Paint Brush	Uses a large graphical symbol of a paintbrush to "paint" the picture on screen starting along the left side of the screen and moving from bottom to top
Shade	Also uses a graphical symbol—this one a window shade—that appears to be drawn up, revealing the page underneath
Curtains	Uses the old movie-curtains symbol that first close and then open on the presentation page (reminiscent of Monty Python)
Text Top	Shows the page background and then scrolls the text in from the top (at varying speeds, depending on their text level)
Text Bottom	Shows the background and moves text in from the bottom
Text Left	Shows the background and moves text in from the left
Text Right	Shows the background and moves text in from the right

Setting the Timing of Page Display

One major consideration in the effectiveness of an on-screen display is the amount of time you leave the page in front of your viewers. You may have to play with this setting in order to get just the right effect. Some screens, such as those that have quite a bit of text, might demand longer display times than others. Others, even if they have only a line or so of text, may require more time so you can add some information orally.

T I P

Timing doesn't have to be an issue. If you like a less defined type of presentation, you may prefer to set the timing to Manual so that you can advance to the next screen when you're good and ready. That way, you're not controlled by upcoming special effects and the second-by-second countdown between displays.

To set automatic timing for your presentation, click in the Display page for box and type the number of seconds you want the page (or all pages) to be displayed. You can select the Apply time to all pages box to apply the number of seconds you specify to all pages. Otherwise, the setting is used only for the current page.

The Advance screen show area in the bottom left corner of the Edit Screen Show dialog box enables you to determine whether you want to manually control the timing of the page advancement or you want Freelance to do it automatically. If you select Automatic, the Display page for box is dimmed so that you cannot select it. You can enter the number of pages you want to include and elect whether you want the screen show to run continuously or to stop at the final page display.

TIP

At any time in the process, you can start the screen show by clicking the Run Show button.

Drawing On-Screen

Did you ever have one of those professors who could never complete a syllable without pounding the chalk on the chalkboard? She would have loved Freelance—not only for its ability to stop and start as often as she'd like, but because she could actually draw on the screen, underlining, circling, and pointing out to her little heart's content.

The draw options appear on another screen, which is displayed when you click the Options button. The Screen Show Options dialog box appears, as shown in Figure 16.4. Instructions for drawing are shown right up at the top; and you can choose the color and line width of your scribbles by choosing the appropriate box in the On screen drawing area. (The color displayed by default is chosen by Freelance in order to contrast with your background color.)

When you click Color, the familiar color palette is displayed. Make your selection by clicking on the color you want. Likewise, the Width box displays a drop-down list of eight different line widths—from very thin to very wide. Click on your selection.

During the on-screen presentation, you can use the mouse pointer as you would a pencil or highlighter, underlining important points, drawing circles around key points, or emphasizing certain elements that might otherwise escape attention.

FIGURE 16.4

The Screen Show
Options dialog box

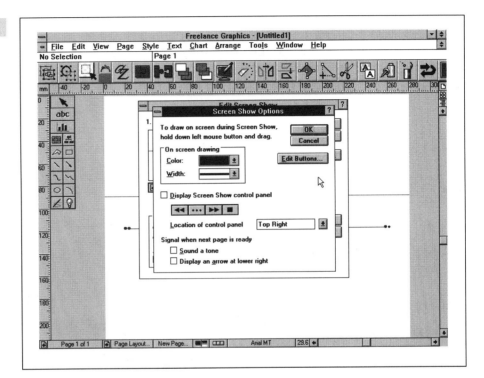

Displaying the Screen
Show Control Panel

Also in the Screen Show Options dialog box, you can elect to display the
screen show control panel. If you've set the display to Manual (as opposed
to Automatic, in which the next slide is displayed after a certain number
of seconds), you can add a control panel that allows you to tell Freelance
when to display the next or previous screen.

To turn on the control panel, click the Display Screen Show control panel button in the center of the Screen Show Options box. Then move the pointer to the Location of control panel option and click ↓. A drop-down list of locations appears as shown in Figure 16.5. Choose where you want the control panel to be displayed by clicking on your choice.

The last two items—*Signal when next page is ready* and *Display an arrow at lower right*—provide you with other options for succeeding page display. You may want to experiment with these options to see whether either fits your presentation style.

Using the control panel in the midst of your presentation is as simple as pushing a button on a VCR. The backward triangles display the previous page; the forward triangles display the next page; the three dots display the List Pages dialog box so you can choose the page you want; and the black rectangle button ends the screen show.

FIGURE 16.5

Choosing a position
for the control panel

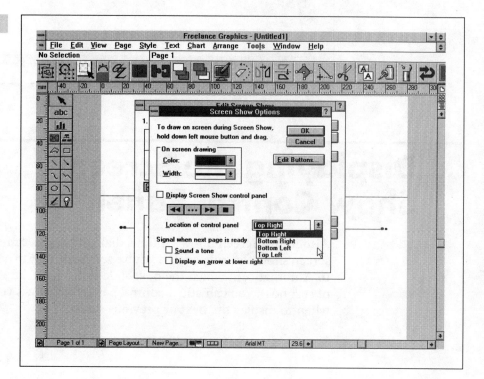

Adding Screen Show Buttons

Your screen show can also become a link to other programs, screen pages, or multimedia applications. Before you can add a button to your screen show, however, you must click on the item you want to use as a button. The item could be a symbol, a text box, or a chart—literally any item you've added to your presentation page.

Next, open the View menu and choose Screen Show. When the submenu appears, select the Create/Edit Button command. The Create Screen Show Button dialog box is then displayed, as shown in Figure 16.6.

FIGURE 16.6

The Create Screen Show Button dialog box

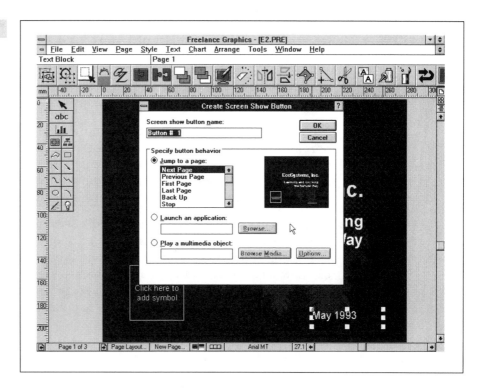

Freelance names the button for you (in this case, Button #1), but you can click in the box and enter a different name, if you like. You then have a decision to make: Do you want this button to perform a certain action within the presentation (such as take you to another page) or do you want to launch another program or play a multimedia video or sound bite?

Your answer will determine what you do next. If you want the button to control page movement within the screen show, click on the Jump to a page option. Then, in the Specify button behavior area, use the scroll bar to display the various actions you can have your button perform. Make your selection by clicking on the one you want.

If you want to launch an application, click that radio button. You can click the Browse button to display the Find Application to Launch dialog box, in which you specify which file you want to open with the screen show button. For example, you could open another screen show by linking it to the button you're working with. Click on the file name you want (or, if necessary, click the Drives and Directories windows to find the file you need). Finally, click OK. (If you want to make sure that information isn't written back to the file you launch, you can click the Read Only box before clicking OK.)

Using Multimedia

Multimedia—the merging of sound and video files—is of particular importance to people who rely heavily on presentations and cutting-edge technology. One of the new enhancements with Windows Version 3.1 was its built-in multimedia support. And now, Freelance Graphics, Version 2.0 has been enhanced to make the most of those new features.

If you decide to incorporate multimedia files in your screen show (first make sure you have plenty of memory), click on the Play a multimedia object button. The Browse Media and Options buttons darken, meaning you can now select them. When you click the Browse Media button, the Lotus Media Manager dialog box appears, allowing you to choose a multimedia file you want to link to the button you're creating (see Figure 16.7).

FIGURE 16.7

The Lotus Media
Manager

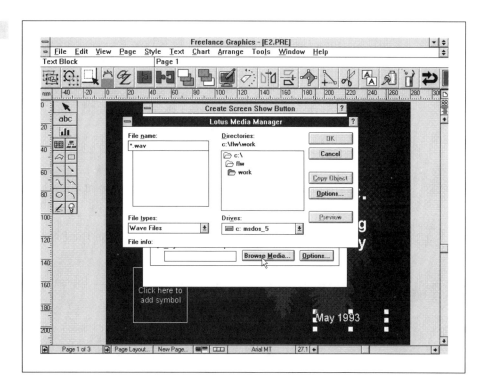

In the File name box, specify the name of the file you want to incorporate. You can use Wave files, MIDI files, or Movies in your screen show presentation. Click on the *Drives:* box and the *Directories:* area to find the file you want to incorporate. Also click the *File types:* box to display the type of file you want to use.

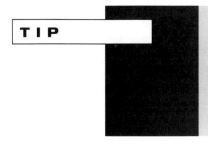

TIP

To find sample multimedia files, click on the C:\ symbol in the *Directories:* box to display the directories on the root directory. Then double-click *lotusapp.* Finally, double-click *multimed.* A list of multimedia files appears in the file name box. Click on the file you want to select it, then click OK.

Click the Options button in the Lotus Media Manager dialog box to display another dialog box. This box lets you control the number of times the multimedia segment is played, and specify whether or not the segment is actually included in the Freelance file or whether a tag is placed in the Freelance file to go out and read the multimedia file. When you've set the options the way you want them, click OK. You are returned to the Create Screen Show Button screen.

The name of the multimedia file you've selected is displayed in the Play a multimedia object box. You can click on the Options button at the far end of that row to choose when you want the file to be called into action. The Multimedia Button Options dialog box, shown in Figure 16.8, appears. Number 10, At button location, causes the multimedia file (in this case, a sound file) to be used each time the button location is clicked.

FIGURE 16.8

The Multimedia Button
Options dialog box

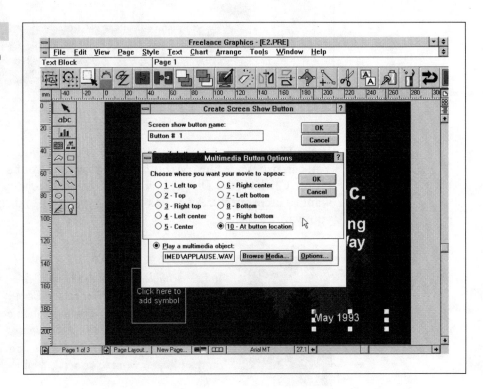

Running the Screen Show

When you're ready to run the screen show, simply open the View menu, choose Screen Show, and select Run. (Or, if you prefer, press Alt-F10.) Remember, if you've set the timing to Automatic, the pages will turn automatically, and the special effect used will be the one (or ones) you selected in the special effects list box.

If you chose Manual timing, Freelance will wait for you to click the mouse button or press PgDn or Enter before advancing the page. Additionally, if you elected to display the control panel, you should see it in the location you specified.

Finally, if you created a button and linked an action, application, or a multimedia file to it, it should be fully functional during the screen show if you have the right equipment (like a sound board) and enough memory to support it.

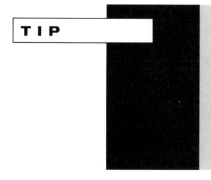

T I P

Remember how memory-intensive Freelance Graphics for Windows tends to be and, when you're creating screen shows for practice, try to keep them small. Also remember how easily anything in Freelance Graphics can be changed. Don't be afraid to be daring and go boldly where few presentations have gone before (within the bounds of good taste, of course).

This chapter finishes up Part Five—and the book, for that matter. In this chapter, you've learned about one of the more exciting aspects of Freelance Graphics for Windows: the display capabilities. With screen show, you can bring your presentations to life in full color, with animation features and special screen effects. And now, with the advent of multi-media capabilities, you can import video and sound files so that the limit of your presentation is only restricted by your hardware.

Here's one of my favorite quotes: "If you can dream it, you can do it," (attributed to Walt Disney over a generation ago). With our software—at least with Freelance Graphics for Windows—we're beginning to see our dreams edging toward reality. Good luck.

APPENDIX A

Installing
Freelance
Graphics for
Windows 2.0

LIKE everything else in Freelance Graphics, installing the program is easy. First and foremost, the installation procedure has the same look and feel as all the installation procedures for Windows products.

Before you do anything else, make copies of the Lotus Freelance Graphics for Windows program disks. This may be an extensive process, and you'll probably need a ton of disks, but making a copy now is a lot less painful than regretting it later.

When you're ready to start the installation procedure, follow these steps:

1. Start Windows and display the Program Manager.

2. Place the copy of the first installation disk in drive A or B (depending on the disk size you are using).

3. Open the Program Manager's File menu by pressing Alt-F or by clicking on the menu name.

4. Select the **Run** command by highlighting it or by clicking on it (see Figure A.1).

5. Type a: (if the program disk is in drive A) or b: (if the disk is in drive B).

6. Type install (see Figure A.2).

7. Click OK or press Enter.

FIGURE A.1

Selecting the Program
Manager's Run
command

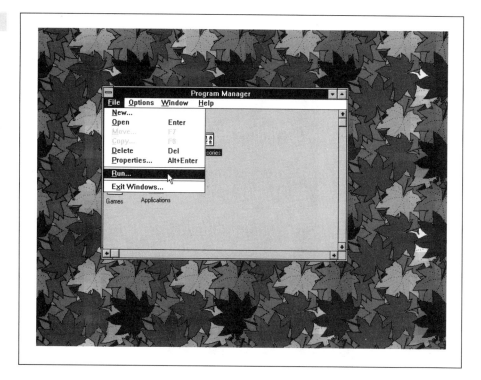

Freelance Graphics then takes over. You will be prompted when to insert which disk, and a series of questions will be displayed, asking for you to verify the directory names Freelance will create.

One important screen asks you whether you want to install *all* of Freelance Graphics for Windows or only selected portions of the program. For maximum performance, including all multimedia files, symbol files, and SmartMaster sets, choose the full version (if your hard disk can support it—you'll need up to 19 megabytes!). If you can't afford the room on your hard drive, you can install only portions of the program.

FIGURE A.2

Starting the
installation process

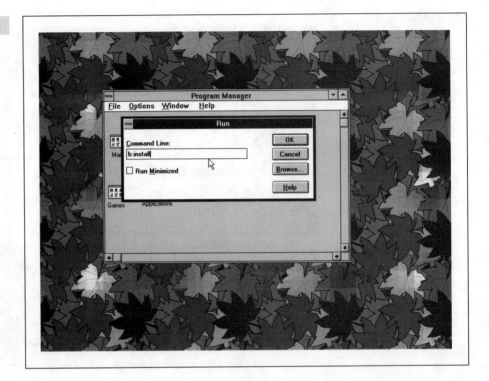

Freelance will copy the files to the hard disk, creating and naming directories as necessary. The entire installation should take around 20 minutes
for the full version, less for a partial installation.

APPENDIX B

New Features
with Version 2.0

THIS appendix lists the changes new with Version 2.0. Many of the features—while not completely new—have been enhanced to make this user-friendly and extremely intuitive program even easier to use than before.

TABLE B.1: Version 2.0 enhancements

CATEGORY	DESCRIPTION
Overall Enhancements	QuickStart Tutorial is more intuitive than ever, offering user-controlled options
	Easy custom page layouts make it simple to create your own text and symbol boxes
	DDE (Dynamic Data Exchange) support for links with other Windows applications
	A new Color/B&W button allows you to change between color and black and white displays with the click of a button
	A click of the right mouse button displays options for the selected element
SmartMasters	Twelve new SmartMasters are included, two with multimedia features
	SmartMasters are now available in black and white and color
	Organizational charts have been added to the SmartMaster Page Layout list
	Table charts have been added to the SmartMaster Page Layout list

TABLE B.1: Version 2.0 enhancements (continued)

CATEGORY	DESCRIPTION
Text	Tip buttons provide information about bullet placement and paragraph styles
	Speaker notes give users the option of adding notes to presentation pages
	Printable outlines—from the Outliner—help ensure logical progression of ideas
	The Outliner now allows you to move blocks of text easily from one page to another
	Collapse or expand outlines with the simple click of a button
	Support for Word and Ami Pro outlines
	Ability to assign page layouts in Outliner view
	Automatic build feature allows you to create several slides from a single bulleted list
	Now users can rotate and curve text in a variety of shapes
	Rather than the traditional bullet styles, any symbol in Freelance's symbol library can be used as a bullet character
Charts	Radar chart type
	3-D line and area charts
	Easy linking with Lotus 1-2-3 for Windows and Ami Pro
Graphics	New freehand tool allows you to draw original art
	Shapes now have a drop-shadow and position option
	On-screen drawing rulers help ensure accurate placement of graphics

TABLE B.1: Version 2.0 enhancements (continued)

CATEGORY	DESCRIPTION
Screen Show	New multimedia support
	The ability to create hot buttons that can carry out actions, launch applications, or start multimedia routines
	Special effects such as transitional fades and wipes that add a professional touch to presentations
	The option of adding a control panel for manual page turning

GLOSSARY

**G**lossary

Arrowheads. The small arrow symbols on the end of the arrow tool in the graphics tool box.

Annotating. The process of adding notes or callouts to charts.

Attributes. Specific text or chart options, such as font size, style, and color.

Axis. The line along which the horizontal and vertical data items (X and Y, respectively) are plotted in a chart

Backup. The process of making a copy of the current, or an original, file or disk.

Background. The page area on which art—SmartMaster or original—is applied to all pages in a presentation.

Bar chart. A type of chart drawn with the use of bars in a variety of styles, such as traditional bars, stacked bars, and 3-D bars.

Bezier curve. A type of curve created in object-oriented graphics (specifically Freelance Graphics) that uses a calculation to draw the curve and prevent distortion.

Bitmap. A type of graphic that is actually a pattern of dots, or pixels, on the screen.

Build pages. A series of pages that build one upon another, based on a bulleted list.

Bulleted lists. A list of items, each highlighted with a symbol.

Buttons. Buttons—such as OK, Cancel, and Print—that allow you to carry out actions with the click of a mouse. You can add your own buttons in the screen show utility.

Charts. A type of graphic that illustrates data comparisons and helps communicate numeric information.

Checkboxes. A type of option in dialog boxes that enables you to turn an item on and off by clicking in the box.

Clip art. Professionally drawn art. Freelance includes many symbols which could accurately be referred to as clip art.

Clipboard. The invisible Windows clipboard, which is used to store data that is copied, cut, or pasted.

Control panel. In the screen show utility, you can add a control panel that allows you to move manually through displayed pages.

Current page view. The presentation page view in which the Smart-Master page is displayed as it will be printed.

Data sets. In the chart feature, a data set is one series of data items that relate to a specific range. A bar chart, for example, might include several data sets, each compared against the other.

Demote button. In the Outliner or in a text box, the demote button subordinates the entered text one level.

Dialog boxes. Pop-up boxes in Freelance Graphics that enable you to enter settings for a command you've chosen.

Drawing tools. The set of art tools along the left edge of the work area.

Dynamic Data Exchange (DDE). A new linking technology that allows you to link charts based on data imported from other applications. When the information in the originating file changes, the chart is automatically updated as soon as you open the application.

Edge attributes. The color, width, and style settings applied to the line that edges a shape, chart, or symbol.

Flipping. Used in graphics, the Flip command will flip the selected graphic from left to right or top to bottom.

Graduated patterns. A shaded or mixed pattern that uses two colors and gradually fades one into another.

Grouping objects. The process of combining lines or objects into one object.

Handles. The small black squares that appear along the perimeter of a selected object.

Handouts. A special print format that allows you to print 2, 4, or 6 presentation pages per printed page.

Icons. Also called SmartIcons, the line of graphical buttons stretching across the screen beneath the menu bar. You can carry out commands by clicking on the SmartIcon you need.

Importing data. The process of copying data from a non-Freelance application into Freelance.

Justification. The alignment of text in a text box. You can choose left-justified, centered, right-justified, or full-justified text.

Landscape orientation. The print (or display) specification of choice for charts and presentation graphics, produces the page in 11-by-8½ format.

Launching applications. Version 2.0 of Freelance allows you to start an application from a button you add in a screen show.

Legend. The key to a chart, explaining chart data sets and color and pattern codes.

Lotus Media Manager. A utility included with Freelance that allows you to work with and access multimedia files for use in the screen show.

Millimeters. The default unit of measurement chosen by Freelance Graphics.

Multimedia. A relatively new technology that allows you to integrate video and sound clips in presentations.

Number grids. A charting option that gives you the choice of displaying a number grid in place of values along an axis.

Object. Any text, chart, or graphic item that can be selected and manipulated with the selection tool.

Online help. The portion of the help system that is always available with the press of F1.

Organization chart. A type of chart new with Version 2.0 that allows you to illustrate a corporate structure or project flow, starting with a main level and breaking into subordinate levels.

Orientation. A setting that controls the way the page is printed or displayed. Landscape prints horizontally (11 by 8½) and portrait prints vertically (8½ by 11).

Outliner. A feature that allows you to enter and edit text in outline fashion.

Page layouts. The type of page you select from the SmartMaster Page Layout dialog box that gives you the template for creating the current page.

Paragraph styles. A typeface, style, alignment, color, and size that is applied to a particular level of text.

Picas. A unit of measurement available in Freelance.

Points mode. In graphics, points mode allows you to add and move small points on a created graphic.

Portrait orientation. A standard, 8½-by-11 business-document format for printing or display.

Previewing. The process of seeing how your changes will look before you accept them.

Radar charts. A new type of chart with Version 2.0 that allows you to plot points on crossed X and Y axes.

Replicating. The process of making a copy and placing the copy immediately on the page.

Rotating. In graphics mode, you can rotate a selected item in any angle.

Rulers. In text mode, rulers can be displayed in text boxes. In graphics mode, drawing rulers appear along the left and top borders of the work area.

Screen show. An on-screen display of created pages in a presentation.

SmartMasters. Predesigned, interactive templates that take all the guesswork out of presentation design.

Speaker notes. A feature new with Version 2.0 that allows you to add notes to your presentation pages.

Special effects. In a screen show, special effects like fades, wipes, and scrolls add professional appeal to your presentations.

Spelling checker. A utility included with Freelance Graphics that allows you to check the spelling in your presentation.

Symbols. Over 100 pieces of predrawn, professional art you can use in your presentations as illustrations or buttons.

Transitional effects. Another phrase for special effects between screen show pages.

Undo. Freelance will allow you undo the last ten operations you performed.

Views. Freelance Graphics provides you with several different views from which you can display your presentation: current page view, Page Sorter view, Outliner view, and SmartMaster page view.

Work area. The central area of the screen on which you create pages for your presentation.

X-axis. The horizontal axis in most chart types.

Y-axis. The vertical axis in most chart types.

Zoom In. The process of magnifying the screen area to get a closer look at an object or layout.

Zoom Out. Reducing the page area and displaying the page from a "far out" vantage point, enabling you to see more accurately how items are placed in proportion to the page.

INDEX

Note: In this index, entries referring to a major discussion are printed in **bold**; entries referring to a figure are printed in *italics*.

A

About Freelance Graphics help option, 42
active tools, 353
Add Point command, 394
Add Point SmartIcon, 345, *345*
Add Symbol to Page dialog box, 78, *79*, **319–325**, *322*
Add To Dictionary button, 154
Add to Symbol Library command, 328
Adjust color library for color printing option, 458
Adobe Type Manager, help for, 42
Advance screen show options, 460–461, *461*, 465
Align command, 387
Align Objects dialog box, 387–388, *388*
aligning
    graphics, **347–349**, *349*
    headers and footers, **438–439**
    objects, **387–388**
    text, **165–168**, *166*
All Chart Text command, 283, 294
All Chart Text dialog box, 294–295, *295*
Alt key, 61
angles
    for bar shadows, 289
    for graphics, 350–351
animals, symbol files for, 317–318
animation in tutorial, 18
annotating charts, 351
Apply time to all pages box, 465
arc tool, *336*, 351, **357–358**, *359–360*
area charts, **245**, *245*
area color of objects, 374
Area command, 304

Arial font for Outliner view, 214
Arrange menu, 65
arranging objects, **385–387**
arrow keys
    for editing text, 133
    in Outliner view, 119
arrow tool, *336*, 351
art tools, **336–337**, *336*
at signs (@) in headers and footers, 439
ATM help option, 42
attributes, editing
    for charts, **285–289**, **293–297**
    for graphics, **371–377**
Attributes command, 282
Attributes menu, 272
audience considerations in presentations, **22**
audience notes, printing, 445
automatic timing for screen shows, 465
axes in charts, 241, 256
    editing, 284
    labels and titles on, **257–259**, *258–260*, 265, 283
    text attributes for, 293
    tickmarks on, 282, 297–298
Axis Titles & Labels command, 283, 293
Axis Titles section, 265, *265*

B

background colors, 408–409
Background command
    on Chart menu, 282
    for graphics, 338
background for charts, 301
backing up program disks, 476

Beyond the basics.

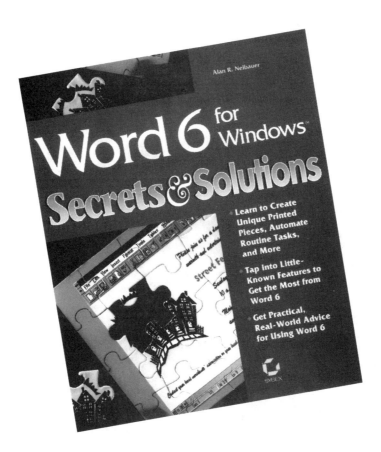

Word Processing guru Alan Neibauer brings Windows users a gold mine of basic information and exotic tips on harnessing the phenomenal power of Word 6. Peppered with real-world examples from the type of work you do.

CREATE YOUR FIRST DATABASE IN A SINGLE EVENING!

Bestselling author Alan Simpson's feature-packed guide to Access 2 covers the new interface, button bars, Wizards, macros, and more— even includes a complete guide to designing a model application!

WINDOWS HAS NEVER BEEN CLEARER.

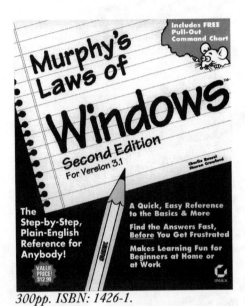

GET A FREE CATALOG JUST FOR EXPRESSING YOUR OPINION.

Help us improve our books and get a **FREE** full-color catalog in the bargain. Please complete this form, pull out this page and send it in today. The address is on the reverse side.

Name _____ **Company** _____

Address _____ **City** _____ **State** ___ **Zip** _____

Phone ( ) _____

1. How would you rate the overall quality of this book?

❑ Excellent
❑ Very Good
❑ Good
❑ Fair
❑ Below Average
❑ Poor

2. What were the things you liked most about the book? (Check all that apply)

❑ Pace
❑ Format
❑ Writing Style
❑ Examples
❑ Table of Contents
❑ Index
❑ Price
❑ Illustrations
❑ Type Style
❑ Cover
❑ Depth of Coverage
❑ Fast Track Notes

3. What were the things you liked *least* about the book? (Check all that apply)

❑ Pace
❑ Format
❑ Writing Style
❑ Examples
❑ Table of Contents
❑ Index
❑ Price
❑ Illustrations
❑ Type Style
❑ Cover
❑ Depth of Coverage
❑ Fast Track Notes

4. Where did you buy this book?

❑ Bookstore chain
❑ Small independent bookstore
❑ Computer store
❑ Wholesale club
❑ College bookstore
❑ Technical bookstore
❑ Other _____

5. How did you decide to buy this particular book?

❑ Recommended by friend
❑ Recommended by store personnel
❑ Author's reputation
❑ Sybex's reputation
❑ Read book review in _____
❑ Other _____

6. How did you pay for this book?

❑ Used own funds
❑ Reimbursed by company
❑ Received book as a gift

7. What is your level of experience with the subject covered in this book?

❑ Beginner
❑ Intermediate
❑ Advanced

8. How long have you been using a computer?

_____ years
_____ months

9. Where do you most often use your computer?

❑ Home
❑ Work

❑ Both
❑ Other _____

10. What kind of computer equipment do you have? (Check all that apply)

❑ PC Compatible Desktop Computer
❑ PC Compatible Laptop Computer
❑ Apple/Mac Computer
❑ Apple/Mac Laptop Computer
❑ CD ROM
❑ Fax Modem
❑ Data Modem
❑ Scanner
❑ Sound Card
❑ Other _____

11. What other kinds of software packages do you ordinarily use?

❑ Accounting
❑ Databases
❑ Networks
❑ Apple/Mac
❑ Desktop Publishing
❑ Spreadsheets
❑ CAD
❑ Games
❑ Word Processing
❑ Communications
❑ Money Management
❑ Other _____

12. What operating systems do you ordinarily use?

❑ DOS
❑ OS/2
❑ Windows
❑ Apple/Mac
❑ Windows NT
❑ Other _____

13. On what computer-related subject(s) would you like to see more books?

_____

_____

_____

_____

14. Do you have any other comments about this book? (Please feel free to use a separate piece of paper if you need more room)

_____

_____

_____

_____

- - - - - - - - - - PLEASE FOLD, SEAL, AND MAIL TO SYBEX - - - - - - - - - -

SYBEX INC.
Department M
2021 Challenger Drive
Alameda, CA
94501

Drawing Tools

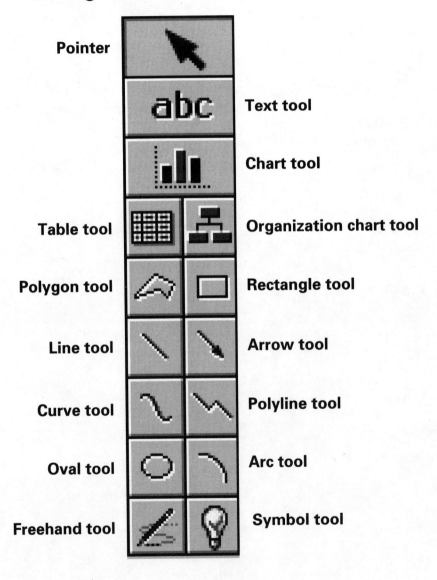

Pointer

Text tool

Chart tool

Table tool

Organization chart tool

Polygon tool

Rectangle tool

Line tool

Arrow tool

Curve tool

Polyline tool

Oval tool

Arc tool

Freehand tool

Symbol tool